BLOOM'S

HOW TO WRITE ABOUT

Shakespeare's Histories

NEIL HEIMS

Introduction by **HAROLD BLOOM**

BLOOM'S
LITERARY CRITICISM
An imprint of Infobase Publishing

Bloom's How to Write about Shakespeare's Histories

Bloom's Literary Criticism
An imprint of Infobase Publishing
132 West 31st Street
New York NY 10001

Library of Congress Cataloging-in-Publication Data
Heims, Neil.
  Bloom's how to write about Shakespeare's histories / Neil Heims ; introduction by Harold Bloom.
    p. cm. — (Bloom's how to write about literature)
  Includes bibliographical references and index.
  ISBN 978-1-60413-721-7 (hardcover)
  1. Shakespeare, William, 1564–1616—Histories. 2. Historical drama, English—History and criticism. 3. Criticism—Authorship. I. Bloom, Harold. II. Title.
  PR2982.H45 2010
  822.3'3—dc22   2010015751

Bloom's Literary Criticism books are available at special discounts when purchased in bulk quantities for businesses, associations, institutions, or sales promotions. Please call our Special Sales Department in New York at (212) 967-8800 or (800) 322-8755.

You can find Bloom's Literary Criticism on the World Wide Web at
http://www.chelseahouse.com

Text design by Annie O'Donnell
Cover design by Ben Peterson
Composition by Mary Susan Ryan-Flynn
Cover printed by Art Print, Taylor, PA
Book printed and bound by Maple Press, York, PA
Date printed: October 2010
Printed in the United States of America

10 9 8 7 6 5 4 3 2 1

All links and Web addresses were checked and verified to be correct at the time of publication. Because of the dynamic nature of the Web, some addresses and links may have changed since publication and may no longer be valid.

CONTENTS

SERIES INTRODUCTION

BLOOM's How to Write about Literature series is designed to inspire students to write fine essays on great writers and their works. Each volume in the series begins with an introduction by Harold Bloom, meditating on the challenges and rewards of writing about the volume's subject author. The first chapter then provides detailed instructions on how to write a good essay, including how to find a thesis; how to develop an outline; how to write a good introduction, body text, and conclusion; how to cite sources; and more. The second chapter provides a brief overview of the issues involved in writing about the subject author and then a number of suggestions for paper topics, with accompanying strategies for addressing each topic. Succeeding chapters cover the author's major works.

The paper topics suggested within this book are open-ended, and the brief strategies provided are designed to give students a push forward in the writing process rather than a road map to success. The aim of the book is to pose questions, not answer them. Many different kinds of papers could result from each topic. As always, the success of each paper will depend completely on the writer's skill and imagination.

HOW TO WRITE ABOUT SHAKESPEARE'S HISTORIES: INTRODUCTION

by Harold Bloom

S HAKESPEARE'S SUPREMACY over all Western writers has several aspects: language, cognition, originality, and vitalism among them. To me, the salient Shakespearean uniqueness is the godlike ability to create human beings: a hundred major figures and a thousand minor ones, almost all of whom feel, think, speak, and act as sharply distinct individuals. Other major authors can create character: Homer, the Yahwist, Dante, Chaucer, Molière, Racine, Milton, Jane Austen, George Eliot, Tolstoy, Flaubert, Henry James, Proust, and Mann among them. But only a few can people a world with personalities: Cervantes, Dickens, and Balzac come closest to Shakespeare's florabundance, but his preternatural exuberance in forging lives is beyond even them.

As a teacher and critic of Shakespeare, I consciously follow after the precursors who most illuminate Shakespeare's personalities for me: Maurice Morgann, Dr. Samuel Johnson, Samuel Taylor Coleridge, William Hazlitt, A. C. Bradley, and the American Harold Goddard. Bradley noted that the four Shakespearean characters "inexhaustible to meditation" were Falstaff, Hamlet, Iago, and Cleopatra. Only one of these—the magnificent Falstaff—is not a tragic protagonist. He is the world's foremost comic personage, but he inhabits histories not comedies.

Shakespeare rarely confines himself to genre, and Falstaff's plays—*Henry IV*, parts 1 and 2—form a single drama that is both history and tragicomedy. One could argue that what I call "the Falstaffiad" also includes Mistress Quickly's Cockney prose elegy for Sir John in *Henry V*, a history haunted by Falstaff's absence.

I recommend writing about Shakespeare's histories by meditating on their major characters: the Bastard Faulconbridge in *King John*, Richard II, Prince Hal/Henry V, Hotspur, Richard III, and, above all, Falstaff. Faulconbridge is the first Shakespearean character so rammed with life that he is too large for his play. Richard II, narcissist and masochistic whiner, is also a metaphysical poet. Hal, after Falstaff, provokes profound thinking, since his complex nature has so many contraries held in balance. Falstaff's student rather than his father's, Henry V emotionally destroys the great comedian by rejecting him.

Hotspur is everything that attracts an audience, but his spectacular "honor" is exposed by Falstaff as a societal hypocrisy, part of the drive for power. That drive nightmarishly is best exemplified by Richard III, a persuasive monster.

Falstaff stands apart, not only by his comic genius, but because more than any other person in Shakespeare he bears the Blessing, in the biblical sense of "more life." To write about Sir John Falstaff, you need to invoke the heroic vitalists of Western literature: Chaucer's Wife of Bath, Panurge in Rabelais, Sancho Panza in *Don Quixote*. Yet that is only a start in apprehending Falstaff. Like the biblical contenders for the Blessing—Jacob and David, in particular—Falstaff, disreputable and extravagant, incarnates the secrets of human joy, of what it might mean to live on into a time without boundaries.

HOW TO WRITE
A GOOD ESSAY

By Laurie A. Sterling and Neil Heims

WHILE THERE are many ways to write about literature, most assignments for high school and college English classes call for analytical papers. In these assignments, you are presenting your interpretation of a text to your reader. Your objective is to interpret the text's meaning in order to enhance your reader's understanding and enjoyment of the work. Without exception, strong papers about the meaning of a literary work are built upon a careful, close reading of the text or texts. Careful, analytical reading should always be the first step in your writing process. This volume provides models of such close, analytical reading, and these should help you develop your own skills as a reader and as a writer.

As the examples throughout this book demonstrate, attentive reading entails thinking about and evaluating the formal (textual) aspects of the author's works: theme, character, form, and language. In addition, when writing about a work, many readers choose to move beyond the text itself to consider the work's cultural context. In these instances, writers might explore the historical circumstances of the time period in which the work was written. Alternatively, they might examine the philosophies and ideas that a work addresses. Even in cases where writers explore a work's cultural context, though, papers must still address the more formal aspects of the work itself. A good interpretative essay that evaluates Charles Dickens's use of the philosophy of utilitarianism in his novel *Hard Times*, for example, cannot adequately address the author's treatment of the philosophy without firmly grounding this discussion in the book itself. In other words, any analytical paper about a text, even one that seeks to evaluate the work's cultural context, must also have a firm handle on the work's themes, characters, and language. You must look for and evaluate these aspects of a work, then, as you read a text and as you prepare to write about it.

WRITING ABOUT THEMES

Literary themes are more than just topics or subjects treated in a work; they are attitudes or points about these topics that often structure other elements in a work. Writing about theme therefore requires that you not just identify a topic that a literary work addresses but also discuss what the work says about that topic. For example, if you were writing about the culture of the American South in William Faulkner's famous story "A Rose for Emily," you would need to discuss what Faulkner says, argues, or implies about that culture and its passing.

When you prepare to write about thematic concerns in a work of literature, you will probably discover that, like most works of literature, your text touches upon other themes in addition to its central theme. These secondary themes also provide rich ground for paper topics. A thematic paper on "A Rose for Emily" might consider gender or race in the story. While neither of these could be said to be the central theme of the story, they are clearly related to the passing of the "old South" and could provide plenty of good material for papers.

As you prepare to write about themes in literature, you might find a number of strategies helpful. After you identify a theme or themes in the story, you should begin by evaluating how other elements of the story—such as character, point of view, imagery, and symbolism—help develop the theme. You might ask yourself what your own responses are to the author's treatment of the subject matter. Do not neglect the obvious, either: What expectations does the title set up? How does the title help develop thematic concerns? Clearly, the title "A Rose for Emily" says something about the narrator's attitude toward the title character, Emily Grierson, and all she represents.

WRITING ABOUT CHARACTER

Generally, characters are essential components of fiction and drama. (This is not always the case, though; Ray Bradbury's "August 2026: There Will Come Soft Rains" is technically a story without characters, at least any human characters.) Often, you can discuss character in poetry, as in T. S. Eliot's "The Love Song of J. Alfred Prufrock" or Robert Browning's "My Last Duchess." Many writers find that analyzing character is one of the most interesting and engaging ways to work with a piece of literature and to shape a paper. After all, characters generally are human, and we all know something about being human and living in the world. While it is always important to remember that these figures are not real people but creations of the writer's imagination, it can be fruitful to begin evaluating them as you might evaluate a real person. Often you can start with your own response to a character. Did you like or dislike the character? Did you sympathize with the character? Why or why not?

Keep in mind, though, that emotional responses like these are just starting places. To truly explore and evaluate literary characters, you need to return to the formal aspects of the text and evaluate how the author has drawn these characters. The 20th-century writer E. M. Forster coined the terms *flat* characters and *round* characters. Flat characters are static, one-dimensional characters that frequently represent a particular concept or idea. In contrast, round characters are fully drawn and much more realistic characters that frequently change and develop over the course of a work. Are the characters you are studying flat or round? What elements of the characters lead you to this conclusion? Why might the author have drawn characters like this? How does their development affect the meaning of the work? Similarly, you should explore the techniques the author uses to develop characters. Do we hear a character's own words, or do we hear only other characters' assessments of him or her? Or, does the author use an omniscient or limited omniscient narrator to allow us access to the workings of the characters' minds? If so, how does that help develop the characterization? Often you can even evaluate the narrator as a character. How trustworthy are the opinions and assessments of the narrator? You should also think about characters' names. Do they mean anything? If you encounter a hero named Sophia or Sophie, you should probably think about her wisdom (or lack thereof), since *sophia* means "wisdom" in Greek. Similarly, since the name Sylvia is derived from the word *sylvan,* meaning "of the wood," you might want to evaluate that character's relationship with nature. Once again, you might look to the title of the work. Does Herman Melville's "Bartleby, the Scrivener" signal anything about Bartleby himself? Is Bartleby adequately defined by his job as scrivener? Is this part of Melville's point? Pursuing questions such as these can help you develop thorough papers about characters from psychological, sociological, or more formalistic perspectives.

WRITING ABOUT FORM AND GENRE

Genre, a word derived from French, means "type" or "class." Literary genres are distinctive classes or categories of literary composition. On the most general level, literary works can be divided into the genres of drama, poetry, fiction, and essays, yet within those genres there are classifications that are also referred to as genres. Tragedy and comedy, for example, are genres of drama. Epic, lyric, and pastoral are genres of poetry. *Form,* on the other hand, generally refers to the shape or structure of a work. There are many clearly defined forms of poetry that follow specific patterns of meter, rhyme, and stanza. Sonnets, for example, are poems that follow a fixed form of 14 lines. Sonnets generally follow one of two basic sonnet forms, each with its own distinct rhyme scheme. Haiku is another example of poetic form, traditionally consisting of three unrhymed lines of five, seven, and five syllables.

While you might think that writing about form or genre might leave little room for argument, many of these forms and genres are very fluid. Remember that literature is evolving and ever changing, and so are its forms. As you study poetry, you may find that poets, especially more modern poets, play with traditional poetic forms, bringing about new effects. Similarly, dramatic tragedy was once quite narrowly defined, but over the centuries playwrights have broadened and challenged traditional definitions, changing the shape of tragedy. When Arthur Miller wrote *Death of a Salesman,* many critics challenged the idea that tragic drama could encompass a common man like Willy Loman.

Evaluating how a work of literature fits into or challenges the boundaries of its form or genre can provide you with fruitful avenues of investigation. You might find it helpful to ask why the work does or does not fit into traditional categories. Why might Miller have thought it fitting to write a tragedy of the common man? Similarly, you might compare the content or theme of a work with its form. How well do they work together? Many of Emily Dickinson's poems, for instance, follow the meter of traditional hymns. While some of her poems seem to express traditional religious doctrines, many seem to challenge or strain against traditional conceptions of God and theology. What is the effect, then, of her use of traditional hymn meter?

WRITING ABOUT LANGUAGE, SYMBOLS, AND IMAGERY

No matter what the genre, writers use words as their most basic tool. Language is the most fundamental building block of literature. It is essential that you pay careful attention to the author's language and word choice as you read, reread, and analyze a text. Imagery is language that appeals to the senses. Most commonly, imagery appeals to our sense of vision, creating a mental picture, but authors also use language that appeals to our other senses. Images can be literal or figurative. Literal images use sensory language to describe an actual thing. In the broadest terms, figurative language uses one thing to speak about something else. For example, if I call my boss a snake, I am not saying that he is literally a reptile. Instead, I am using figurative language to communicate my opinions about him. Since we think of snakes as sneaky, slimy, and sinister, I am using the concrete image of a snake to communicate these abstract opinions and impressions.

The two most common figures of speech are similes and metaphors. Both are comparisons between two apparently dissimilar things. Similes are explicit comparisons using the words *like* or *as*; metaphors are implicit comparisons. To return to the previous example, if I say, "My boss, Bob, was waiting for me when I showed up to work five minutes late today—the snake!" I have constructed a metaphor. Writing about his experiences fighting in World War I, Wilfred Owen begins his poem "Dulce et decorum est" with a string of similes: "Bent double, like old beggars under sacks, / Knock-kneed, coughing like hags, we cursed through sludge." Owen's goal was to undercut clichéd notions that war and dying in battle were glorious. Certainly, comparing soldiers to coughing hags and to beggars underscores his point.

"Fog," a short poem by Carl Sandburg, provides a clear example of a metaphor. Sandburg's poem reads:

> The fog comes
> on little cat feet.
>
> It sits looking
> over harbor and city
> on silent haunches
> and then moves on.

Notice how effectively Sandburg conveys surprising impressions of the fog by comparing two seemingly disparate things—the fog and a cat.

Symbols, by contrast, are things that stand for, or represent, other things. Often they represent something intangible, such as concepts or ideas. In everyday life we use and understand symbols easily. Babies at christenings and brides at weddings wear white to represent purity. Think, too, of a dollar bill. The paper itself has no value in and of itself. Instead, that paper bill is a symbol of something else, the precious metal in a nation's coffers. Symbols in literature work similarly. Authors use symbols to evoke more than a simple, straightforward, literal meaning. Characters, objects, and places can all function as symbols. Famous literary examples of symbols include Moby Dick, the white whale of Herman Melville's novel, and the scarlet *A* of Nathaniel Hawthorne's *The Scarlet Letter.* As both of these symbols suggest, a literary symbol cannot be adequately defined or explained by any one meaning. Hester Prynne's Puritan community clearly intends her scarlet *A* as a symbol of her adultery, but as the novel progresses, even her own community reads the letter as representing not just *adultery,* but *able, angel,* and a host of other meanings.

Writing about imagery and symbols requires close attention to the author's language. To prepare a paper on symbolism or imagery in a work, identify and trace the images and symbols and then try to draw some conclusions about how they function. Ask yourself how any symbols or images help contribute to the themes or meanings of the work. What connotations do they carry? How do they affect your reception of the work? Do they shed light on characters or settings? A strong paper on imagery or symbolism will thoroughly consider the use of figures in the text and will try to reach some conclusions about how or why the author uses them.

WRITING ABOUT HISTORY AND CONTEXT

As noted above, it is possible to write an analytical paper that also considers the work's context. After all, the text was not created in a vacuum. The author lived and wrote in a specific time period and in a specific cultural context and, like all of us, was shaped by that environment. Learning more about the historical and cultural circumstances that surround the author and the work can help illuminate a text and provide you with productive material for a paper. Remember, though, that when you write analytical papers, you should use the context to illuminate the text. Do not lose sight of your goal—to interpret the meaning of the literary work. Use historical or philosophical research as a tool to develop your textual evaluation.

Thoughtful readers often consider how history and culture affected the author's choice and treatment of his or her subject matter. Investigations into the history and context of a work could examine the work's relation to specific historical events, such as the Salem witch trials in 17th-century Massachusetts or the restoration of Charles II to the English throne in 1660. Bear in mind that historical context is not limited to politics and world events. While knowing about the Vietnam War is certainly helpful in interpreting much of Tim O'Brien's fiction, and some knowledge of the French Revolution clearly illuminates the dynamics of Charles Dickens's *A Tale of Two Cities,* historical context also entails the fabric of daily life. Examining a text in light of gender roles, race relations, class boundaries, or working conditions can give rise to thoughtful and compelling papers. Exploring the conditions of the working class in 19th-century England, for example, can provide a particularly effective avenue for writing about Dickens's *Hard Times.*

You can begin thinking about these issues by asking broad questions at first. What do you know about the time period and about the author? What does the editorial apparatus in your text tell you? Similarly, when specific historical events or dynamics are particularly important to understanding a work but might be somewhat obscure to modern readers, textbooks usually provide notes to explain historical background. With this information, ask yourself how these historical facts and circumstances might have affected the author, the presentation of theme, and the presentation of character. How does knowing more about the work's specific historical context illuminate the work? To take a well-known example, understanding the complex attitudes toward slavery during the time Mark Twain wrote *Adventures of Huckleberry Finn* should help you begin to examine issues of race in the text. Additionally, you might compare these attitudes to those of the time in which the novel was set. How might this comparison affect your interpretation of a work written after the abolition of slavery but set before the Civil War?

WRITING ABOUT PHILOSOPHY AND IDEAS

Philosophical concerns are closely related to both historical context and thematic issues. Like historical investigation, philosophical research can provide a useful tool as you analyze a text. For example, an investigation into the working class in Dickens's England might lead you to a topic on the philosophical doctrine of utilitarianism in *Hard Times*. Many other works explore philosophies and ideas quite explicitly. Mary Shelley's famous novel *Frankenstein,* for example, explores John Locke's tabula rasa theory of human knowledge as she portrays the intellectual and emotional development of Victor Frankenstein's creature. As this example indicates, philosophical issues are more abstract than investigations of theme or historical context. Some other examples of philosophical issues include human free will, the formation of human identity, the nature of sin, or questions of ethics.

Writing about philosophy and ideas might require some outside research, but usually the notes or other material in your text will provide you with basic information, and often footnotes and bibliographies suggest places you can go to read further about the subject. If you have identified a philosophical theme that runs through a text, you might ask yourself how the author develops this theme. Look at character development and the interactions of characters, for example. Similarly, you might examine whether the narrative voice in a work of fiction addresses the philosophical concerns of the text.

WRITING COMPARISON AND CONTRAST ESSAYS

Finally, you might find that comparing and contrasting the works or techniques of an author provides a useful tool for literary analysis. A comparison and contrast essay might compare two characters or themes in a single work, or it might compare the author's treatment of a theme in two works. It might also contrast methods of character development or analyze an author's differing treatment of a philosophical concern in two works. Writing comparison and contrast essays, though, requires some special consideration. While they generally provide you with plenty of material to use, they also come with a built-in trap: the laundry list. These papers often become mere lists of connections between the works. As this chapter will discuss, a strong thesis must make an assertion that you want to prove or validate. A strong comparison/contrast thesis, then, needs to comment on the significance of the similarities and differences you observe. It is not enough merely to assert that the works contain similarities and differences. You might, for example, assert why the similarities and differences are important and explain how they illuminate the works' treatment of theme. Remember, too, that a thesis should not be a statement of the obvious. A comparison/contrast paper that focuses only on very obvious similarities or differences does little to illuminate the connections between the works. Often, an effective method of shaping a strong thesis and argument is to begin your paper by noting the similarities between the works but then to develop a thesis that asserts how these apparently similar elements are different. If, for example, you observe that Emily Dickinson wrote a number of poems about spiders, you might analyze how she uses spider imagery differently in two poems. Similarly, many scholars have noted that Hawthorne created many "mad scientist" characters, men who are so devoted to their science or their art that they lose perspective on all else. A good thesis comparing two of these characters—Aylmer of "The Birth-mark" and Dr. Rappaccini of "Rappaccini's Daughter," for example—might initially identify both characters as examples of Hawthorne's mad scientist type but then argue that their motivations for scientific experimentation differ. If you strive to analyze the similarities or differences, discuss significances, and move beyond the obvious, your paper should move beyond the laundry list trap.

PREPARING TO WRITE

Armed with a clear sense of your task—illuminating the text—and with an understanding of theme, character, language, history, and philosophy, you are ready to approach the writing process. Remember that good writing is grounded in good reading and that close reading takes time, attention, and more than one reading of your text. Read for comprehension first. As you go back and review the work, mark the text to chart the details of the work as well as your reactions. Highlight important passages, repeated words, and image patterns. "Converse" with the text through marginal notes. Mark turns in the plot, ask questions, and make observations about characters, themes, and language. If you are reading from a book that does not belong to you, keep a record of your reactions in a journal or notebook. If you have read a work of literature carefully, paying attention to both the text and the context of the work, you have a leg up on the writing process. Admittedly, at this point, your ideas are probably very broad and undefined, but you have taken an important first step toward writing a strong paper.

Your next step is to focus, to take a broad, perhaps fuzzy, topic and define it more clearly. Even a topic provided by your instructor will need to be focused appropriately. Remember that good writers make the topic their own. There are a number of strategies—often called "invention"—that you can use to develop your own focus. In one such strategy, called *freewriting*, you spend 10 minutes or so just writing about your topic without referring back to the text or your notes. Write whatever comes to mind; the important thing is that you just keep writing. Often this process allows you to develop fresh ideas or approaches to your subject matter. You could also try *brainstorming*: Write down your topic and then list all the related points or ideas you can think of. Include questions, comments, words, important passages or events, and anything else that comes to mind. Let one idea lead to another. In the related technique of *clustering*, or *mapping*, write your topic on a sheet of paper and write related ideas around it. Then list related subpoints under each of these main ideas. Many people then draw arrows to show connections between points. This technique helps you narrow your topic and can also help you organize your ideas. Similarly, asking journalistic questions—Who? What? Where? When? Why? and How?—can lead to ideas for topic development.

Thesis Statements

Once you have developed a focused topic, you can begin to think about your thesis statement, the main point or purpose of your paper. It is imperative that you craft a strong thesis, otherwise, your paper will likely be little more than random, disorganized observations about the text. Think of your thesis statement as a kind of road map for your paper. It tells your reader where you are going and how you are going to get there.

To craft a good thesis, you must keep a number of things in mind. First, as the title of this subsection indicates, your paper's thesis should be a statement, an assertion about the text that you want to prove or validate. Beginning writers often formulate a question that they attempt to use as a thesis. For example, a writer exploring the theme of honor in Shakespeare's *1 Henry IV* might ask, Why is the question of honor so important in *1 Henry IV*? While a question like this is a good strategy to use in the invention process to help narrow your topic and find your thesis, it cannot serve as the thesis statement because it does not tell your reader what you want to assert about honor and the role of honor in the play. You might shape this question into a thesis by instead proposing an answer to that question: In *1 Henry IV*, many of the characters are deeply concerned with the problem of honor. The way a character feels about honor and what he is willing to do in the name of honor, in fact, make honor a matter of life and death. But in *1 Henry IV*, Shakespeare does not present honor as a clearly desirable value. Because of Falstaff's eloquent disdain for honor, the very value that motivates the other leading characters is called into question. Notice that this thesis provides an initial plan or structure for the rest of the paper, and notice, too, that the thesis statement does not necessarily have to fit into one sentence, nor is it necessarily the first sentence in your paragraph. In this example, the thesis sentence is the third sentence. After discussing King Henry's, Prince Hal's, Hotspur's, and, perhaps, Owen Glendower's sense of honor, you would examine Falstaff's views on honor and from there move to the way Shakespeare has built into his play an apparent ambivalence to the concept of honor as a guiding value. That observation would then lead you to consider why. What is the effect of this ambivalence on a reader's evaluation of characters such as Hal, Hotspur, Glendower, and King Henry himself and their attitudes and enterprises?

Second, remember that a good thesis makes an assertion that you need to support. In other words, a good thesis does not state the obvious. If you tried to formulate a thesis about honor by simply saying, Honor is important in 1 Henry IV, you have done nothing but rephrase the obvious. Since Shakespeare's play culminates with Falstaff's great catechism on honor and in the battle of antagonists for honor, there would be no point in spending three to five pages supporting that assertion. You might try to develop a thesis from that point by asking yourself some further questions: What does it mean to put honor above everything else? What effect does Falstaff's disdain for honor have on the way we think and feel about Hal and Hotspur and their values? Does the play seem to support or to challenge accepted ideas about the value of honor? Such a line of questioning might lead you to a more viable thesis, like the one in the preceding paragraph.

As the comparison with the road map also suggests, your thesis should appear near the beginning of the paper. In relatively short papers (three to six pages) the thesis almost always appears in the first paragraph. Some writers fall into the trap of saving their thesis for the end, trying to provide a surprise or a big moment of revelation, as if to say, "TA-DA! I've just proved that in *1 Henry IV* Shakespeare uses the concept of honor to cast doubt on the values of the leading characters in the play." Placing a thesis at the end of an essay can seriously mar the essay's effectiveness. If you fail to define your essay's point and purpose clearly at the beginning, your reader will find it difficult to assess the clarity of your argument and understand the points you are making. When your argument comes as a surprise at the end, you force your reader to reread your essay in order to assess its logic and effectiveness.

Finally, you should avoid using the first person ("I") as you present your thesis. Though it is not strictly wrong to write in the first person, it is difficult to do so gracefully. While writing in the first person, beginning writers often fall into the trap of writing self-reflexive prose (writing *about* their paper *in* their paper). Often this leads to the most dreaded of opening lines: "In this paper I am going to discuss . . ." Not only does this self-reflexive voice make for very awkward prose, but it frequently allows writers boldly to announce a topic while completely avoiding a thesis statement. An example might be a paper that begins as follows: Shakespeare's Richard III tells the story of a scheming man's lust for power. In this essay, I am going to discuss how the people around Richard III responded to his schemes. The author of this paper has done little more than announce a general topic for the paper (Richard III's lust for power and how the people around him responded to him). While the two sentences might contain the germ of a thesis, the writer fails to present an opinion about the significance of the responses or even what they were. To improve this "thesis," the writer would need to back up a couple of steps. First, the announced topic of the paper is too broad; it very vaguely summarizes the events in the play, without saying anything about the ideas in the play. The writer should highlight what she considers the meaning of the story: What is the story about? The writer might conclude that the force of personality of a man who lusts for power not only intoxicates the person who lusts for power, but it even can seduce his victims despite themselves. When Richard decides to ensnare an enemy—Lady Anne, for example—he has the power to focus on her deepest needs and use her virtue against her and to his own advantage. From here, the author could show the means by which Shakespeare has Richard undermine Anne's resolve by playing on her deeply embedded Christian charity, showing the weakness of virtue when confronted by cunning vice. A writer who chooses to explore the techniques of cunning that are associated with Richard might, for example, craft a thesis that reads, *Richard III* is a play that explores the use of cunning in Richard's quest for the English throne and the kinds of manipulative techniques that he employed to gain people's confidence and how he ultimately was defeated.

Outlines

While developing a strong, thoughtful thesis early in your writing process should help focus your paper, outlining provides an essential tool for logically shaping that paper. A good outline helps you see—and develop—the relationships among the points in your argument and assures you that your paper flows logically and coherently. Outlining not only helps place your points in a logical order but also helps you subordinate supporting points, weed out any irrelevant points, and decide if there are any necessary points that are missing from your argument. Most of us are familiar with formal outlines that use numerical and letter designations for each point. However, there are different types of outlines; you may find that an informal outline is a more useful tool for you. What is important, though, is that you spend the time to develop some sort of outline—formal or informal.

Remember that an outline is a tool to help you shape and write a strong paper. If you do not spend sufficient time planning your supporting points and shaping the arrangement of those points, you will most likely construct a vague, unfocused outline that provides little, if any, help with the writing of the paper. Consider the following example.

Thesis: *Richard III* is a play that explores the effects of physical and moral deformity on one man and how he compensates for his weakness by the pursuit of power through the exercise of cunning. The play examines the kinds of manipulative techniques that he employs and how they ultimately fail.

    I. Introduction and thesis

   II. Richard
      A. Opening Speech

  III. Deformity
      A. False prophecy
      B. Hypocrisy
      C. Diabolical wit
      D. Charm
      E. Cunning

   IV. Lady Anne (Wooing)

    V. Failure
      A. Buckingham
      B. Richmond

  VI. Conclusion
      A. Richard's physical and moral deformities are at the root of his quest for power, but we see how they fail because,

> despite his cunning, he cannot escape
> the vengeance of his enemies or his own
> guilty conscience

This outline has a number of flaws. First, the major topics labeled with the Roman numerals are not arranged in a logical order. If the paper's aim is to show how Richard is affected by his deformities, the writer should establish what they are before showing how he responds to them. Similarly, the thesis makes no reference to Lady Anne or to Buckingham and Richmond, but the writer includes each of them as major sections of this outline. As one of his victims, Lady Anne may well have a place in this paper, but the writer fails to provide details about her place in the argument. Buckingham and Richmond, too, are significant players, each in his own way, in Richard's downfall, but as the writer is designing the paper, they do not logically merit a major section. The writer could, however, discuss the importance of each of these characters for Richard's rise and fall and how they provide Shakespeare with the opportunity to show the workings of his character in other sections of the essay. Third, the writer labels section III with the heading "Deformity," but letters B, C, D, and E all refer to Richard's specific Machiavellian character traits, and letter A refers to a false prophecy without explaining its content or context at all. None of them can properly be subsumed in the category of "deformity." The writer could argue that hypocrisy, diabolical wit, and charm are all weapons of cunning Richard uses in his attempt to overcome the sense of weakness he feels because of his deformities, and she could explain that Richard has managed to have his brother Clarence imprisoned by falsely interpreting a prophecy to make it appear that the king's life is in danger because of Clarence. Then, the use of false prophecy can be shown to be one example of Richard's cunning, and all these points might be itemized under the heading of "Manipulative techniques." A fourth problem is the inclusion of a section A in sections II and VI. An outline should not include an A without a B, a 1 without a 2, and so forth. The final problem with this outline is the overall lack of detail. None of the sections provides much information about the content of the argument, and it seems likely that the writer has not given sufficient thought to the content of the paper.

A better start to this outline might be the following:

Thesis: *Richard III* is a play that explores the effects of physical and moral deformity on one man and how he compensates for his weakness and exclusion from the pleasures and rewards of society and fellowship by the pursuit of power through the exercise of cunning. The play examines the kinds of manipulative techniques that he employs in addition to commissioned murders and how they ultimately fail.

   I. Introduction and thesis

  II. Richard's recognition of his exclusion from society's pleasures because of his moral and physical deformities
    1. His misshapen body
    2. His inability to be a sportsman, a gallant courtier, or a fashionable lover
    3. His determination "to prove a villain"

 III. Manipulative techniques
    1. Richard manipulates a prophecy to secure the imprisonment of his brother Clarence who is nearer in line for the throne than Richard is
    2. Richard behaves with hypocrisy, pretending to sympathize with Clarence when he speaks with him as Clarence is led to the tower
    3. Richard uses his diabolical wit and charm to bend those whom he has harmed to his will

  IV. Richard's failure
    1. Richard's sense of his own power is so tenuous that even after he becomes king he does not feel secure in his power
      a. He continues to murder his enemies

      b. He continues to manipulate others
         against their wills to achieve his
         ends
      c. He becomes confused
    2. He is overcome by his own sense of guilt

V. Conclusion

This new outline would prove much more helpful when it came time to write the paper.

An outline like this could be shaped into an even more useful tool if the writer fleshed out the argument by providing specific examples from the text to support each point. Once you have listed your main point and your supporting ideas, develop this raw material by listing related supporting ideas and material under each of those main headings. From there, arrange the material in subsections and order the material logically.

For example, you might begin with one of the theses cited above: In *1 Henry IV*, many of the characters are deeply concerned with the problem of honor. The way a character feels about honor and what he is willing to do in the name of honor, in fact, makes the pursuit of honor a matter of life and death. But in *1 Henry IV*, Shakespeare does not present honor as a clearly desirable value. Because of Falstaff's eloquent disdain for honor, the very value that motivates the other leading characters is called into question. As noted above, this thesis already gives you the beginning of an organization: Start by supporting the notion that many of the characters are preoccupied with the concept of honor and then explain how Shakespeare uses this as a means of analyzing the nature of honor and the striving to attain it. Be sure to include references to parts of the text that help build your case.

An informal outline might look like this:

Thesis: In *1 Henry IV*, Shakespeare does not present honor as a clearly desirable value. Although many of the characters are deeply concerned with the pursuit of honor, and although the pursuit of honor in the play is often portrayed as a matter of life and death, because of Falstaff's eloquent disdain for honor, and because of the ambiguity with which Shakespeare portrays the motives of the characters who are dedicated to the pursuit of honor, the actual value of honor is called into question by the play.

1. Honor or the want of honor is shown to be the essential factor in the quality and dynamics of every significant relationship in *1 Henry IV*
   - Honor is a major factor in Prince Hal's relationship with his father
     - Hal's apparent disdain for honor taints his relationship with his father
     - King Henry envies Northumberland "a son who is the theme of honor's tongue" and wishes that "some night-tripping fairy had exchanged / . . . our children where they lay, / and called mine Percy, his Plantagenet" [1.1.80ff.]
   - Apparent disdain for his own honor characterizes Hal's relationship with Falstaff and dishonors his royal obligations as the Prince of Wales
     - Falstaff is a thief and a drunkard, notable for his cowardice, lechery, and lying
     - Percy disparages Hal, calling him "that . . . sword and buckler Prince of Wales" whom he would "have . . . poisoned with a pot of ale." [1.3.228,231]
     - Falstaff imagines influencing Hal when he becomes king
     - "Do not thou, when thou art king, hang a thief." [1.2.64]

- ○ "Rob me the exchequer the first thing thou doest, and do it with unwashed hands, too." [3.3.189]
- Henry Percy is guided in everything he does by his sense of the importance of honor
  - ○ Percy justifies rebellion against King Henry by arguing that by rebellion his father and his uncle "may redeem/ Your banished honors" [1.3.179–180]
  - ○ He complains that Henry "disgraced me in my happy victories" [4.3.97]
  - ○ Percy's desire to participate in the rebellion is fueled by dreams of winning honor (1.3.199ff.)
  - ○ He is called "the king of honor." [4.1.10]
- Owen Glendower defines himself by his sense of being honored by Nature
  - ○ Glendower is enraged when Hotspur refuses to give him the honor he believes is his due by right of birth
- Vernon boasts that when he is moved to action in the service of honor he is without fear

2. Attitudes toward honor: How honor is used and valued
  - Describe how each character uses the concept of honor to define himself and the value he places upon it
    - ○ Henry is manipulative; in his opening address, promises to go on a crusade to the Holy Land, an enterprise full of honor, as opposed to the recent civil strife, as a way of mobilizing support for himself and distracting opinion from the questionable way in which he gained the crown; in his reproach to Prince Hal, he characterizes Hal

as God's punishment; in his account of how he manipulated his image so that when he was seen, "like a comet, I was wondered at" [III.ii.47], places expediency over honor; betrays the trust of those who supported him

○ Hal manipulates others' perception of his relation to honor in order to be able to present himself to his best advantage later; in his challenge to Hotspur, seeks and gains honor in his combat with Percy by defeating him and, thereby, transferring Percy's reputation for honor to himself

○ Hotspur glories in it and lives for it

○ Falstaff dismisses honor, disdains it; mocks honor; by boasting about his deeds of valor when he exaggerates how many robbers assailed him; acts without regard for honor; is shameless in speech and act; values his life above his honor

3. The pursuit of honor presented as self-serving, a relative, conditional or ambiguous virtue and honor itself of questionable value

• The characters in the play who espouse and pursue honor do not necessarily have spotless motives; the pursuit of honor is often the pursuit of power, glory, self-aggrandizement

○ Henry demands honor in others but does not as a rule behave honorably; broke his word in pursuit of power and continued to break it when his power was challenged

○ Hal, in seeking honor, uses Falstaff and his other tavern companions for his own ends; he is ready to sacrifice them; regarding Falstaff: ("I do. I will"); Hal's challenge to Hotspur and victory over Hotspur serve the purpose of increasing his own honor

○ Hotspur's regard for honor is shown as a result of his hotheadedness; his regard for his honor comes at the expense of his regard for his wife and for life itself

○ Falstaff is a braggart and a liar with no concern for honor but not a dissembler; when he takes the poorest for soldiers, it is a parody of what others do without admitting what he admits, that soldiers are "food for powder" [4.2.67]; when he does lie, everyone knows it; his "catechism" on honor makes sense, as does his earlier remark on seeing the corpse of Sir Walter Blunt, "There's honor for you." [5.3.32]

○ Vernon, at Worcester's request, agrees to lie to Hotspur about the King's agreement to make peace

4. Conclusion: Although at first glance *1 Henry IV* seems to be a heroic pageant in praise of honor, the subversive message of the play is that the pursuit of honor is a pursuit of power, which involves slaughter rather than nurture. It is pursued by men with self-serving motives. Shakespeare reveals the contradictions inherent in the concept of honor and apparent in the pursuit of honor in *1 Henry IV* and continues to do so in *Henry V,* which can be read as an even stronger paean to patriotism and honor, when Prince Hal, now King Henry V, with a ragged band of English soldiers, defeats the French at

the battle of Agincourt and secures the English claim to France. Like *1 Henry IV, Henry V* seems to glorify battle and the pursuit of honor but scattered throughout are suggestions of the suffering that war entails and the brutality it engenders and, most significantly, despite the rhetoric of honor and patriotism that supports Henry's war effort, Shakespeare has framed the events of *Henry V* in Henry IV's parting speech to Hal at his death in *2 Henry IV* when he tells him that because his hold on the crown is not entirely secure, since he won it by overthrowing and murdering Richard II, the best way to substantiate his royal authority is to fight a foreign war. Indeed, after Henry has conquered France, in *Henry VI*, English political strife breaks out again and the lust for power rises to the surface and swamps any idea of honor.

You would set about writing a formal outline with a similar process, though in the final stages you would label the headings differently. A formal outline for a paper that argues the thesis about *Richard III* previously cited—that the play examines how Richard compensates for his exclusion from social pleasures and fellowship because of his physical and moral deformities with a cruel and cunning pursuit of power—might look like this:

> I. Introduction and thesis
>
> *Richard III* is a play that explores the effects of physical and moral deformity on one man and how he compensates for his deformity and exclusion from the pleasures and rewards of society and fellowship by the pursuit of power through the exercise of cruelty, craft, and cunning. The play examines the kinds of manipulative techniques that the

king employs in addition to commissioned murders and how they ultimately fail

II. Richard's recognition of his exclusion from society's pleasures because of his moral and physical deformities
   A. His misshapen body
   B. His inability to be a sportsman, a gallant courtier, or a fashionable lover
   C. His determination "to prove a villain" [1.1.30]

III. Manipulative techniques
   A. Richard manipulates and falsifies a prophecy to secure the imprisonment of his brother Clarence who is nearer in line for the throne than Richard
   B. He behaves with hypocrisy
      1. Pretends to sympathize with Clarence when he speaks with him as Clarence is led to the tower
      2. Accuses Queen Elizabeth of having provoked Clarence's arrest
      3. Pretends to be more interested in sacred study than in monarchical power
   C. He uses his diabolical wit and charm to bend those whom he has harmed to his will
      1. In the case of Lady Anne
         a. He plays on her virtue, knowing she will not be able to kill him when he offers to let her
         b. He assumes a penitential manner
      2. In the case of Queen Elizabeth
         a. He admits his faults in killing her sons

           b. He promises that by marrying her daughter he will make amends

IV. Richard's failure and continuing insecurity
    A. Even after he becomes king, Richard's sense of his own power is tenuous
        1. He senses that "my kingdom stands on brittle glass" [4.2.59.]
        2. He continues to murder his enemies
        3. He continues to manipulate others in order to achieve his ends
        4. He is unable to trust his followers
           a. Buckingham
           b. Stanley
    B. He becomes confused
        1. Catesby [4.4.440]
        2. Ratcliffe [4.4.453ff.]
    C. He is overcome by a sense of guilt.
        1. He is plagued by conscience [5.3.180, 307ff.]
        2. He has bad dreams

V. Conclusion

Although throughout the centuries of Shakespeare criticism, many critics have complained that Shakespeare's tragedies lack a clear moral conclusion, in which good does not decisively triumph over evil, in *Richard III* Shakespeare presents a situation in which a character really does reap what he sows and in which virtue, in the form of Richmond, definitively triumphs over vice. The forces of history and of personal conscience overwhelm the power of individual will and supreme cunning and dissembling. Richmond's victory over Richard serves as an emblem of the victory of the English monarchy over disorder.

As in the previous example outline, the thesis provided the seeds of a structure, and the writer was careful to arrange the supporting points in a logical manner, showing the relationships among the ideas in the paper.

Body Paragraphs

Once your outline is complete, you can begin drafting your paper. Paragraphs, units of related sentences, are the building blocks of a good paper, and as you draft you should keep in mind both the function and the qualities of good paragraphs. Paragraphs help you chart and control the shape and content of your essay, and they help the reader see your organization and your logic. You should begin a new paragraph whenever you move from one major point to another. In longer, more complex essays, you might use a group of related paragraphs to support major points. Remember that in addition to being adequately developed, a good paragraph is both unified and coherent.

Unified Paragraphs

Each paragraph must be centered on one idea or point, and a unified paragraph carefully focuses on and develops this central idea without including extraneous ideas or tangents. For beginning writers, the best way to ensure that you are constructing unified paragraphs is to include a topic sentence in each paragraph. This topic sentence should convey the main point of the paragraph, and every sentence in the paragraph should relate to that topic sentence. Any sentence that strays from the central topic does not belong in the paragraph and needs to be revised or deleted. Consider the following paragraph about honor in the world of *1 Henry IV*. Notice how the paragraph veers away from the main point that honor is presented as a questionable value in the play:

> In *1 Henry IV*, Shakespeare presents honor as a questionable value, and the pursuit of honor is not shown as always being virtuous or a good thing, rather as motivated by a desire for power. Honor is difficult to define. Honor probably has something to do with power. And everybody in *1 Henry IV* wants power. The fight between Hotspur and Glendower, after all, is the result of Hotspur's refusal to grant that Glendower really has the supernatural power that he boasts of possessing. Glendower maintains that at his birth the heavens were on fire. That seems to mean that there was a raging storm, with thunder and lightning. Hotspur thinks Glendower's boast is ridiculous and that his

> birth had nothing to do with the kind of weather there was on that day. He scoffs at it. Glendower is a funny character. His language is very high blown and pompous. It is very realistic that someone like Hotspur should clash with him. Hotspur is very down to earth. He is impulsive in his behavior and a great soldier who puts his own honor above everything. That makes the contest between Hotspur and Prince Hal even greater, because it is ultimately about who will be England's ruler, Hotspur or Prince Hal. It is a contest for ultimate power. When Hal defeats Hotspur and kills him, then Hal has won honor because he has proved his power in mortal combat.

Although the paragraph begins solidly, and the opening sentence provides the central idea of the paragraph, the author soon goes on a tangent. If the purpose of the paragraph is to demonstrate that the pursuit of honor is not shown as a virtue, the sentences about Hotspur's quarrel with Glendower are at best tangential here, and the sentences about combat between Prince Hal and Hotspur, although they might be more to the point, are undeveloped and unfocused. The matter in regard to Glendower may find a secondary place later in the paper, but it should be deleted from this paragraph, and the point about combat needs to be refocused in order to illustrate the thesis.

Coherent Paragraphs

In addition to shaping unified paragraphs, you must also craft coherent paragraphs, paragraphs that develop their points logically with sentences that flow smoothly into one another. Coherence depends on the order of your sentences, but it is not strictly the order of the sentences that is important to paragraph coherence. You also need to craft your prose to help the reader see the relationship among the sentences.

Consider the following paragraph about the value of honor in *1 Henry IV.* Notice how the writer uses the same ideas as the paragraph above yet fails to help the reader see the relationships among the points.

> Falstaff's dismissal of honor as something to strive for makes a lot of sense. It can be contrasted with the devotion to honor that we see in Prince Hal and

in Hotspur. All honor finally leads to is death. And what good is that? Even if you die heroically and earn a great reputation, you are not around to enjoy that reputation. Look at what Percy says about being food for worms when he dies. He can't even finish his sentence. Prince Hal has to finish it for him. Once he's dead, even Hal forgets about him. He does not even care that Falstaff claims to have killed him. Hotspur has become a worthless corpse. Besides, Falstaff says, reputation does not last very long. So it's like a tombstone, which people forget about and only visit now and then. Honor can't achieve anything positive. It can't heal an injury, and it belongs to the dead. The point is reinforced when Falstaff sees Sir Walter Blunt lying dead on the battlefield. Moreover, his point is worth considering when he says that "There's not three of my hundred and fifty left alive," of his men. That does not reflect well on him, but it does not really work to contradict his argument. No one expects Falstaff to be honorable. The play shows that valiant soldiers as well as the raggedy kind that Falstaff has recruited get "peppered." So in the end, it does not matter. Falstaff just does more openly what everyone does. He may not value honor, but he represents honesty.

This paragraph demonstrates that unity alone does not guarantee paragraph effectiveness. The argument is hard to follow because the author fails both to show connections between the sentences and to indicate how they work to support the overall point.

A number of techniques are available to aid paragraph coherence. Careful use of transitional words and phrases is essential. You can use transitional flags to introduce an example or an illustration (*for example, for instance*), to amplify a point or add another phase of the same idea (*additionally, furthermore, next, similarly, finally, then*), to indicate a conclusion or result (*therefore, as a result, thus, in other words*), to signal a contrast or a qualification (*on the other hand, nevertheless, despite this, on the contrary, still, however, conversely*), to signal a comparison (*likewise, in comparison, similarly*), and to indicate a movement in time *(afterward, earlier, eventually, finally, later, subsequently, until)*. But be careful that you use these tags appropriately, that when you say, *nevertheless*, for example, you really are adding something that is valid despite something you just have said that seems to indicate otherwise.

In addition to transitional flags, careful use of pronouns aids coherence and flow. If you were writing about *The Wizard of Oz*, you would not want to keep repeating the phrase *the witch* or the name *Dorothy*. Careful substitution of the pronoun *she* in these instances can aid coherence. A word of warning, though: When you substitute pronouns for proper names, always be sure that your pronoun reference is clear. In a paragraph that discusses both Dorothy and the witch, substituting *she* could lead to confusion. Make sure that it is clear to whom the pronoun refers. Generally, the pronoun refers to the last proper noun you have used.

While repeating the same name over and over again can lead to awkward, boring prose, it is possible to use repetition to help your paragraph's coherence. Careful repetition of important words or phrases can lend coherence to your paragraph by reminding readers of your key points. Admittedly, it takes some practice to use this technique effectively. You may find that reading your prose aloud can help you develop an ear for effective use of repetition.

To see how helpful transitional aids are, compare the paragraph below to the preceding paragraph about the importance of honor in *1 Henry IV*. Notice how the author works with the same ideas and quotations but shapes them into a much more coherent paragraph whose point is clearer and easier to follow.

```
Falstaff's dismissal of honor as something worth striving
for makes sense. Although Falstaff himself is far from
being the embodiment of honor, nevertheless, what he
says about honor cannot but affect a reader's attitude
toward it. Honor, Falstaff says, is only "a word." It
gives a person nothing. It cannot heal a wound or offer
consolation for grief. Only the dead have honor, and they
cannot enjoy it, he says. Their reputation, after their
death, moreover, quickly fades. Consequently, honor,
Falstaff says, is an uncertain monument, depending on
the fickle memory and disposition of the living. This
observation is confirmed in the death of Hotspur. As
```

he is dying, Hotspur says his loss of honor to Prince Hal pains him more than his loss of life, but then he adds that he is "dust, / And food for. . . ," but death prevents him from finishing the sentence. Prince Hal finishes it for him by saying, "for worms." And then Hal adds: "Ill-weaved ambition, how much art thou shrunk!" He notes that when Percy was alive, "a Kingdom" was not big enough for him, "but now two paces of the vilest earth / Is room enough." As if in confirmation of how insignificant Percy has become, despite the honor he had earned in life, Hal does not even protest when Falstaff, typically taunting Hal, falsely claims to have killed him. Hotspur has become a worthless corpse. Similarly, when Falstaff sees the corpse of Sir Walter Blunt on the battlefield, he says, "There's honor for you." He refers to death as "grinning honor." The objection that Falstaff is himself far from an honorable character, however true, does not, in itself, render his negative reflections about the pursuit of honor false. If Falstaff, for example, is responsible for the death of ill-equipped soldiers, war itself, not Falstaff, bears the ultimate responsibility for the deaths of all the soldiers, the worthy as well as Falstaff's "rag of muffins." Falstaff gives voice to what a concern for honor prevents others from saying. He many not value honor, but he represents honesty.

Similarly, the following paragraph from a paper on Richard's feelings of inferiority and exclusion in *Richard III* demonstrates both unity and coherence. In it, the author argues that at the same time that Richard's first soliloquy shows how he intends to take revenge on others for his deformities and for his consequent exclusion from the pleasures and rewards of society through the exercise of cruelty and cunning, it also introduces Richard as a captivating character whose psychology is as dramatically compelling as his actions.

By opening *Richard III* with a 41-line soliloquy, Shakespeare gives the play an added dimension, a psychological depth. Shakespeare presents a portrait of Richard that allows him to charm the audience watching the play almost as effectively as he charms all the persons within the play. Even as the spectators realize Richard is cunning, evil, and dangerous, he is insinuating his way into their sympathies because he is fascinating. He is more interesting than anyone else who appears in the play, and he makes everyone else interesting because of what he does to them and how he drives them to respond to him. Richard, in other words, is a consummate actor who brings the passions of the others to life as he bends them to his will and destroys them. His opening soliloquy presents, explores, and accounts for this destructive power, as it also reveals its peculiar charm. It shows how Richard's personality, his moral deformity, which is manifest in his wicked pursuit of power, is rooted in his physical deformity. "I . . . am not shaped for sportive tricks," he says, after describing the pleasurable pastimes of peace that now may be enjoyed at the court by erstwhile warriors and their ladies. He is ugly, he says, and "Not made to court an amorous looking glass." This is not only his courtly way of saying that he has no pleasure in looking at himself in the mirror because what he sees is his misshapen body, he also personifies the mirror and gives it the capacity to feel. It is an "amorous looking glass." The mirror will not give him love. He conceives of the mirror not only as it reflects him; he makes it represent what he feels to be the world's attitude toward him. The mirror rejects him. With biting honesty, Richard proceeds to anatomize himself. He is ugly, dwarfed, lame, "curtailed . . . cheated of good feature . . . deformed, unfinished . . . scarce half made up." As he used the mirror to represent the world's reaction to him, Richard also uses the reactions of dogs to him to represent how he feels about himself. He is so repulsive "that dogs bark at me as I halt by them." When he sees his own shadow, he says, all he is moved to do, like the mirror and the dogs, is to notice his own ugliness. He is obsessed with his own ugliness and with a self-pity and self-hatred that he turns against everybody else. Since he feels excluded from love and fellowship and cannot enter into the joys of the world and gain recognition for himself—"since I cannot prove a lover/To entertain these fair well-spoken days"—he is "determined to prove a villain and hate the idle pleasures of these days." He will exclude instead of be excluded. With this psychological foundation laid down, his spite and self-hatred revealed from the start, Richard then begins the action of the play by telling the spectators about the plot he has hatched against his brother.

Introductions

Introductions present particular challenges for writers. Generally, your introduction should do two things: capture your reader's attention and explain the main point of your essay. In other words, while your introduction should contain your thesis, it needs to do a bit more work than that. You are likely to find that starting that first paragraph is one of the most difficult parts of the paper. It is hard to face that blank page or screen, and as a result, many beginning writers, in desperation to start somewhere, start with overly broad statements. While it is often a good strategy to start with more general subject matter and narrow your focus, do not begin with sweeping statements such as Everybody at some time or other in his or her life has felt excluded. Such sentences are nothing but empty filler. They begin to fill the blank page, but they do nothing to advance your argument. Instead, you should try to gain your readers' interest. Some writers like to begin with a pertinent quotation or with a relevant question. Or, you might begin with an introduction of the topic you will discuss. If you are writing about the importance of the opening soliloquy in *Richard III*, for instance, you might begin by talking about why, at first glance, the introduction might seem unnecessary. Another common trap to avoid is depending on your title to introduce the author and the text you are writing about. Always include the work's author and title in your opening paragraph.

Compare the effectiveness of the following introductions:

1. Richard is power mad. That is obvious from everything he does. Power is about action, and the play is full of action. That is what makes it exciting. Anything that slows down the action, therefore, ought to be eliminated for dramatic effect so that the audience can feel the excitement of the story and how Richard claws his way to the crown. So it is a really good question to ask why Shakespeare would waste the opening minutes of the play with a soliloquy of more than 40 lines where one character is alone on the stage just talking to himself.

2. The need to have power and to exercise it without check and as one pleases is generally regarded as so fundamental and so common a human characteristic that it hardly seems to need explanation. Consequently, its presentation on the stage as the subject of a drama hardly needs justification. Similarly, the propensity for human cruelty and self-centeredness is so widespread, and instances are so readily available both historically and in everyone's daily experience, that such behavior, too, hardly elicits any need for explanation. It does not appear, therefore, that there is any dramatic necessity for Shakespeare to have begun *Richard III* with Richard's mischievous and brooding opening soliloquy, "Now is the winter of our discontent."

The first introduction begins with a true, but obvious sentence and pretends to substantiate it by offering the same idea in other words. It continues with several shaky and unsubstantiated assertions and finally arrives at a weak statement of the thesis as a question. Notice, too, how a reader deprived of the paper's title does not know the title of the play that the paper will analyze. The second introduction works with the same material and thesis but provides more detail and is consequently much more interesting. It begins by offering solid social and psychological observations and moves logically to the statement of the thesis, which includes both the author and the title of the work to be discussed.

The paragraph below provides another example of an opening strategy. It begins by introducing the author and the text it will analyze, and then it moves on by briefly introducing relevant details of the story in order to set up its thesis.

Shakespeare's history play *1 Henry IV*, the second in a series of eight plays that trace the struggle for the English throne that was waged between several royal factions over the course of the fifteenth century and called the War of the Roses, examines and challenges the idea of honor. For King Henry IV; his son, Prince Hal; and the young Harry Percy, called Hotspur, one of the leaders of a rebellion against King Henry, the importance of honor is a driving force and a matter of life and death. King Henry covets honor. He wants to be the focus and recipient of honor both as a king and as a father. In both instances, however, he feels himself to be on shaky ground. He became king by toppling his predecessor, Richard II, and was complicit in his murder. As a father, he is slighted rather than honored. His son, Hal, the prince of Wales, the heir to his throne, rather than honoring him with his love and obedience, spends most of his time in a tavern with dissolute companions. Although the prince declares in his first soliloquy that he "will awhile uphold" his "unyoked humor," in other words, that he will continue his wild behavior a little longer and that he plans ultimately to cast it off so that when the time comes he will shine more brightly in his subjects' eyes, nevertheless, Hal seems ambivalent in regard to the pursuit of honor. He seems to be forcing, by an act of will, his sense of royal duty to overcome a fundamental inclination. Hotspur has no such ambivalence but eagerly seeks to be, as one of his allies in the rebellion calls him, "the king of honor." Falstaff, Hal's tavern companion, also has no ambivalence in regard to honor. He dismisses it with contempt, calling it a "mere scutcheon," a decoration given to the dead. He will have none of it and prefers life. If Falstaff's repudiation does not entirely subvert the value of honor in 1 Henry IV, it does, nevertheless, seriously call Hotspur's, Hal's, and King Henry's idealization of honor into question.

Conclusions

Conclusions present another series of challenges for writers. No doubt you have heard the adage about writing papers: "Tell us what you are going to say, say it, and then tell us what you've said." While this formula does not necessarily result in bad papers, it does not often result in good ones, either. It will almost certainly result in boring papers (especially boring conclusions). If you have done a good job establishing your points in the body of the paper, the reader already knows and understands your argument. There is no need merely to reiterate. Do not just summarize your main points in your conclusion. Such a boring and mechanical conclusion does nothing to advance your argument or interest your reader. Consider the following conclusion to the paper about the effect of physical deformity on Richard III's character and career:

In conclusion, Shakespeare has drawn a picture of a spiteful man bent on destroying everyone else because he feels that he has been left out. His physical deformity is one thing. Many people suffer from one handicap or another. But many people overcome a limitation without becoming bitter and wishing to punish others because of it. But in Richard, Shakespeare has given us a man who has fallen into the trap of becoming bitter. In consequence, what was, as bad as that is, at first a physical deformity—which, by the way, did not prevent Richard from doing all the destructive things he did—became a moral deformity. That is his tragedy.

Besides starting with a mechanical transitional device, this conclusion does little more than reiterate the main points of the outline (and it does not even touch on all of them). It is incomplete and uninteresting (and a little too moralistic).

Instead, your conclusion should add something to your paper. A good tactic is to build upon the points you have been arguing. Asking "why?" often helps you draw further conclusions. For example, in the paper on *Richard III* you might speculate or explain how opening with a soliloquy by Richard in which he describes his mental and emotional state affects the way audiences view the rest of the play. What is the effect of making the audience Richard's confidant? Another method for successfully concluding a paper is to speculate on other directions in which to take your topic by tying it into larger issues. You might do this by envisioning your paper as just one section of a larger paper. Having established your points in this paper, how would you build upon this argument? Where would you go next? In an alternate conclusion to the paper on *Richard III*, the author might recall some of the main points of the paper, for example, Richard's Machiavellian cunning and hypocrisy and his address to the audience, in order to consider how such manipulation functions in Shakespeare's other history plays—for example, in Prince Hal's soliloquy at the end of act 1, scene 2 in *1 Henry IV* or how Shakespeare uses it in the tragedies of *Othello* and *King Lear,* where Iago and Edmund are fascinating diabolical figures who, like Richard, speak engagingly to the audience:

In these 41 lines, Shakespeare does more than just effectively deal with the problem of narrative exposition and set the scene for the action that follows. He gives a psychological portrait of his villainous hero. By doing so, he gives the story a special focus and a strong center. By transforming the story from a historical chronicle into a psychological study, Shakespeare directs the focus of the play away from a narrative that many spectators or readers can find hopelessly confusing and possibly tedious in its pileup of atrocities. He involves the spectators in the narrative by making the way Richard influences history through his villainous machinations and the sufferings they produce the center of concern because of the opening soliloquy. That it is Richard himself who offers that psychological self-analysis, rather than one of the other characters talking about him, makes him an even more fascinating character. He is fascinating just because Shakespeare has made him a repulsive character who is, nevertheless and paradoxically, attractive. Taking the spectators into his confidence makes the spectators—to the degree that they are charmed by Richard, to the degree that they are enthralled by Richard's crafty insights and by the cunning operation of his mind, to the extent that they wish to see Richard practice his diabolical art—his victims, too, as well as complicit in his villainies, as many of the characters in the play are. Even against their wills, they are charmed by him, subdued by him, or even brought to the heights of despair and the depths of self-defining grief as he practices his cruelty on them.

Similarly, in the following conclusion to a paper on honor in *1 Henry IV,* the author draws a conclusion about what the play is saying about honor more broadly, extending an examination of the way Shakespeare uses the theme of honor in several of his other history plays:

Although at first glance *1 Henry IV* seems to be a heroic argument in praise of honor, the subversive message underlying the two coming-of-age stories that dominate the plot, Hal's and Hotspur's, as Falstaff reveals in his catechism on honor, is that the pursuit of honor is a pursuit of power, vanity, and death. It involves slaughter, whether the slaughter of others or of one's own inclinations, rather than nurture. Shakespeare continues to explore the contradictions inherent in the concept of honor and apparent in the pursuit of honor that he examines in *1 Henry IV* in *Henry V*. *Henry V* can be read as an even stronger homage to patriotism and honor than *1 Henry IV*. In it, Prince Hal, now King Henry V, with a ragged band of English soldiers and a series of brilliantly stirring speeches, defeats the French at the battle of Agincourt and secures the English claim to France. Like *1 Henry IV*, *Henry V* seems to glorify battle and the pursuit of honor, but scattered throughout are images and examples of the heartlessness and suffering that war entails and the brutality it engenders. Of great significance, too, is that Shakespeare has given the heroic action of *Henry V* a Machiavellian overture at the conclusion of *2 Henry IV*. In Henry IV's dying speech to Hal, he advises him that the best way to ensure the security of his possession of the crown is to find a foreign war to fight. *Henry V* is the story of that war, ostensibly fought for the glory of England but actually contrived to ensure the reign of Henry V. Once Henry has conquered France, and after his death, English political strife breaks out again and, beginning in *1 Henry VI*, the lust for power rises to the surface and swamps any idea of honor.

Citations and Formatting

Using Primary Sources

As the examples included in this chapter indicate, strong papers on literary texts incorporate quotations from the text in order to support their points. It is not enough for you to assert your interpretation without providing support or evidence from the text. Without well-chosen quotations to support your argument, you are, in effect, saying to the reader, "Take my word for it." It is important to use quotations thoughtfully and selectively. Remember that the paper presents *your* argument, so choose quotations that support *your* assertions. Do not let the author's voice overwhelm your own. With that caution in mind, there are some guidelines you should follow to ensure that you use quotations clearly and effectively.

Integrate Quotations

Quotations should always be integrated into your own prose. Do not just drop them into your paper without introduction or comment. Otherwise, it is unlikely that your reader will see their function. You can integrate textual support easily and clearly with identifying tags, short phrases that identify the speaker. For example:

> He is so repulsive, he says "that dogs bark at me as I
> halt by them."

While this tag appears before the quotation, you can also use tags after or in the middle of the quoted text, as the following examples demonstrate:

> "I . . . am not shaped for sportive tricks," he says,
> after describing the pleasurable pastimes of peace that
> now may be enjoyed at the court by erstwhile warriors
> and their ladies.

> Although the prince declares in his first soliloquy
> that he "will awhile uphold" his "unyoked humor," that
> he will continue his wild behavior a little longer and
> that he plans ultimately to cast it off so that when the
> time comes he will shine more brightly in his subjects'
> eyes, nevertheless, Hal seems ambivalent in regard to
> the pursuit of honor.

You can also use a colon to introduce a quotation formally:

> Hotspur's thirst for glory is obvious: "O, would the
> quarrel lay upon our heads, / And no man might draw
> short breath today / But I and Harry Monmouth!"

When you quote brief sections of poems (three lines or fewer), use slash marks to indicate the line breaks in the poem:

> Since he feels excluded from love and fellowship, cannot
> enter into the joys of the world and gain recognition
> for himself—"since I cannot prove a lover / To entertain
> these fair well-spoken days"—he is "determined to prove
> a villain / And hate the idle pleasures of these days."

Longer quotations (more than four lines of prose or three lines of poetry) should be set off from the rest of your paper in a block quotation. Double-space before you begin the passage, indent it 10 spaces from your left-hand margin, and double-space the passage itself. Because the indentation signals the inclusion of a quotation, do not use quotation marks around the cited passage. Use a colon to introduce the passage:

Falstaff makes clear his doubts about the value of honor and his reluctance to pursue honor in his battlefield meditation on honor:

> Can honor set to a leg? no: or an arm? no: or take away the grief of a wound? no. Honor hath no skill in surgery, then? no. What is honor? a word. What is in that word honor? What is that honor? air. A trim reckoning! Who hath it? he that died o' Wednesday. Doth he feel it? no. Doth he hear it? no. 'Tis insensible, then. Yea, to the dead. But will it not live with the living? no. Why? detraction will not suffer it. Therefore I'll none of it. Honor is a mere scutcheon: and so ends my catechism.

However impressed a reader might have been with Hal or Hotspur and their quests for honor, Falstaff's speech cannot but cause some doubt about just how much value ought really be attached to pursuing honor.

The very opening lines of Richard's soliloquy show that he is a master rhetorician and brilliant ironist:

> Now is the winter of our discontent
> Made glorious summer by this sun of York;
> And all the clouds that lour'd upon our house
> In the deep bosom of the ocean buried.
> Now are our brows bound with victorious
>   wreaths;
> Our bruised arms hung up for monuments;
> Our stern alarums chang'd to merry meetings,
> Our dreadful marches to delightful measures.
> Grim-visag'd war hath smooth'd his wrinkled
>   front;
> And now,—instead of mounting barbed steeds

```
To fright the souls of fearful adversaries,—
He capers nimbly in a lady's chamber
To the lascivious pleasing of a lute.
```

```
Shakespeare immediately establishes that whatever other
power Richard has or lacks, he clearly commands the
power of words.
```

It is also important to interpret quotations after you introduce them and explain how they help advance your point. You cannot assume that your reader will interpret the quotations the same way that you do.

Quote Accurately

Always quote accurately. Anything within quotations marks must be the author's exact words. There are, however, some rules to follow if you need to modify the quotation to fit into your prose.

1. Use brackets to indicate any material that might have been added to the author's exact wording. For example, if you need to add any words to the quotation or alter it grammatically to allow it to fit into your prose, indicate your changes in brackets:

    ```
    "Why, Percy I killed myself, and saw thee
    [Falstaff] dead."
    ```

    ```
    He is so repulsive, he says "that dogs bark at
    [him] as [he] halt[s] by them."
    ```

2. Conversely, if you choose to omit any words from the quotation, use ellipses (three spaced periods) to indicate missing words or phrases:

    ```
    "I . . . am not shaped for sportive tricks," he
    says.
    ```

    ```
    He is ugly, dwarfed, lame, "curtailed of  . . .
    fair proportion / Cheated of feature  . . . /
    Deformed, unfinished . . . scarce half made up."
    ```

3. If you delete a sentence or more, use the ellipses after a period:

> In defense of himself, Falstaff says: "But to
> say I know more harm in him than in myself,
> were to say more than I know. . . . If to be
> fat be to be hated, then Pharaoh's lean kine are
> to be loved."

4. If you omit a line or more of poetry, or more than one paragraph of prose, use a single line of spaced periods to indicate the
   omission:

> Now is the winter of our discontent
> Made glorious summer by this sun of York;
> And all the clouds that lour'd upon our
>   house
> In the deep bosom of the ocean buried.
> . . . .
> Our bruised arms hung up for monuments;
> Our stern alarums chang'd to merry meetings,
> Our dreadful marches to delightful measures.

Punctuate Properly

Punctuation of quotations often causes more trouble than it should.
Once again, you just need to keep these simple rules in mind.

1. Periods and commas should be placed inside quotation marks,
   even if they are not part of the original quotation:

> The first line of Richard's opening soliloquy,
> "Now is the winter of our discontent," plays
> with ambiguity because the line ending and the
> ending of the sentence are not the same

The only exception to this rule is when the quotation is followed by a parenthetical reference. In this case, the period
or comma goes after the citation (more on these later in this
chapter):

```
Richard grabs our attention by saying "Now is
the winter of our discontent" (1.1.1).
```

2. Other marks of punctuation—colons, semicolons, question marks, and exclamation points—go outside the quotation marks unless they are part of the original quotation:

```
Why does Falstaff say: "'Tis no sin for a man to
labor in his vocation"?
```

```
After Worcester tells the king, he has "not
sought the day of this dislike," Henry rebukes
him by demanding, "How comes it then?"
```

Documenting Primary Sources

Unless you are instructed otherwise, you should provide sufficient information for your reader to locate material you quote. Generally, literature papers follow the rules set forth by the Modern Language Association (MLA). These can be found in the *MLA Handbook for Writers of Research Papers* (sixth edition). You should be able to find this book in the reference section of your library. Additionally, its rules for citing both primary and secondary sources are widely available from reputable online sources. One of these is the Online Writing Lab (OWL) at Purdue University. OWL's guide to MLA style is available at http://owl.english.purdue.edu/owl/resource/557/01/. The Modern Language Association also offers answers to frequently asked questions about MLA style on this helpful Web page: http://www.mla.org/style_faq. Generally, when you are citing from literary works in papers, you should keep a few guidelines in mind.

Parenthetical Citations

MLA asks for parenthetical references in your text after quotations. If you were working with prose (short stories, novels, or essays), you would include page numbers, in the parentheses, from the text you are citing, as in this example from John Steinbeck's story "The Chrysanthemums":

```
Henry's effort with Elisa is clear: "You've got a strong
new crop coming" (2).
```

When you are quoting poetry or prose from Shakespeare's plays, include line numbers:

```
Hal notes that when Percy was alive, "a Kingdom" was
not big enough for him, "but now two paces of the vilest
earth/Is room enough." (5.4.86-91)
```

Works Cited Page

These parenthetical citations are linked to a separate works cited page at the end of the paper. The works cited page lists works alphabetically by the authors' last name. An entry for the above reference to Shakespeare's *1 Henry IV* would read:

```
Shakespeare, William. Henry IV, Part One. New York:
    Signet, New American Library, 1965. 148.
```

The *MLA Handbook* includes a full listing of sample entries, as do many of the online explanations of MLA style.

Documenting Secondary Sources

To ensure that your paper is built entirely upon your own ideas and analysis, instructors often ask that you write interpretative papers without any outside research. If, on the other hand, your paper requires research, you must document any secondary sources you use. You need to document direct quotations, summaries or paraphrases of others' ideas, and factual information that is not common knowledge. Follow the guidelines above for quoting primary sources when you use direct quotations from secondary sources. Keep in mind that MLA style also includes specific guidelines for citing electronic sources. OWL's Web site provides a good summary: http://owl.english.purdue.edu/owl/resource/557/09/.

Parenthetical Citations

As with the documentation of primary sources, described above, MLA guidelines require in-text parenthetical references to your secondary sources. Unlike the research papers you might write for a history class, literary research papers following MLA style do not use footnotes as a means of documenting sources. Instead, after a quotation, you should cite the author's last name and the page number:

> "Empson sees Falstaff as a potential mob leader" (Bloom 294).

If you include the name of the author in your prose, then you would include only the page number in your citation. For example:

> Harold Bloom is clear about his admiration for Falstaff: "Critics regularly have called Sir John one of the lords of language, which beggars him: he is the veritable monarch of language, unmatched whether elsewhere in Shakespeare or in all Western literature" (294).

If you are including more than one work by the same author, the parenthetical citation should include a shortened yet identifiable version of the title in order to indicate which of the author's works you cite. For example:

> Harold   Bloom   points   out   that   "Shakespeare's contemporaries did not moralize against Falstaff, who immediately became the most popular of all Shakespearean characters" (Introduction, STA, xii).

Similarly, and just as important, if you summarize or paraphrase the particular ideas of your source, you must provide documentation:

> Falstaff is a mixture of elements. Readers can find things to admire in him without respecting him. Readers can disapprove of him, but it is hard to dislike him. He can always provoke laughter (Johnson, Notes, STA, 59).

Works Cited Page

Like the primary sources discussed above, the parenthetical references to secondary sources are keyed to a separate works cited page at the end of your paper. Here is an example of a works cited page that uses the examples cited above. Note that when two or more works by the same author are listed, you should use three hyphens followed by a period in the subsequent entries. You can find a complete list of sample entries in the *MLA Handbook* or from a reputable online summary of MLA style.

WORKS CITED

Bloom, Harold. *Shakespeare: The Invention of the Human.* New York, NY: Riverhead Books, 1998.

———. "Introduction." *Bloom's Shakespeare through the Ages. Henry IV, Part I,* Neil Heims, volume editor. New York: Infobase Publishing, 2008.

Johnson, Samuel. "Notes on Shakespeare's Plays." *Bloom's Shakespeare through the Ages. Henry IV, Part I,* Neil Heims, volume editor. New York: Infobase Publishing, 2008.

Plagiarism

Failure to document carefully and thoroughly can leave you open to charges of stealing the ideas of others, which is known as plagiarism, and this is a very serious matter. Remember that it is important to include quotation marks when you use language from your source, even if you use just one or two words. For example, if you wrote, Falstaff is the monarch of language, you would be guilty of plagiarism, since you used Bloom's distinct language without acknowledging him as the source. Instead, you should write: Falstaff can make words do whatever he likes. He is "the monarch of language," and it is evident whenever he speaks (Bloom 294). In this case, you have properly credited Bloom.

Similarly, neither summarizing the ideas of an author nor changing or omitting just a few words means that you can omit a citation. Maynard Mack's introduction to the Signet edition of *1 Henry IV* contains the following passage about Shakespeare's use of English history in writing the play:

The reconciliation of Prince and King touched on in the chronicles and dramatized briefly in the Famous Victories as occurring in Henry's later years, he moved forward to a position before Shrewsbury, in order to enhance the human drama of father and son and further sharpen our anticipation of Hal's meeting with Hotspur.

Below are two examples of plagiarized passages:

> Shakespeare moved the renewal of friendship between Prince Hal and his father to an earlier period of time than history indicated so that it could happen before the Battle of Shrewsbury. He did this in order to exploit the drama of a reunion between a father and son and to give added excitement to Prince Hal's encounter with Hotspur.

> Shakespeare moved the reconciliation between Prince Hal and King Henry forward so that it could happen before Hal's meeting with Hotspur at Shrewsbury in order to enhance the drama of a father and son reconciling and in order to increase the excitement we feel about this upcoming encounter (Mack xxx).

While the first passage does not use Mack's exact language, it does list the same ideas he proposes as the reasons for Shakespeare's changes in the actual historical time sequence without citing his work. Since this interpretation is Mack's distinct idea, this constitutes plagiarism. The second passage has shortened his passage, changed some wording, and included a citation, but some of the phrasing is Mack's. The first passage could be fixed with a parenthetical citation. Because some of the wording in the second remains the same, though, it would require the use of quotation marks, in addition to a parenthetical citation. The passage below represents an honestly and adequately documented use of the original passage:

> According to Maynard Mack, Shakespeare "moved" "the reconciliation between Prince [Hal] and King [Henry]" that is "touched on in the chronicles and dramatized briefly in the Famous Victories . . . forward to a position before Shrewsbury" so that he could "enhance the human drama" of the father/son relationship and create a sense of "anticipation" about Hal's encounter with Hotspur (Mack xxx).

This passage acknowledges that the interpretation is derived from Mack while appropriately using quotations to indicate his precise language.

While it is not necessary to document well-known facts, often referred to as "common knowledge," any ideas or language that you take from someone else must be properly documented. Common knowledge generally includes the birth and death dates of authors or other well-documented facts of their lives. An often-cited guideline is that if you can find the information in three sources, it is common knowledge. Despite this guideline, it is, admittedly, often difficult to know if the facts you uncover are common knowledge or not. When in doubt, document your source.

Sample Essay

Raymond McCarthy
Mr. La Fonte
English II
April 2, 2010

HONOR AS A VALUE IN *1 HENRY IV*

Shakespeare's *1 Henry IV* is the second in a series of eight history plays—chronologically, although not in the order of its composition—that Shakespeare wrote between 1589 and 1599. These plays trace the struggle for the English throne that was waged between two royal factions throughout most of the fifteenth century. That long conflict was called the War of the Roses because one faction, the House of York (to which Richard III belonged), chose a white rose for its emblem and the other faction, the House of Lancaster (to which the Henrys belonged), chose a red rose for theirs. As it recounts an unsuccessful rebellion against King Henry IV, *1 Henry IV* examines and challenges the idea and the value of honor. For King Henry IV; for his son, Prince Hal; and for the young Harry Percy, called Hotspur, one of the leaders of the rebellion, the attainment of honor is a driving force and a matter of life and death. King Henry covets honor. He wants to be the focus and recipient of honor both as a king and as a father. He wishes to present himself to his subjects as an honorable man, and he is in quest of further honor.

To that end, he vows, as the play begins, to lead a crusade against the "pagans" (1.1.24) in the Holy Land. He also wishes to enjoy the gratification that a father experiences in learning of his son's honor and to be honored by his son. In both instances, however, he feels himself to be on shaky ground. He became king by toppling his predecessor, Richard II, and was complicit in his murder. As a father, he is slighted rather than honored. His son, Hal, the prince of Wales, the heir to his throne, rather than being the recipient of honor and honoring his father with his love and obedience, spends most of his time in a tavern with dissolute companions and a surrogate father, Sir John Falstaff. Although the prince declares in his first soliloquy that he "will awhile uphold" his "unyoked humor," (1.2.199-200)—that he will continue his friendship with unsavoury companions and pursue his wild behavior a little longer and that he plans ultimately to cast it off so that when the time comes for him to assume the power that he clearly does desire, he will shine more brightly in his subjects' eyes—nevertheless, he seems ambivalent in regard to the pursuit of honor. Hal seems to be forcing himself, by an act of will, to live up to his sense of royal duty and to overcome a fundamental rebellious inclination. Yet, he seems, too, to be disgusted with himself for that inclination to deviate from the pursuit of honor and turns that disgust angrily against Falstaff in act 2, scene 4, lines 444-481, in the scene where he, Hal, playing the role of his own father, reproaches and abuses Falstaff, who is playing the prince. Hotspur has no such ambivalence but eagerly seeks to be, as Douglas, one of his allies in the rebellion against King Henry IV, calls him, "the king of honor" (4.1.10). He dreams of "pluck[ing] bright honor from the pale-faced moon" or "div[ing] into the bottom of the deep" and "pluck[ing] up drowned honor" so that he "might wear / Without corrival all [honor's] dignities" (1.3.200-205). Falstaff, Hal's tavern companion, also has no ambivalence when it comes to honor. He dismisses it with contempt, calling it a "mere scutcheon" (5.1.140), that is, a decoration given to the dead. He will have none of it and prefers life. If Falstaff's repudiation does not entirely subvert the value of honor in *1 Henry IV*, it does, nevertheless, seriously call Hotspur's, Hal's, and King Henry's idealization of honor into question.

Falstaff's dismissal of honor as something to strive for makes sense. Although Falstaff himself is far from being a recognizable embodiment of honor or any other commonly esteemed virtue, nevertheless, what he says about honor cannot but affect a reader's attitude toward honor. Honor, Falstaff says, is only "a word" (1.1.134). It gives a person nothing. It cannot heal a wound or offer consolation for grief or deaden the perception of pain. Only the dead have honor, and they cannot enjoy it, he says. Their reputation, after their death, moreover, quickly fades. Consequently, honor, Falstaff says, is an uncertain monument, depending on the fickle memory and disposition of the living. This observation is confirmed in the death of Hotspur. As he is dying, Hotspur says that his loss of honor to Prince Hal pains him more than his loss of life, but then he adds that he is "dust,/And food for . . ." (5.4.85), but death prevents him from finishing the sentence. Prince Hal finishes it for him by saying, "for worms" and adds perfunctory praise calling him "brave" and "great heart." But despite his honor, Percy is reduced to nothing, and Hal adds: "Ill-weaved ambition, how much art thou shrunk!" He notes that when Percy was alive, "a Kingdom" was not big enough for him, "but now two paces of the vilest earth / Is room enough" (5.4.86-91). As if in further confirmation of how insignificant Percy has become, despite the honor he had earned in life, Hal hardly protests when Falstaff, typically taunting Hal, totes Percy's corpse on his back, claims to have killed him himself, and reproaches Hal for lying when Hal says, astonished, "Why, Percy I killed myself, and saw thee [Falstaff] dead" (5.4.142). Hotspur has become a worthless corpse. Similarly, when Falstaff sees the corpse of Sir Walter Blunt on the battlefield, he says, "There's honor for you" (5.3.33-34). He refers to death as "grinning honor" (5.3.59). The objection that Falstaff is himself far from an honorable or an honored man, however true, does not, in itself, render his negative reflections about the pursuit of honor false. If Falstaff, for example, is to be blamed for the death of the poor lot of soldiers that he led into battle and for being cavalier about their death, war itself, not Falstaff, bears the ultimate responsibility for the deaths of those, as of all soldiers, the worthy as well as Falstaff's "rag of muffins" (5.3.36). All commanders lead their troops into battle with a sure knowledge that death awaits them, and pious incantations about the honor of the fallen do nothing to restore them to life. In his "catechism" (5.1.141) against honor, Falstaff gives voice to what a concern for their honor, careers, or station in society prevents other captains from saying. He may not value honor, but he represents honesty.

Although at first glance, 1 Henry IV seems to be a spectacle offering an argument by examples in praise of honor, the subversive message underlying the two coming-of-age stories that dominate the plot, Hal's and Hotspur's, as Falstaff reveals in his "catechism" against honor, is that the pursuit of honor is actually a desire for power, vanity, and death. The pursuit and practice of honor involves slaughter, whether the slaughter of others or of one's own lively inclinations, rather than nurture. Falstaff affirms this when he sees what he calls "grinning honor" on the face of the battlefield corpse of Sir Walter Blunt and says, "Give me life" (5.4.58-59). Nor can anything make the absurdity of honor clearer than Hotspur's giddy pledge as he prepares for the dubious battle with King Henry: "Doomsday is near. Die all, die merrily" (4.1.133).

Shakespeare continued to explore the contradictions inherent in the concept of honor and apparent in the pursuit of honor that he examined in *1 Henry IV* in *Henry V*. *Henry V* can be read as an even stronger homage to patriotism, heroism, and honor than *1 Henry IV*. In it, Prince Hal, now King Henry V, with a ragged band of English soldiers and a series of brilliantly stirring speeches, defeats the haughty French at the battle of Agincourt and secures the English claim to France. Like *1 Henry IV*, *Henry V* seems to glorify battle and the pursuit of honor, but scattered throughout are images and examples of the heartlessness that war demands, the suffering that it exacts, and the brutality that it engenders and on which it thrives. Of great significance, too, in arguing that the celebration of honor is suspect in *Henry V*, is the fact that Shakespeare has given the heroic action of the play a Machiavellian overture. At the conclusion of *2 Henry IV*, in King Henry IV's dying speech to Hal, the king advises his son that the best way to ensure the security of his possession of the crown is to find a foreign war to fight. It will deflect the energy of criticism at home away from him and harness that energy in a patriotic wish for his victory over a common enemy. *Henry V* is the story of that war, ostensibly fought for the glory of England but actually contrived to ensure the reign of Henry V and the continuance of the House of Lancaster. Once Henry has conquered France and after his death, English political strife breaks out again and, beginning in *1 Henry VI*, the clawing lust for power rises to the surface. In the renewed conflict between the Houses of York and Lancaster, the exigencies of power erase any coloring of honor.

WORK CITED

Shakespeare, William. *Henry IV, Part One*. Maynard Mack, volume editor. New York: Signet, New American Library, 1965.

HOW TO WRITE ABOUT SHAKESPEARE'S HISTORIES

PEOPLE HAVE been writing about Shakespeare for more than 400 years. The amount being written, over that time, has not diminished. Each generation seems to find itself reflected in Shakespeare, and every generation seems to find Shakespeare, as it understands him, relevant to its own times and contemporaneous concerns. In addition, every generation seems to find that approaches to Shakespeare that have preceded its own must be challenged, or defended, or revised. Consequently, each generation seems to find still more to write about Shakespeare's work and about what has previously been written about Shakespeare's work than its predecessors.

The earliest critical words written about Shakespeare appeared in 1592 as an allusion in a pamphlet by Robert Greene, an actor and playwright associated with a group of literary men and scholars called University Wits who were schooled at Oxford and Cambridge universities. Greene introduced Shakespeare to the world of commentary as "an upstart crow, beautified with our feathers, that, with his Tygers heart wrapt in a Players hide, supposes he is as well able to bumbast out a blanke verse as the best of you; and being an absolute Johannes Factotum, is in his owne conceit the onely Shake-scene in a countrie." Greene not only offers in "Shake-scene" a contemptuous pun on Shakespeare's name, but the first time there is a mention of Shakespeare in print, he is associated with his history plays. The denigrating phrase, "Tygers heart wrapt in a Players hide" suggests York's invective against Margaret, the line from Shakespeare's *3 Henry VI*, 1.4.137: "O tiger's heart wrapp'd in a woman's hide!" In December of the same year, three months after Greene's death, Henry Chettle, the publisher and printer of Greene's testy pamphlet, *A Groatsworth of Wit*, issued a public apology for the pamphlet and repudiated Greene's attack. The long conversation about Shakespeare in writing had begun.

In 1598, Frances Meres published *Palladis Tamia, Wits Treasury*, a commonplace book he kept. A commonplace book is a kind of diary. In it, Meres noted that he had seen several plays by Shakespeare. Among them he lists *Richard II* and *Richard III*, *King John*, and *1 Henry IV*. Twenty-five years later, in 1623, and seven years after Shakespeare's death in 1616, two of Shakespeare's friends and fellow actors in his troupe, the King's Men, John Heminge and Henry Condell, published the First Folio, a collection of Shakespeare's plays. Dedicatory matter prefacing this seminal publication included testimony from Shakespeare's contemporary, the poet and playwright Ben Jonson.

Little was written about Shakespeare for the rest of the seventeenth century. The theaters were shut down by the Puritans in 1642 and remained closed until 1660, when the English monarchy was restored and Charles II returned from exile in France and assumed the English throne. When the theaters were reopened, it was on a different world from the one for which Shakespeare had written. One significant change was that women were permitted on the stage and men no longer took women's parts; but the change in taste went further than that. Heroic spectacles and fashionable comedies of manners predominated. Shakespeare was generally regarded as old-fashioned. When his plays were presented, they were usually entirely or partially revised or rewritten to suit the times.

In 1692, the first official critical writing about Shakespeare appeared with the publication of Thomas Rhymer's *A Short View of Tragedy*. In it, Rhymer dismissed *Othello* as a "bloody farce." In 1709, Nicholas Rowe published "Some Account of the Life &c. of Mr. William Shakespear" as an introduction to his edition of Shakespeare's plays, *The Works of Mr. William Shakespear*. Inaccurate as the biography has proved to be, it exerted great influence on how generations of writers and readers thought about Shakespeare's life. Rowe's edition of the plays is noteworthy for his introduction of act and scene divisions to the original texts.

While Shakespeare's plays continued to hold the stage in revised or distorted forms that reflected the tenor, stage technology, and sensibilities of the times, critics and editors turned their attentions to the original texts, trying to make sense of obscure or heavily altered passages through interpretation, emendation, and interpolation, explicating the plays, and focusing on themes, characters, motives, dramatic devices, historical events, Elizabethan printing practices, and events from the purported biography of Shakespeare himself. At the same time, a lively written criticism of Shakespeare's plays grew and multiplied. Like the stage practitioners, the critics, too, reflected the spirit of their times in their criticism and, as a result, influenced succeeding views of Shakespeare's plays. As Harold Jenkins wrote in 1951 in the introduction to *Shakespeare Survey* 6, "the nineteenth century's conception of [the ten English history plays] was in some measure the result of its predilection. For an age of industrial and commercial progress, of growing nationalisms and imperialist expansion, the most obvious thing about Shakespeare's history plays was their expression of a national spirit. Together they formed an 'immortal epic' of which England was the true protagonist." A survey of what has been written about Shakespeare includes a survey of the greatest names in letters, among them Samuel Johnson, Samuel Taylor Coleridge and August Wilhelm von Schlegel, as well as encounters with writers who would remain entirely unknown had they not written about Shakespeare.

"What," a student faced with the task of writing about Shakespeare might demand, "can I possibly write about, after 400 years of so many people saying so much about Shakespeare?" The answer is simpler than might be expected. Write about what interests you. The secret to discovering what interests you as a writer is finding what interests you as a reader. That means paying careful and lively attention as a reader to what you are reading. You do not have to approach reading Shakespeare as if you were reading a foreign language. Not only will such a view prevent you from being able to enjoy reading a play, but you will have to strain just to begin to understand it. You should not expect to "get" everything on the first or even on the third reading of a particular play. Shakespeare is multidimensional and inexhaustible and offers new and various riches with each of our encounters, but he is not aloof. What we get from Shakespeare depends, moreover, as much on what we bring to Shakespeare as what is in Shakespeare. He grows as we age. The more complex or nuanced our view of the world becomes, the more complex we recognize his to be. To be a good reader, to pay careful and lively attention, means to believe in yourself as a reader, to trust your responses as you read, and to let yourself be surprised, puzzled, or enraptured by what you read.

We have been trained as readers and as viewers to respond to narrative suspense. "What happens next?" is a question that keeps a reader turning pages. For most readers and viewers, plot is the most important element. Something has to happen. Plot, after all, is important. The opposite of suspense perhaps is contemplation. While suspense propels us forward and makes us yearn for revelation and resolution, contemplation holds us in place by the presence of something absorbing enough to prompt pause and consideration. Contemplation is an aesthetic experience. It focuses our attention on the aspects of whatever is before us, allowing us to trace its beauties, puzzle over its mysteries, examine its unity, and appreciate its complexity.

The unfolding present, in Shakespeare, as in all literature, is composed of words, phrases, and sentences. What is special about Shakespeare and a few other masters of literature is that these elements can form environments of their own, within the overall environment of the entire work, within which we can dwell and contemplate. Consider two examples that are by no means among the greatest examples of Shakespeare's writing and are not taken from Shakespeare's greatest plays. Begin with the opening line of *1 Henry VI:*

Hung be the heavens with black, yield day to night!

The function of a first line usually is to lead to the second line; but not here. The perplexing and ambiguous syntax demands that the reader stay put. "Hung be the heavens with black." Does that mean the heavens are hung with black? Is this an image of the sky that compares it to a room that has been darkened by black curtains? Grammatical analysis suggests there is something more. This is a command implied as well: *let* the sky be covered in black. The second part of the line authorizes this reading. It is an injunction. Something like a prayer or an invocation is being uttered, a demand being made: Let the heavens be hung with black and let day yield to night. Who is making this demand? The text indicates someone named Bedford. Who he exactly is the reader does not yet know. Why is he making this invocation? Again, it is not clear. All the reader knows for certain at this point is a tone, one of gloom, grief, despair, and darkness: "Hung be the heavens with black, yield day to night!" The following lines,

> Comets, importing change of times and states,
> Brandish your crystal tresses in the sky,

seem to offer no more information than the first, but the syntax has become more straightforward. The person who has called for the heavens to be dark now invokes comets, calling on them to appear in the sky, and he paints the picture of their flight across the heavens by describing their trails of light as "crystal tresses," as diamond strands of hair. Within the tableau of these three lines, there is, nevertheless, an indication of movement. Comets indicate "change of times and states," where the word *states* refers both to nation-states, like England, and to conditions, like, we will learn, the death of a king. The word *brandish* suggests the threatening motion of a sword being waved. This sense is, indeed, realized in the fourth line:

> And with them scourge the bad revolting stars.

The comets' crystalline strands of hair are ordered to scourge like swords, to whip the stars, which are characterized as "bad" and rebellious. What began as the moody rendering of a disturbed night sky has now become a call for a clash of elements, for an elemental conflict. The fifth line gives the reason. The stars, as the astrological determinants of earthbound events, "have consented unto Henry's death!" Bedford's speech ends with the revelation that England's heroic king, Henry V, has just died. What we are reading is a dirge or a funeral oration.

As the dirge continues, the speaker changes from Bedford to Gloucester, a figure equally undefined for the reader as Bedford, but the reader understands now that she is reading a dirge for a dead king, a lamentation for his loss and a celebration of his greatness. Intermixed with the glorious language of tribute are actual details of Henry's life, particularly his victories over the French. Between lines 32 and 33, however, there is a dramatic shift in the nature of what is being presented in the text or on the stage. At line 32, Winchester, one of the mourners, says in tribute, "The Church's prayers made him so prosperous." A viewer, unlike a reader, would see that Winchester is wearing the garments of a bishop. In line 33, Gloucester, who is dressed like a lord, although he is undoubtedly carrying his staff of secular office indicating his role as protector, responds,

> The church! where is it? Had not churchmen pray'd,
> His thread of life had not so soon decay'd:

This passage suggests the churchmen had some culpability in the death, desired it perhaps. This is no longer a dirge for the dead king but an argument, a jockeying for authority between two of his survivors, between ecclesiastical and secular powers. Gloucester continues with this accusation:

> None do you like but an effeminate prince,
> Whom, like a school-boy, you may over-awe.

Here he intimates that the churchmen have an eye on gaining civil power and favor a weak king, like the infant Henry VI, rather than a strong monarch like Henry V. Winchester counters, identifying his interlocutor as protector of the realm, with a set of accusations of his own:

> Gloucester, whate'er we like, thou art Protector,
> And lookest to command the Prince and realm.
> Thy wife is proud; she holdeth thee in awe,
> More than God or religious churchmen may.

They continue their quarrel and, as they do, reiterate historical information that would be familiar to an Elizabethan audience, that the death of Henry V brings to the throne his infant son and, consequently, a struggle for power between factions belonging to the church and the nobility. This conflict ushers in a period of bloody civil war in England that comes to be known as the War of the Roses. Thus a reader absorbed in the language that opens the play can realize the dramatic shift from dirge to conflict and see the stage being set for the bloody contentions that will be the subject of the three *Henry VI* plays and *Richard III*. A reader familiar with the *Henry VI* plays will recognize Winchester's remarks about Gloucester's wife, Eleanor, as the prelude to a plot against Gloucester. That plot succeeds, in *2 Henry VI*, in toppling him from his office. A writer interested in discussing several of the history plays might examine how events or remarks in one play are foreshadowed by events or remarks in another or how accurately remarks in one play reflect conditions in another. Considering Gloucester's words about the church's preference for a weak king, a writer might examine the opening scenes of *Henry V* to see what was the actual relation between the bishops and the king at the time the play is set.

To explore another example, here are the opening lines of *King John*. Entirely expository, they stand in sharp contrast to the dirge that begins *1 Henry VI*. However, they, too, require the reader to figure out what is happening:

> *King John:* Now, say, Chatillon, what would France with us?
> *Chatillon:* Thus, after greeting, speaks the King of France
> In my behavior to the majesty,
> The borrow'd majesty, of England here.
> *Queen Elinor:* A strange beginning: 'borrow'd majesty!'
> *King John:* Silence, good mother; hear the embassy.

Here characters and their relationships are immediately identified. The courtier Chatillon is delivering a message sent from the king of France to the king of England. The words *borrowed majesty* convey the challenge to the English king's legitimacy, and, in case the reader has not noticed that particular phrase, Shakespeare has Elinor react to it. Here, contained in Elinor's line of dialogue are the major themes of a play in which a character called Bastard possesses the fullest degree of majesty of all the characters. What, in the world of the play, constitutes majesty? What constitutes legitimacy? John's response to Elinor gives the reader the further information that she is his mother in a play in which the maternity and the realm of mothers is of great concern.

While the opening of *1 Henry VI* may be, at first, too figural and allusive for a reader accustomed to forthright narrative to grasp what is happening, the opening of *King John* may be too spare. A careful reader of Shakespeare must adjust to the fact that narrative in Shakespeare is advanced through the drama of language rather than through simple exposition. Dramatic writing tells what is happening only by showing or presenting it as it is happening. One helpful way to approach any reading of Shakespeare is to give in to the text but not to strain for a close reading. As the Shakespearean scholar Thomas McFarland once remarked, like the pyramids, Shakespeare's texts can be looked at both up close and from a distance. Each perspective offers its own rewards, and each enriches the other. A good grasp of details contributes to an appreciation of the whole, and a good sense of the whole advances an appreciation of and concern for the details.

Look at the beginning of one other of Shakespeare's English history plays, in this case, one of Shakespeare's masterworks, *Henry IV, Part 1*. A reader cannot be faulted if she responds blankly to a first encounter with the opening address Henry IV delivers at court. The speech draws the reader immediately into the heart of the action, in the middle of events that are described with the king's rhetorical subjectivity. His speech seems eloquent, but it is also wordy and disjointed. He welcomes peace and calls for war. He says one thing and then unsays it. Is this deliberately murky or imprecise writing on Shakespeare's part or what? Only after at least one reading of the play will Henry's opening speech begin to make sense and will the reader be able to see how explicitly it fits his character and his purposes. Shakespeare's characters always speak from within a given context. Those contexts must be discovered and reconstructed through readings of the play. Still, an imprecise initial impression of Henry's speech ought not to keep a reader from noting and appreciating Henry's oratorical skill, even if the exact point and intention of his rhetorical style is not entirely evident in this or his successive utterances. In fact, rereadings of it will reveal that in all likelihood, in our first reading of Henry's speech, we read it as he intended it to be heard, without an awareness of his motives and manipulations, with just the naiveté he could wish in his hearers. So Shakespeare is not a murky or imprecise writer. He is rendering the complexity of political rhetoric and a politician's equivocations.

The first reading of a passage, scene, or play often yields that distant view of the pyramids McFarland referred to, an overall impression of the object of contemplation. We get only a general sense of what is occurring but know that as we read on our understanding will increase. The problems we encounter in understanding the play we are reading, the things that puzzle or challenge us as much as the things that please and interest us, become subjects for closer examination. One of the ways of closely examining a specific aspect of Shakespeare's plays is by writing about it, by focusing on a problem or a particular interest in a play and turning that isolated element into a thesis.

Writers discussing Shakespeare often look for themes, images, or characterizations that repeat and develop throughout the plays, seeing his work as a series or a set of themes and variations. Works can be regarded as variations of or responses to one another. The idea of theme and variation can be especially rewarding when applied to Shakespeare's English history plays because of their narrative and thematic interrelations. Of the 10 history plays, eight form a unified narrative and an ongoing meditation on such themes as loyalty, treachery, majesty, succession, war, and virtue. An understanding of each, thus, contributes to an understanding of the others.

Of the two plays that do not relate directly or sequentially to Shakespeare's other historical dramas, *King John,* the first chronologically, is furthest removed from the historical narrative of the English histories, and *Henry VIII,* the last chronologically of the histories, is outside the main historical narrative because, in it, the fundamental concerns related to the issues of power and succession are treated as if they are resolved. *Henry VIII* is a history play that suggests that English history has been resolved and that Henry governs in a posthistorical era. The eight plays that form the essence of the English histories, however, present a unified narrative beginning with *Richard II,* continuing through the two *Henry IV* plays, through *Henry V,* the three *Henry VI* plays, and culminating with the victory of Henry VII at the end of *Richard III.* Thus some of the difficulty a reader might have with Henry IV's opening words in *1 Henry IV* will be resolved if he or she is familiar with *Richard II,* the play that sequentially precedes it. In addition, a writer may choose not to confine herself to writing about only one play but might consider instead the evolution and development of the character of Henry IV from *Richard II* through *2 Henry IV.*

These eight plays swarm with characters, events, intrigues, plots and counterplots, enmities and alliances, wars and rebellions, orations, lamentations, heroism, cowardice, tragedy, comedy, loyalty, and betrayal. Beyond these similarities, these plays can be divided into two major sections. The first section is composed of the four plays beginning with *Richard II* continuing through the two *Henry IV* works and ending with

Henry V; the second includes the three *Henry VI* plays and *Richard III.* The plays of the second group, although they chronologically follow the plays in the first group, were written before the plays in the first group. The second group of plays, just because they are among Shakespeare's first works, are, more than the first group of works, chronicle plays, following and sometimes distorting the course of historical events and the actions of historical characters. They are not marked by the complex study of character, meaning, values, and identity that has come to define Shakespeare's work or by the unfathomable quality that Shakespeare's mature language achieved that allowed it to penetrate and to define human experience. Looked at in one way, the English histories trace the narrative of English history. Looked at in another way, the English histories construct a narrative of Shakespeare's development as a poet and dramatist.

Reading the eight plays in their historical order ought to help a reader follow the course of events and the growth of the characters. The king's opening speech in *1 Henry IV* will make more sense and have more resonance for a reader familiar with what the character undergoes in *Richard II.* The real advantage, nonetheless, will belong to the reader familiar with the two parts of *Henry IV* who then returns to the opening of the first part. Only then, for example, will the double irony of Henry's intention to go to Jerusalem become evident and the rationale of his rhetoric be revealed. Similarly, the opening of *1 Henry VI* will immediately bear more weight—if only because of the continuity or sense of narrative continuum that is created—to the reader who has just completed *Henry V.* The king that Bedford, Gloucester, Exeter, and Winchester are memorializing will still be vivid as well in the mind of the reader.

It seems unlikely if not imprudent that most readers of Shakespeare's English histories, and especially readers who have not read them a number of times, will choose to write about the entire group. It is probable that some readers will find it useful to trace certain themes or characters they find running through several of the plays. The ramifications of having recurring characters in multiple plays present one strong possible essay topic. Bolingbroke over the course of three plays becomes Henry IV. Prince Hal, over the course of three plays, changes from the apparently unruly prince into Henry V, the steadfast monarch who overwhelms the French with a small and ill-equipped army. Richard II, although he appears only in the play named for him, is more than once recalled in subsequent plays, and attitudes about his reign, his temperament, and his legitimacy are revisited and revised. Henry VI is a weak monarch whose indecisive presence defines the climate in which the events of his reign unfold. Richard, Duke of Gloucester, who ascends to the title Richard III in the play of that name, is first introduced in *2 Henry VI*. He is not only presented as his own independent entity in the work; he is also inescapably the son of Richard Plantagenet, Duke of York, who first appears in *1 Henry VI* and plays a significant part in the rivalries and conflicts that are the subject of the three *Henry VI* plays until his grim execution in act 1, scene 4 of *3 Henry VI*. Richard Plantagenet's father, Richard, Earl of Cambridge, in turn appears in *Henry V*, where he is ordered executed for treason by Henry before the king sails for France. It is with the Earl of Cambridge that the Yorkist quarrel with the House of Lancaster begins.

One of the qualities that makes a work of art identified as such is that it is a unified whole rather than a combination of disordered or unrelated utterances. It is always useful for a writer to show the unity and integrity of a work, and it is usually with that purpose in mind that writers argue for the place and importance of particular themes, patterns of imagery, nature of characters, or pervasive ideas and philosophies in a particular work. These elements unify a work of literature and show what diverse parts have in common or how those diverse parts work together to form something that has its own completeness and integrity. These elements can also span several works in order to give the impression of an organized and ordered sequence. The theme of loyalty and the idea of legitimacy, along with their opposites, the theme of treachery and the idea of illegitimacy or usurpation, are central to the English history plays and especially important in the eight plays from *Richard II* through *Richard III*. The imagery of blood runs through the three *Henry VI* plays and *Henry V*, suggesting the metaphors of lineage and violence. The question of what constitutes a legitimate king pervades all eight of the plays and *King John*.

Although the nature and the problems of romantic relationships or relationships between the sexes do not seem to be fundamental issues in the English history plays, nevertheless, a reader interested in tracing the variety of those relationships or the distribution of power as applied to gender might look at the relationship between the female characters and the men they are attached to: Richard II and his queen in *Richard II;* Hotspur and Kate in *1 Henry IV;* Falstaff and Doll Tearsheet in *2 Henry IV;* King Harry and Katherine of France in *Henry V;* the French king, Charles, and Joan of Arc and John Talbot and the Countess of Auvergne in *1 Henry VI;* Suffolk and Margaret and Henry VI and Margaret in the *Henry VI* plays; and Richard III and Anne and Richard and his mother in *Richard III.* Are there any generalizations about love, power, or gender-specific characteristics that can be drawn by examining, comparing, and contrasting these relationships? What is the significance of the relative absence of women in the plays? What is the picture presented in the plays of women's place and roles in the social order? Queen Margaret, as traced through the three *Henry VI* plays and *Richard III,* can provide a focal point for several essays, whether about treachery, cruelty, power, defeat, or how experience and fortune shape character.

After studying Shakespeare's English histories, a writer might choose to demonstrate that what serves most clearly to unite all 10 of them is not the narrative arc that ties most of them together but the way, taken together, they contribute to a philosophical exploration and contemplation of the meaning of kingship. A writer choosing such a topic can explore the concept of the ruler as it is presented in the plays, showing how Shakespeare examines the topic in a variety of aspects, from a vision of the king as God's proxy to the idea that the king is a man who has mastered the fundamentals of Machiavellian statecraft. To develop and enrich the discussion, a writer may find it useful to touch on a number of the themes that occupy Shakespeare in these plays, considering, among other problems, the nature of virtue, courage, cowardice, loyalty, masculinity, power, honor, glory, shame, brutality, and community or nationalism.

TOPICS AND STRATEGIES
Themes

Each of the history plays explores its own self-contained themes and thematic preoccupations. Given the historical continuum many of the history plays chart, naturally there are themes that a writer may find running through several, and sometimes all, of the works. It may be useful to examine how a theme highlighted in one play resonates in or is transformed by its treatment and handling in another work.

Sample Topics:

1. **Honor in the *Henry* plays:** The theme of honor is central to *1 Henry IV*. How significant is it in the Henry plays that follow?

   Referring to the way Shakespeare concentrates on honor in *1 Henry IV*, you might want to consider how Henry V is or is not a paragon of honor or how he uses the concept of honor rhetorically to advance his political and military agendas. Alternately, you might want to consider what happens to the idea of honor by the time the series comes to *Richard III*.

2. **Loyalty:** Like honor, loyalty is a complex value whose worth is determined by its object. How does Shakespeare explore and represent this quality in the history plays?

   What is the role of loyalty in the history plays? What are its several objects? You might consider Prince Hal's conflict, his loyalty divided between his father and Falstaff and interpret the meaning of that division. What is the impact of his divided loyalties on Hal as a character? What other characters are forced to choose sides or form an allegiance?

Character

Issues, themes, philosophies, and intrigues all are significant aspects of Shakespeare's histories, but for nearly all readers, characters predominate. Shakespeare leaves a reader primarily with a sense of his people, opening up any number of avenues for a thoughtful exploration of how characterization functions in the history plays.

Sample Topics:

1. **The presentation of Hotspur:** When Hotspur is onstage, in a play with such strong characters as Falstaff, Hal, and King Henry, he, nevertheless, manages to hold his own as a compelling character.

   To explain how Shakespeare accomplishes this, a writer might look at Hotspur's impulsiveness, his impatience, his sense of humor, his pride, and his speech patterns, particularly their peculiarities and how they are conveyed. All these are made apparent in the way he interacts with other characters and speaks of them.

2. **Richard III presented as a frightening villain:** Without the title character, *Richard III* would have no substance as a play. Richard is responsible for the play's past and present. In other words, he is responsible for the combination of misery and terror that define the play. He is himself frightening and the cause of fear in others.

To examine how Shakespeare makes him so frightening, a reader may study Richard's soliloquies, his interactions with others, and what others say about him. A reader can also move backward from *Richard III* and look not only at how Richard behaves in the preceding *Henry VI* plays but at how his father behaves and how he is treated. Another fruitful approach would be examining the paradox of Richard's charm and consider that his seductiveness is one of his most frightening aspects.

History and Context

In these works, historical context is a consideration that cannot be avoided. The plays taken together suggest that history has meaning, that it is shaped by human actors and their actions. Shakespeare's task in part was to take historical fact and to ground it within the reality of his play, the motives of the characters he has created and the situations and decisions they face.

Sample Topics:

1. **Richard II, Bolingbroke, Prince Hal, Henry VI, or Richard III as fashioners of historical context:** A writer may choose any one of these characters or another to consider the context in which history shapes and influences their characters as it forms their choices and opportunities and how they, by their dispositions and actions, in turn form history and direct its

course. It is not a matter of whether they ultimately succeed or fail but how they steer their course.

Writers may ask why Richard III is a "better" king than Henry VI, although arguably the worst example of a human being, or how Prince Hal's father and family history determined his character, or how the historical role of Hotspur's family's contributed to who he is, as represented in the plays.

2. **Context and intertexuality:** Each of the history plays is an account of a certain period of time, a work complete unto itself, presenting its own self-contained concerns and preoccupations. Given their historical subjects, however, the plays also form a continuum, a collective context each individual work can be seen as responding to.

A writer may consider any of the plays in relation, not in comparison, to any of the others. How, for example, does Henry IV reflect his youthful history as a usurper? How does Henry V reflect his youthful history as a rebellious son? How does Richard III reflect the consequences of his father's and his grandfather's deaths? What is the role of the church in the Henry plays?

Form and Genre

Despite being grouped in the general category of history plays, the individual works are formally various. A writer may consider how the form of a play contributes to its meaning and achieves its desired effects.

Sample Topics:

1. *Henry V* **as a pageant:** From its opening through its last lines, *Henry V* is presented as a pageant of English history.

How does the play use pageantry to glorify England? A writer may look at language and diction, at dramatic devices such as the Chorus, or at the national and regional composition of its characters. Is there any contrast in the way Shakespeare portrays the French and French history?

2. *1 Henry IV* **as comedy:** Although it continues the historical course established in *Richard II, 1 Henry IV* functions dramatically as a comedy, not least because of Falstaff's central if not overwhelming presence.

A student writing about the play as a comedy, of course, could focus on Falstaff and on what makes him a comic character and what his comic persona and commentary bring to the historical aspect of the play. Can a play be a history and a comedy as well or successfully reflect elements of each? Focusing on Hal or Hotspur can also be a useful strategy for an essay on this topic, for there are strong comic elements in each.

Language, Symbols, and Imagery

Characters, plots, themes, images—what are they but constellations of words arranged in particular patterns and rhythms yielding specific and sometimes multiple or ambiguous meanings? A work of literature is a deliberately arranged presentation of language. A play's script is a blueprint for the dramatization the actors will perform onstage by conveying the words and the gestures those words conjure to an audience.

Shakespeare's drama is a drama of poetry, of words that can penetrate below the surface of their manifest content to reveal dimensions of latent meanings and relationships. The history plays are made up of a language of symbols and images as well as of propositions, presumptions, and hypotheses.

Sample Topics:

1. Recurrences: Are there any words, images, symbols, or grammatical constructions that recur throughout several of the histories?

A writer might examine how Shakespeare uses a word like *blood* or *crown* or *horse* and how its meaning changes from one play to another or remains the same. How does the varying or consistent meaning of a specific term contribute to the way we understand and interpret a play or a group of plays?

2. **Language and the formation of character:** Characters are defined no only by what others say about them but how they use language to describe and represent themselves. The essence of performance in Shakespeare's plays is speech, what a character says and how she or he says it.

Writers might explore individual characters, examine their speech patterns, what they say, and how they speak to themselves and to others. Prince Hal is a potentially strong choice in this regard. He is master of several differing speech strategies. Hotspur, on the other hand, is a practitioner of only one. Richard III is also a master of linguistic shape-shifting or misrepresentation. Alternately, a writer may consider how Richard II develops in his speech to become the poet most readers think he is.

Compare and Contrast Essays

Shakespeare's histories can be defined as much by what they are not as by what they are. One of the ways of seeing what a play is or is not can be by comparing it to another play.

Sample Topics:

1. **Comparing *Richard II* through *Henry V* with the three *Henry VI* plays and *Richard III*:** The middle eight history plays are composed of two groups. The first group (*Richard II*, the two parts of *Henry IV*, and *Henry V*) was written after the second (the three *Henry VI* plays and *Richard III*) but precedes it chronologically. The second group, written first, historically precedes the first.

A writer may examine how these groups compare with each other as works in their complexity, in their sense of the relation of the individual to history and of history to the individual. An essay could also focus on the use of language in each cycle and how the historical record informs and dictates the course of the work.

2. Comparing *King John* and *Henry VIII* with the middle eight history plays: *King John* and *Henry VIII* fall outside the narrative framework of the eight middle histories. The first was produced relatively early in Shakespeare's career. The other comes at the end and may not have been entirely written by him.

Writers interested in considering these plays might compare them to one another as a way of seeing how Shakespeare looked on monarchy at the start and at the end of his career. A writer might also compare a work's dramatic structures, character portrayal, or use of language with any of the other histories.

Bibliography and Online Resources

Auden W. H. *"Henry VI, Parts One, Two, and Three,"* October 9, 1946. *"Richard III,"* October 16, 1946. In *Lectures on Shakespeare.* Ed. Arthur Kirsch. Princeton University Press, 2000. http://press.princeton.edu/chapters/s1_6910.html
(*Auden constructs readings of these four plays guided by the principle that "In the chronicle play, which is historical, not myth or fiction, the central interest is the search for cause and pattern, a depiction not merely of the event, but of the cause of it and its effect."*)

Dutton, Richard, and Jean E. Howard, eds. *A Companion to Shakespeare's Works, Volume II: The Histories.* Blackwell Publishing, 2005. Blackwell Reference Online. 31 August 2009 http://www.blackwellreference.com/public/book?id=g9781405136068_9781405136068
(*This is a collection of 22 essays analyzing individual history plays, groups of them, and important themes in and the historical events surrounding them.*)

Hoenselaars, Ton, ed. *Shakespeare's History Plays: Performance, Translation and Adaptation in Britain and Abroad.* Cambridge: Cambridge University Press, 2004.
(*Hoenselaars introduces the essays in this collection by noting that they "address the different attitudes to Shakespeare's English history plays in Britain and abroad, from the early modern period to the present day." He presents a survey of how the works were read and performed throughout Europe.*)

Howard, Jean E., and Phyllis Rackin. *"Engendering a Nation: A Feminist Account of Shakespeare's English Histories."* London and New York: Routledge, 1997. *(Howard and Rackin consider the scarcity of women in the histories and the roles of those who do appear as contributing to the idea of what the English nation ought to be and how women normatively ought to be regarded.)*

Saccio, Peter. *Shakespeare's English Kings: History, Chronicle, and Drama.* Oxford University Press, 2000. *(Saccio reads Shakespeare's histories with reference to the source material that Shakespeare consulted, written by the Tudor historians, and with reference to modern historical accounts of that period in an attempt to distinguish historical myths from facts and to clarify and sort out the issues and characters that the plays present.)*

Shakespeare Survey, Volume 6: *The Histories.* Ed. Allardyce Nicoll. Cambridge University Press, 1953. Cambridge Collections Online. Cambridge University Press. 08 September 2009 DOI:10.1017/CCOL0521064198.001
Shakespeare Survey, Volume 38: *Shakespeare and History.* Ed. Stanley Wells. Cambridge University Press, 1986. Cambridge Collections Online. Cambridge University Press. 07 September 2009 DOI:10.1017/ CCOL0521320267.001
(These two issues, beginning with criticism from 1900, feature a number of essays on the English history plays.)

Taylor, Gary. *Reinventing Shakespeare: A Cultural History from the Restoration to the Present.* Oxford University Press, 1991. *(Taylor surveys the way that Shakespeare was written about, thought about, and performed from the time of his death until the present.)*

Tillyard, E.M.W. *Shakespeare's English History Plays,* Chatto & Windus, 1944. *(Tillyard is known for having supplied a narrative arc to the English histories by considering them as an unfolding of a "Tudor Myth" that postulates the ·vents of English history following the deposition and murder of an ongoing process of punishment and expiation for that event.)*

KING JOHN

READING TO WRITE

*K*ING *JOHN*, believed to have been written sometime between 1594 and 1597, is among the least known of Shakespeare's plays. This fact could potentially recommend it all the more as the subject of a strong, incisive essay on an overlooked Shakespeare work. A close reading reveals the play to be a veiled indictment of the nature and practice of political power and a wry examination of the vicissitudes of political allegiances and the allegiance to politics and power. *King John* examines the maneuvers of the rulers and those around them who either propel or are caught in the operations of power and politics. Within the context of this general plotline, the play is difficult to characterize in terms of genre. Ostensibly a historical drama, it mixes historical narrative, comedy, tragic melodrama, and spectacle. There is a suggestion of the supernatural at work in the play, too, as curses and prophecies are fulfilled and retribution for guilt is effected. The tone of the play mixes malice with innocence, desperation with hope, sardonic irony with pathetic exhortation, and pity with horror. Rather than allowing its sharp shiftings to frustrate interpretation, a reader can profit by investigating the play's fluid nature. In beginning to think about the play and to find a topic, a writer approaching the work might ask how *King John* questions rather than celebrates conventional sources of political authority and the use of political power. How do the play's peculiarities, rather than serving to obscure it, help define the work?

King John does not closely resemble many of the esteemed tragedies Shakespeare produced in his lifetime. It does not have the compelling plots and characters of the great tragedies. Rather than coherence and unity, it seems to offer a scattering of set pieces: a mother's mad scene, the torture of a child, the clawing exchanges between Eleanor and Constance, Faulconbridge's sardonic commentaries on the action and characters of the play, and the king's agonizing death. The beauty and passion of romance, the drama of soul-wrenching confrontation, the intensity of tragedy, the richness of character, the rhythm of narrative, the subtle emotional coloring, and the intricate comic wit that define Shakespeare's dramatic writing are not to be abundantly found in *King John* in all their astonishing Shakespearean richness and fullness. Nor has *King John* the extraordinary poetry and prose that distinguish most of what Shakespeare wrote. The language can seem rhetorical, bombastic, and complicated. Characters declaim long, seemingly endless speeches and soliloquies. Why did Shakespeare choose this style over dialogue or briefer monologues?

Following the action of *King John* depends heavily on tracing the discursiveness and verbal wanderings of the characters. Conventionally, novels and short stories have narrators who unify the text, identifying the characters and describing the actions being recounted. Most dramas written after Shakespeare's time have stage directions, too, which can also give readers a sense of orientation and clarity. In the absence of these clarifying elements and verbal cues from the author, *King John* offers countless directions for exploring the nature of Elizabethan drama: finding points of light in the dark, unravelling the threads that make up the fabric of the play, finding connections between individual scenes, finding the life in a character who at first appears as only an amalgam of words. You need to know what is going on, who is doing what, what the issues are, and how they are handled by the people of the play and its author in order to formulate any kind of thesis about the play.

If, in your reading of *King John*, you think something is funny, strange, or tedious, trust yourself and your reactions. Perhaps it is meant to be. Consider, for example, act 2, scene 1. You may perhaps initially feel overwhelmed by the long and bombastic speeches as the two kings, John of England and Philip of France, each lay siege to the city of Angiers, in France. Each claims it, and each claims to be England's rightful king. Each king also threatens to destroy Angiers unless its citizens recognize him as their rightful sovereign. It is a perplexing problem and a double bind for the citizens: No matter which king they choose to accept, the other will be enraged. Rather than becoming the victims of the royal power clash, however, the citizens transcend it, pledging to yield to whichever power prevails over the other in battle. This is very near farce. The two armies fight; the result is a draw; the problem is no nearer resolution than before. When Faulconbridge, the Bastard (the natural son of the dead king, Richard the Lionhearted), suggests the two rulers unite to destroy Angiers and resume hostilities once the city is subdued, farce becomes absurdity. The proposal does not mark the episode's conclusion, however. When Hubert, the spokesman for the people of Angiers, hears the threat, rather than reacting in fright, he defies both kings and offers a fairy tale solution: Let the niece of the king of England marry the son of the king of France, he says, thereby joining the two powers in amity. The military encounter and all the bluster seem to have been for nothing. Instead, a happy ending takes the place of conflict. This sort of comedy is not what a reader was necessarily expecting. But is it really the absurdist comedy it seems; did Shakespeare intend the scene to be possibly or partially interpreted in that light?

Although there is no single unifying narrator in the work, as there would potentially be in a novel, to put events in perspective and guide the reader's response, there is the Bastard, Faulconbridge, who serves throughout the play as a choral figure as well as a dramatic presence. He is often a comic presence too. Yet, he is not a comic figure in essence. He is a rather intricately conceived character and one who suggests the depths of human portraiture that Shakespeare will go on to draw in his great comedies and tragedies. Perhaps disconcertingly, when Faulconbridge appears in the fourth and the fifth acts, he is no longer a vehicle for the sour wit he brings in the first three.

"Here's a stay," he says outside the walls of Angiers, commenting on the apparent resolution to the crisis over which monarch will claim the city. As if speaking for the reader, he describes what many a spectator may well be feeling after all the saber rattling and speechifying:

> Our ears are cudgell'd; not a word of his [Hubert's]
> But buffets better than a fist of France.
> Zounds! I was never so bethump'd with words
> Since I first call'd my brother's father dad.

> (2.1.464–67)

"Bethump'd with words"—that is possibly what the reader is feeling. "Since I first call'd my brother's father dad" or since he began to speak. This is Shakespearean language? Yes, and it is humorous in its apparent circumlocution, funny because of its verbiage and dissonance. Shakespeare is writing about a confrontation of kings, but he is not doing so using a grand or heightened literary style. What, a reader considering topics for a paper on *King John* might wonder, is the purpose of this intrusion of dissonance? An alert reader will realize that these words refer to Faulconbridge's own genealogy and that what appears to be circumlocution is actually concision. The man he had called father, since he is the bastard son of Richard the Lionhearted, who seduced his mother, was not his father but his brother's father. "Since I first called my brother's father dad" thus serves as comic relief after and commentary on the immediately foregoing action. The line also gives voice to an element that ties the parts of *King John* together and reinforces one of the play's recurring motifs: making a perplexing choice. The line recalls the events of the interlude in act 1, scene 1, when the bastard's actual lineage as Richard's son is established, comically, at the expense of his mother's reputation for virtue, and he must choose between two lineages and, consequently, two identities. As in the confrontation before the city of Angiers, between brother kings, over who is the city's legitimate ruler, so in the scene between the bastard Philip Faulconbridge and his (half) brother, the legitimate Robert, the problem of choosing between two claimants to legitimate authority is at issue.

In each case, the problem is settled by what is referred to as a *deus ex machina*. Literally, *deus ex machine* means "god from the machine." Greek tragedies sometimes ended by introducing the device of a god appearing onstage and, with divine authority and power, resolving a situation that was until his arrival insoluble. The term has come to suggest the intervention of a force independent of the facts of the dramatic circumstance that intervenes or is introduced to resolve an impossible conflict and break an impasse. The use of this dramatic trick in the first and second acts of *King John* accomplishes more, however, than merely tying the two acts together. It suggests that, without a new perspective, an existing narrow focus can only perpetuate conflict. The fairy tale solution that Hubert offers and that the kings accept is short lived. As if from nowhere, with no advance dramatic or narrative preparation in *King John*, the spell is broken, the alliance is challenged. The next impossible choice is introduced. Pandulph, the papal legate, enters at line 61 in the first scene of act 3, with no more warning than King Philip's exclamation: "Here comes the holy legate of the Pope." With no advance preparation, a new thread is woven into the plot: a conflict between Pope Innocent III and King John over John's defiance of the papal appointment of Stephen Langdon as archbishop of Canterbury. In the name of the pope, Pandulph demands the alliance between France and England be broken and that France engage in a holy war against England. As a result, the device of *deus ex machina* has been transformed into a *diabolus ex machina*. Rather than concluding the action of the play, the bedevilling Pandulph extends the action and complicates it by opening a new conflict between old rivals. Driving this renewed conflict is the ongoing theme of the struggle to establish authority and the problem of who has and what constitutes legitimate authority. A reader searching for topics to write about might begin by asking if in *King John* Shakespeare is not arguing that history is a series of perplexities that never ends.

TOPICS AND STRATEGIES

Once you have completed your reading or multiple readings of the text and feel you have some comfortable familiarity with *King John,* you might think about you own reactions, your own feelings about the play. Think about what you will potentially write about by sifting through your reactions and asking yourself broad questions that you can begin to narrow and refine. What elements of *King John* presented themselves to you most definitively? Topic headings and lists like the ones presented in this chapter can help you in that narrowing-down process. Which characters did you find most interesting? Which events? Were there any aspects of the play that made you laugh or cry or that aroused feelings of pity or horror? Did you find any ideas or attitudes overtly or implicitly expressed in *King John*? If so, what were they? Of particular importance: Did you notice any recurring elements in the play, even frequently used words? Identify such elements. They can lead you to see dominant themes or other unifying aspects and patterns.

The following suggestions can help you approach the play, bring it into focus, and provide some ways of reading that may help you begin to penetrate this underappreciated Shakespeare work.

Themes

As compelling as strong characters or a powerfully told story can be, the ideas a work expresses, the notions it rests on and embodies, can be just as fruitful avenues to explore in preparing and presenting an essay. The themes of a work—the ideas a work of literature advances, challenges, or sets against one another—also provide some of its primary unifying devices by lending its plot and characters a sense of context, broader implication, and meaning.

Sample Topics:

1. **Conflict:** History is, in general, a story of conflicts: between people; between institutions; between cities, states, and nations; between technologies; between beliefs and ideologies. Conflicts involve power struggles for possession, for property, titles, honor, domination, legitimacy, and authority. Conflict is a common theme in literature that can propel and define its essential action. In *King John,* conflict is basic to the play. It runs throughout and determines the course of the play and the attitudes of its characters.

   A writer can begin by showing that the play begins with a belligerent anticipation of an oncoming challenge. "What would France with us?" King John asks the French envoy, whose answer is a challenge to John's right to rule England. France "lays," according to the envoy, "most lawful claim / To this fair island and the territories" that he proceeds to list. Just as it has begun with the announcement of conflict, the play ends, after England has survived the assaults of Rome and France, with Faulconbridge's defiant declaration almost inviting conflict, "Come the three corners of the world / And we shall shock them." A writer may analyze *King John,* consequently, as an anatomy of conflict.

   A great conflict seldom exists without a host of related, satellite conflicts that it either generates. Examine the numerous conflicts that you note in *King John.* What are their similarities and differences? What defines each of the conflicts? They can manifest in a work in a number of ways: between people, as between Constance and Elinor; between nations, France and England; between authorities, secular or ecclesiastical. Or there are internal conflicts exclusive to a character, as when Hubert agonizes over his commission to blind Arthur. What seems to be at the root of these conflicts? What are their consequences? Does the play, overall, seem to have a point of view about these conflicts? Or are there several points of view expressed within it? Is the play in conflict with itself about the theme of conflict? Make a list of all the major characters. What seems to be the attitude of each in regard to conflict? What conflict or conflicts is he or she committed to? Both kings and both Faulconbridge brothers are first shown caught in conflict. Hubert several times is faced with conflicts and resolves them. What is Pandulph's attitude toward conflict? What is the conflict Blanch faces, and what is its effect on her?

2. **Treachery:** In 1911, the British poet John Masefield, writing about *King John,* argued in regard to its central thesis that "*King John* is an intellectual form in which a number of people with obsessions illustrate the idea of treachery." What is particularly useful to you as a writer on *King John* comes when Masefield elaborates on his thesis: "Perhaps the most interesting of [the illustrations of the idea of treachery] are those subtle ones that illustrate treachery to type, or want of conformity to a standard imagined or established."

In other words, Masefield is suggesting that treachery (or loyalty, for that matter) is not only interpersonal. It does not only relate to a transaction between individuals but can also signify a relationship between an individual and a principle, idea, or standard. For Pandulph, authority lies in the church; for the kings, in military might; for the Bastard, in noble blood and noble action; for Arthur, in love; for Hubert, in his conscience. A good essay on *King John* could argue that treachery to oneself and one's proper allegiances precedes treachery to others.

Character

Characters act and interact and express thoughts and feelings. In that way, they not only reveal aspects of themselves—and frequently of us— but also frame and present themes. Making a sharp distinction between the two categories or considerations of theme and character, in order to anatomize and facilitate the process of writing, while useful, can also become artificial. The theme of identity, for example—what constitutes identity and what are the foundations of identity—can be traced throughout *King John* by a study of the characters in *King John*. Despite the truth in the general critical consensus that the characters in *King John* are not among the most developed or humanly complex characters that Shakespeare ever presented, nevertheless, they are each vivid creations in possession of their own personalities, even as they remain types whose action or suffering is predetermined by their assigned roles.

Sample Topics:

1. **Constance:** Constance is an emblem of the grieving mother whose passion for conquest had blinded her to the grief of war, even after she had, at first, hoped to avoid war (2.1.44–49).

   Writing about Constance may, of necessity, involve writing about the perils of a mother's ambition for her son or the ironic pathos of the consequences of enthusiasm for war. Or it might show how her interest in her son's success puts her at odds with John's flinty, quarrelsome, and domineering mother, Elinor. Considering the two women, a writer may examine how much power Elinor really has and how it is exercised in comparison to Constance's. Or a writer may consider the importance of Constance as a figure in the play, recalling how it is her curse (3.1.13–21), after the engagement of Blanch and Lewis and immediately preceding Pandulph's entrance and announcement of the papal decree against John, that accomplishes her will and destroys the peace.

2. **Blanch:** Writing about Blanch surely will involve commenting on the divisions war inflicts on the human personality, as she laments at 3.1.253ff.:

I am with both: each army hath a hand;
And in their rage, I having hold of both,
They swirl asunder and dismember me.
Husband, I cannot pray that thou mayst win;
Uncle, I needs must pray that thou mayst lose;
Father, I may not wish the fortune thine;
Grandam, I will not wish thy fortunes thrive:
Whoever wins, on that side shall I lose
Assured loss before the match be play'd.

A writer can show that because she is equally bound to characters at war with each other, Blanch's identity is at one with her predicament. Apart from her situation, she has no other identity. Is there a sense of her as a person or a personality otherwise? A writer might consider what sort of personality she ought to be given, most likely by an actress playing her. Is she pathetic? Is she angry? What considerations ought to shape an actress's decision? If you have read or seen Shakespeare's *Antony and Cleopatra*, you may find a resemblance between Blanch and Octavia, Octavius Caesar's sister, and you might ask how Shakespeare's treatment of two women with such a similar grief changes over the course of a decade.

3. **The representation and development of character:** "Faulconbridge is the most interesting character in *King John*." In itself, that observation does not stand as a thesis. It is an opinion. To move from having an opinion to representing a thesis, a writer needs to ask, "What is it that makes Faulconbridge the most striking individual presence in *King John*?"

Sketching an informal outline might be a useful way to develop a response to that question and lay the foundation for a good essay. List the characteristics of Faulconbridge that make him noteworthy. Write down the things he does and says that make him distinctive. How is he presented to the reader that differentiates him from the other characters in the play? He seems to be the only character who has a sense of humor and a sense of perspective about himself. Additionally, he seems to be the only character who evolves, who decides to be one kind of person rather than another, as opposed to a person who simply shifts his allegiances or changes his policy, as others do in the play depending on political expediency. Even though he pledges himself to expediency, which he calls "commodity" in his soliloquy "Mad world! Mad kings!" starting at line 561 of act 2, scene 1, he does not ultimately pursue expediency. Instead, beginning at 4.3.140, in another soliloquy, after Arthur's death, he asserts,

> I am amazed, methinks, and lose my way
> Among the thorns and dangers of this world.
> . . . .
> The life, the right and truth of all this realm
> Is fled to heaven.

He steps forward and stands a little outside the action of the play, yet still in character, addressing himself and the spectators. Faulconbridge is aware of himself as an actor in a world that is his to evaluate as he chooses.

4. **Characters defined by their roles:** Pandulph is an identifiable personality, but his personality is the product of the characteristics he is made to embody and the role he is designed to play. He seems to be a two-dimensional character created to represent the power lust, manipulative techniques, contempt, and treachery of papal authority and ambition. Similarly, Arthur, the innocent victim of other people's striving for political power, has a personality determined by his victimization. An examination of Arthur, Pandulph, and Hubert can show how Shakespeare fashioned characters defined by their roles and fates rather than as authors of their own stories.

To what extent does such a hypothesis appear valid? To what extent, if any, do these characters transcend their roles? What sort of character is John? Does he have any depth, any existence beyond the role he is cast in? How do you regard his decision in the Faulconbridge brothers judgment scene? What does his agony at the end of the play suggest? Is Shakespeare simply playing to a popular taste of the time for ghastly spectacle, or is there something more being represented in his death throes? What does the kind of depiction of characters shown suggest about the view of history presented in *King John?*

History and Context

Shakespeare's history plays were not intended to be historically accurate portraits of the events and periods they present. They are dramas, not documentaries. They rely on and reflect historical persons and events, but they do not record history, nor are all the characters in the history plays actual historical figures. Nevertheless, the plays are rooted in English history. Consequently, a knowledge of English history and of the historical contexts in which the plays were performed can foster a reader's appreciation and understanding of them by revealing the plays' relations to their times and the ways the works offer commentary on their historical settings.

Although it is not the first of the 10 history plays that Shakespeare wrote, *King John* is, chronologically, the first in the series of those plays. King John's reign began in 1199. He died in 1216. In *King John,* Shakespeare does not include and never even alludes to the most famous and historically significant event of John's reign, the signing of the Magna Carta in 1215, one of the foundational documents in the evolution of constitutional democracy. In addition, there are only a few references to one of England's mythic historical figures, Richard the Lionhearted, the famous crusader and John's elder brother.

Sample Topics:

1. **Historical research into Richard's life and death and King John's conflict with his barons:** Some historical research about Richard's life and death or about King John's conflict with his barons over the division of powers that led to the signing of Magna Carta might provide the way to a strong topic on the interrelations of history and artistic license.

The play can be seen as commenting on an international identity crisis as embodied by King Richard, John's brother, an English king who spoke French but not English and spent little time in England before his murder but much of his time in France, in prison, and fighting battles in the Middle East as part of the Crusades.

A writer might also ask what Shakespeare accomplished by ignoring the signing of the Magna Carta, undoubtedly the most important event of John's reign. How does the omission reflect on Shakespeare's interest in history? A writer can explore how it suggests that, even when it comes to history, Shakespeare is concerned with the melodrama of internal torment and external conflict rather than with the evolution of forms of governance.

2. **Pandulph as the personification of the Roman Catholic Church:** The role of the papal legate, Pandulph, might lead a student to research the relations, agreements, and struggles between the papacy and the English monarchy, not only in John's time but up through Queen Elizabeth's reign, the monarch when *King John* was written and performed. It was under her father, King Henry VIII, that the tensions between the papacy and the monarchy came to a head.

How, a writer might ask, did the history of struggle between Rome and England affect the characterization and the role of Pandulph in *King John?* There was an actual, historical figure named Pandulph who was Pope Innocent III's legate to King John, but it is obvious that the man portrayed in the play is represented only in terms of his function, not in terms of his individuality.

3. **Torture in England:** The scene between Hubert and Arthur suggests that torture was practiced by the English monarchy. It was.

A student interested in the role of torture in Elizabethan England might look at the story of two of Shakespeare's contemporaries and fellow playwrights: Christopher Marlowe, who was murdered by Elizabeth's operatives, and Thomas Kyd, who was severely tortured by them for alleged atheist opinions. What are the implications of torture as represented in the play and as practiced in the historical record?

Philosophy and Ideas

Political power is the fundamental and propelling issue in *King John,* and closely associated with that notion is the idea of legitimacy. What gives power legitimacy, in *King John,* is almost a tautology. Power *is* legitimacy, or is it? Power is made legitimate by the ability to exercise it. Its authority is established often by the ability to mobilize and unleash overwhelming destructive force. *King John* shows that kind of power at work, but it also shows both how reluctant people are to summon power and the forces that can overcome that reluctance. Those forces are both interior and exterior. The power to achieve one's will is not only a function of physical strength.

The source of and right to power are repeatedly questioned in *King John.* "From whom hast thou this great commission, France, / To draw my answer from thy articles?" John demands at 2.1.109. At 3.1.77ff., he challenges Pandulph, demanding, "What earthy name to interrogatories / Can task the free breath of a sacred king?" and answers his own question, asserting defiance, "Thou canst not, cardinal, devise a name/ So slight, unworthy and ridiculous, / To charge me to an answer, as the pope." Then, at 5.6.4–5, Hubert returns Faulconbridge's question, "Whither dost thou go?" with this retort, "What's that to thee? Why may not I demand / Of thine affairs, as well as thou of mine?"

Sample Topics:

1. **The power of fear:** The role that Pandulph plays in causing war in *King John* shows that the power of inculcating fear can reside in the spiritual as well as the material realm. The pope's power of excommunication, contingent on the religious belief of the people and the fear of eternal damnation, is strong enough to subdue the king of France to the pope's will and later to frighten John into submission.

A student considering the power of fear can write about how Pandulph instills fear in seemingly powerful people by invoking yet higher authority. A student can consider how he accomplishes this and the role words play in affecting a person's disposition. A student may consider in this respect the power John gives to a prediction of his death. Drawing on these manifestations of the ability of words to provoke fear, a student may consider what *King John* has to say about the sources of actual power and the construction of power through the manipulation of language and symbols.

2. **The power of human sympathy, the questioning intellect, and natural events to undermine power:** In the play, power is mostly represented as a force that can subdue others either through brutality or the creation of fear. Although this is the dominant mode, the weakness of power is also revealed in *King John.*

How is the idea of tenderness, compassion, or pity introduced in 4.1, when Arthur overcomes Hubert, who is about to burn out his eyes? A writer can show how the paradoxical power of vulnerable, loving innocence can cut through to responsive compassion as it does in the case of Hubert. The scene presents an idea that runs counter to the dominant idea of the play.

Another threat to power is what is presented literally as shipwreck in *King John,* but a writer may consider the metaphorical use of shipwreck in the play. Both sides experience the calamity. Consider "Power, for all its pride and brutality, cannot be guaranteed to hold what it grabs" as the basis for an essay on *King John.*

The morality of power is also a question that concerns *King John.* How is it addressed by Faulconbridge in his first soliloquy? What does his self-mockery show about the ways self-interest affects and influences his view of power?

Language, Symbols, and Imagery

An analysis of the mode of communication between characters, of the way they speak to and about one another, can illuminate several aspects of *King John.* Much of the play is written in verse, but the verse is not lyrical, nor is it the kind of dramatic writing that probes the hidden dimensions of the human psyche where language and nonverbal sensation intersect. The language of the play is most often rhetorical and declamatory.

Sample Topics:

1. **Coercion through language:** Can you make a case that the characters are using a coercive language? Do they make speeches in order to bend others to their wills, in order to overwhelm and overcome other characters with bombast?

   You might choose speeches from among the major characters, from King John to Arthur, and from public utterances to prison cell pleadings. How do the setting and word choices influence a given speech's intended purpose?

2. **The use of decoration in language:** The rhetoric of *King John*, no matter who the speaker, is rich in decorative figures of speech or tropes. How does this mode or aspect of the play's language contribute to a greater understanding of the work overall? Here is a sampling of the main rhetorical tropes:

   1) "Though I will not practice to deceive, / yet, to avoid deceit, I mean to learn" 1.1.214–15
   2) "The peace of heaven is theirs that lift their swords / In such a just and charitable war" 2.1. 35–36
   3) "Peace be to England, if that war return / From France to England there to live in peace" 2.1.89–90
   4) "I trust I may not trust thee. . . Believe me, I do not believe thee" 2.2.7ff.
   5) "O then tread down my need, and faith mounts up; / Keep my need up, and faith is trodden down!" 3.1.141–42
   6) "And falsehood falsehood cures" 3.1. 203
   7) "Grief fills the room up of my absent child / Lies in his bed . . ." 2.3.93
   8) "That John may stand, then Arthur needs must fall" III. iii.139
   9) "But if you be afeard to hear the worst, / Then let the worst unheard fall on your head" 4.2.135–36

What do these various tropes suggest about the play? Several instances cited are paradoxes: 1, 2. Some are personifications: 3, 7. Some are chiastic, meaning they have an X-like structure: One side of the sentence is the mirror reflection or inverse of the other, as in 2, 3, 5, 8, and 9. Maurice Hunt, in "Antimetabolic *King John*," argues that the chiastic figures represent in miniature the dramatic structure of the play. Faulconbridge rises as John falls. What possibilities for defining the mood of the play can you find in the paradoxical utterances found in *King John?* How does the rhetorical construction of various utterances challenge political power, the apparent subject of the play? A question to ask in relation to Constance that can illuminate the underlying criticism of the values of the characters in the play is: If she personifies abstractions like grief, is she abstracting, even in her desperate love for him, the person of her son, denying him his actual humanity and turning him into a symbol? Look at her reply to him as Arthur tries to console her after the truce between France and England at Angiers deprives him of the monarchy—act 2, scene 2, 44ff.

Compare and Contrast Essays

A comparison between characters can serve to illuminate the nature of each individual and can help define the tensions that are at the dramatic and thematic heart of a play. Characters may also be contrasted in terms of their attitudes toward a similar conflict or problem.

Sample Topics:

1. **Comparative attitudes about loyalty to others:** Despite their ferocious differences, do Elinor and Constance have anything in common? Does Blanch's response to her plight reflect on them, or for that matter on others, like King John himself? She is torn because she is loyal to all the members of her family.

   Elinor, Constance, and John are selective in their allegiances. Blanch is not and cannot divide herself. Contrast Blanch with John. While she laments her divided loyalties, he has no qualms about murdering his brother's son and only regrets it when it shows itself to be politically inexpedient. Contrast Blanch with Pandulph. While Pandulph thinks only in terms of doctrine, power politics, and the abstract authority that the pope represents, Blanch is moved by human connections, not by political manueverings.

2. **Comparing Faulconbridge with Edmund and Iago:** How can Faulconbridge be read as a precursor to two of Shakespeare's greatest characters, Edmund in *King Lear* and Iago in *Othello?*

Consider Faulconbridge's power of self-reflection, self-analysis, and self-knowledge to Edmund's or Iago's. Contrast his sense of morality and the conclusions he comes to in regard to his role in the drama he finds himself in to that of the other character you choose. Consider how much of a role each plays in creating the drama the people around them are embroiled in.

3. *King John* and *Richard II:* Like *King John, Richard II* tells the story of one man's fall from power and another's rise. Compare and contrast these two history plays, probably written quite close to each other.

Although the trajectories that characters follow are similar, the nature of the characters and our involvement with them are quite different in each case. What makes that difference? What effect does that difference have on the nature, quality, and complexity of each play?

Bibliography and Online Resources for *King John*

Blanpied, John W. "Stalking 'Strong Possession' in *King John*." In *Time and the Artist in Shakespeare's English Histories*, pp. 98–119. Newark: University of Delaware Press, 1983.
(Sees King John *as "cautious, suspicious, coldly analytical," and "sardonic," a history play that does not glorify English history or give the audience a figure around which firmly to secure its patriotic or nationalist emotions.)*

Champion, Larry S. "'Confound Their Skill in Covetousness': The Ambivalent Perspective of Shakespeare's *King John*." *Tennessee Studies in Literature* 24 (1979): 36–55.
*(Argues that "*King John *appears to be the play in which Shakespeare commits himself to the development of [a] powerfully ambivalent perspective for his*

history plays, a perspective combining the elements of depth and breadth, of engagement and detachment, which will ultimately produce Henry IV *and* Henry V.*")*

Grennan, Eamon. "Shakespeare's Satirical History: A Reading of *King John."* *Shakespeare Studies* 11 (1978): 21–37.
(Reads King John *as a transitional work between the earlier* Henry VI *plays and the* Henry IV *plays and* Henry V, *"in which we as audience are vitally implicated in the issues of the stage world and can come to few or no historical conclusions regarding the substance and final meaning of that world.")*

Hobson, Christopher Z. "Bastard Speech: The Rhetoric of 'Commodity' in *King John."* *Shakespeare Yearbook* 2 (Spring 1991): 95–114.
(A close reading of Faulconbridge's "Commodity" speech, "Mad world, mad kings," arguing that, in it, Shakespeare subjects monarchy to an ethical critique.)

Hunt, Maurice. "Antimetabolic King John." *Style,* 34:3 (Fall 2000), pp. 380–401.
(Discusses the way rhetorical tropes in King John *reflect the dramatic structure of the play.)*

Kehler, Dorothea. "'So Jest with Heaven': Deity in *King John."* In King John: *New Perspectives,* edited by Deborah T. Curren-Aquino, pp. 99–113. Newark: University of Delaware Press, 1989.
(Argues that, in King John, *Shakespeare shows that "What matters in the end are not spiritual but military needs, not the soul's but the nation's survival through the common bond of patriotism. The need to worship . . . is dangerous when left unfulfilled. The Bastard's final speech provides an answer to that [need]. . . . Bellicose nationalism is the new faith in Shakespeare's vision of the modern political world.")*

Leggatt, Alexander. "Dramatic Perspective in *King John."* In *English Studies in Canada,* vol. III, no. 1, Spring 1977, pp. 1–17.
(Traces Faulconbridge's role from satirical commentator on events to patriotic spokesman and sees him as guiding the audience's attitude about the events of the play.)

Levin, Carole. "'I Trust I May Not Trust Thee': Women's Visions of the World in Shakespeare's *King John*." In *Ambiguous Realities: Women in the Middle Ages and Renaissance,* edited by Carole Levin and Jeanie Watson, pp. 219–34. Detroit: Wayne State University Press, 1987.
(Argues that "the women characters [in King John*] . . . are far more insightful of the world in which they live [than the men]. The women are also more honest, at least with themselves, than the male characters of the play.")*

Levine, Nina S. "Refiguring the Nation: Mothers and Sons in *King John*." In *Women's Matters: Politics, Gender, and Nation in Shakespeare's Early History Plays,* pp. 123–45. Newark: University of Delaware Press, 1998.
(Reads King John *in the context of the anxiety over succession in England in the 1590s since Elizabeth had no children; Levine argues that "King John suggests that when England is not figured exclusively in the monarch, a space opens up for the nation to reimagine itself in new and sometimes radical ways.")*

McAdam, Ian. "Masculine Agency and Moral Stance in Shakespeare's *King John*." *Philological Quarterly,* 86:1–2 (Winter-Spring 2007), pp. 67–95.
(Argues that in King John, *Shakespeare "catalyzes a debate about masculine agency and morality that . . . raises pressing issues in our current discussions of gender and political control, and of the nature of subjectivity.")*

Moore, Ella Adams. "Moral Proportion and Fatalism in Shakespeare: *King John,* and Conclusion." *Poet Lore* 8 (1986): 139–45.
(Argues that in the depiction of John, Shakespeare has abandoned the true historical model and devised a figure of tragic dimension.)

Rackin, Phyllis. "Patriarchal History and Female Subversion." In *Stages of History: Shakespeare's English Chronicles,* pp. 146–200. Ithaca, N.Y.: Cornell University Press, 1990.
(Suggests that "in King John, *the fathers and husbands are dead, reduced to the status of names in history books, and the mothers survive on Shakespeare's stage to dispute the fathers' wills and threaten their patriarchal legacies." Rackin also argues that "Shakespeare subjects the masculine voices of patriarchal authority to skeptical feminine interrogation.")*

Saeger, James P. "Illegitimate Subjects: Performing Bastardy in *King John.*" *Journal of English and Germanic Philology* 100, no. 1 (January 2001): 1–21. *(Contends that "The Life and Death of King John dramatizes a relationship between personal identity and political legitimacy.")*

Trace, Jacqueline. "Shakespeare's Bastard Faulconbridge: An Early Tudor Hero." In *Shakespeare Studies: An Annual Gathering of Research, Criticism and Reviews,* XIII, J. Leeds Barroll, ed., pp. 59–70. New York: Burt Franklin, 1980. *(Traces the historical sources of Shakespeare's nonhistorical Faulconbridge.)*

Vaughan, Virginia M. *"King John:* A Study in Subversion and Containment." In King John: *New Perspectives,* edited by Deborah T. Curren-Aquino, pp. 62–75. New York: Associated University Presses, Inc., 1989. *(Discusses the historical context in which* King John *is set.)*

King John
http://www.middle-ages.org.uk/king-john.htm

King John Lackland
http://www.nndb.com/people/198/000092919/

King John plot summary
http://www.wsu.edu/~delahoyd/shakespeare/kingjohn1.html

King John Was Not a Good Man
http://www.icons.org.uk/theicons/collection/magna-carta/biography/king-john

Silent film clip, 1899, *King John* death scene
http://www.youtube.com/watch?v=Yr7T4Jn8WgQ

RICHARD II

READING TO WRITE

*R*ICHARD *II* is the first in a series of eight plays that trace the story of the English monarchy from the reign of Richard II (1377–99) through the fall of Richard III (1483–85). Although written in 1595, around the same time as *King John,* in tone, structure, theme, depiction of character, and treatment, *Richard II* differs greatly from that play, although the subject of both is a struggle between two forces for sovereignty over England. *King John* is a patchwork of disparate episodes and a melange of jarring linguistic strategies: Speech is deliberately cast as rhetoric and bombast, and identity is an external characteristic that is determined by one's place in a power hierarchy. *Richard II* presents a unified, deliberately constructed narrative describing the intersecting arcs of one man's fall and one man's rise. It is set entirely in verse, much of it lyrical. Character is not simply determined by historical fortune or external circumstance but springs from an essential interiority that is conveyed by Shakespeare's language.

In *Shakespeare: The Invention of the Human,* Harold Bloom groups *Richard II* with what he calls "The Major Histories"—the two *Henry IV* plays and *Henry V*—as distinct from what he identifies as "The First Histories," *King John,* the three *Henry VI* plays, and *Richard III.* Bloom then revises his assertion somewhat, choosing to include *Richard II* in an alternative triad, removing it momentarily from the histories and grouping it with *Romeo and Juliet* and *A Midsummer Night's Dream,* deriving a categorical unity independent of subject and defined by style. *Romeo and Juliet,* Bloom points out, is a lyrical tragedy; *A Mid-*

summer Night's Dream, a lyrical comedy; and *Richard II,* a lyrical history. Whereas history records the waves of human activity and action as they shape the common, overarching circumstances that determine the conditions under which we live, lyricism is an intensely personal mode that reveals the essential nature of the human character as it works in a given individual. Whereas a reader might construct a thesis arguing that *King John* is "really about" Faulconbridge or the conflict between ecclesiastical and civil authority rather than its eponymous monarch, or that *1 Henry IV* is "really about" Falstaff or the problems of honor and rebellion, *Richard II* is squarely about and centered on Richard. Rather than anatomizing the course of history as it is determined by Richard's actions and personality, or by his rival, Bolingbroke's, *Richard II* uses the historical circumstances that constitute Richard's environment, including Bolingbroke's challenge, as the vehicle for exploring not the historic Richard or Richard's mark on history but the essential, human Richard as he construes himself given the enveloping historical circumstances. It is that attention to the inner Richard, as much as the fact that the play is written entirely in verse, that makes the work a lyrical history. It is that concentration on the inner Richard, too, that justifies the play's full title, which is not *The History of King Richard the Second* but *The Tragedy of King Richard the Second.* The word *tragedy* focuses our attention on something fundamental about the man and his personal history rather than on the broader, historical events surrounding him. Richard's tragedy is the result of a contradiction: He is a bad king who is in rebellion, because of corruption, against his divinely appointed role as king. When he loses his kingship, he becomes a good man, loyal to the existential task of self-discovery. His goodness is not constituted by actions that are, either in motivation or effect, the opposite of his unwholesome actions as king. He does not, after his fall, perform historically and socially good actions as, during his reign, he performed historically and socially wicked ones. His regeneration involves the fact of his resignation to mortality and to his insight into mortality. He becomes worthy of esteem when his consciousness is severed from history and from the possibility of acting inside history. He becomes passive and interior. That is what makes him a lyrical presence. When one says he is a good man, one means he has become authentically human in his quest for personal meaning.

Richard's role in history, as monarch, is to act in the capacity of king. What, according to *Richard II*, is the role of a king, and how is that role defined for the reader? How does the play reveal what a king ought to be? What kind of king is Richard? In large part, the sense of Richard as ruler can be understood through negatives. Drawing on a number of passages from *Richard II*, a writer might propose that "Richard deserved to be deposed." John of Gaunt implicitly lays blame for England's trials on Richard's betrayal of a sacred trust. England is bankrupt because of Richard's policies. The condition of England's financial bankruptcy reflects the deeper condition of Richard's existential or emotional bankruptcy. When Gaunt attributes corruption to Richard's advisers, the "thousand flatterers [who] sit within thy crown," this respectful indirection nevertheless points directly to Richard's failure, a lapse that combines bad judgment in advisers with mortal vanity and a poor sense of his divine responsibility as king. Can you argue that, paradoxically, Richard's failure consists of elevating his political ambition above his divine identity as an anointed king?

Richard is "landlord of England," a managerial function, Gaunt complains, "not [its] king." Richard is not seen as fulfilling the heroic, moral, and metaphysical function of God's steward. Gaunt calls him "[a] lunatic, lean-witted fool," and Richard meets this rebuke with scorn that strongly suggests the truth of Gaunt's accusation.

What is the heroic/moral/metaphysical function that John of Gaunt suggests Richard neglects? The answer is embedded in the action of the text. *Richard II* begins with a trial at which Richard, as king, presides. His first words express the solemnity of the occasion with a formal and ritualistic question. The reader must recall later, when Gaunt calls Richard "[a] lunatic, lean-witted fool," that he first addressed him as "time-honor'd." The juxtaposition signals Richard's political hypocrisy and his unnamed trepidation. Richard's phrase "oath and band," in other words a bond, signals the solemnity and formality of a legal proceeding. We are watching a trial. The adversaries are Gaunt's son Henry Hereford, the plaintiff, and Thomas Mowbray, the defendant. A careful reading of the text will reveal the issues to the reader (which once again argues for the importance of several readings: To understand the beginning of the play, a reader must know what happens later on in the play). These issues, however, are less at the center of the drama, as the play begins, than the confrontation itself and the constellation of plaintiff, defendant, and judge.

As judge, Richard's role is not to adjudicate the issue and decide the matter of right and wrong but to facilitate an established juridical ritual, to serve as the still, focal point at the center of a dizzying swirl of contention. He is the symbol of the divine order, the function Gaunt later complains he has abandoned. He may, however, act as a mediator, asserting the will of heaven, as he attempts to do at 1.1.152 when he advises the "wrath-kindled" adversaries to "be ruled by me." In that passage, he is representing self-interest, not divine order. The duplicity of his intervention is not initially apparent to first-time readers or viewers of the play, although the fact that the contestants will not be ruled by him shows Richard's weakness as a monarch. The dramatic effect, however, is to present Richard sympathetically, whether he warrants sympathy or not. He seems like a wise, disinterested advocate of reconciliation and a peacemaker: They are hotheads; he is temperate. That the combatants refuse his guidance does not tarnish something humanly luminous, if not divine, that appears to be in his nature. The rhyming couplets he speaks make his utterance seem like the final wisdom that can be spoken.

The impression of Richard's wise gentleness is deepened at the second encounter between Bolingbroke and Mowbray. Just as they take their places to begin the combat, Richard breaks it off. Again, he appears to be the most temperate and judicious of the three, a judge who takes to heart his kingdom's peace and his subjects' benefit, even when anger blinds the other two to such considerations. Richard stops the duel with gentle words that seem to show a judicious sovereign's good heart and serious care. They soften the impression that must be made by other Richard utterances that are not so gentle and by John of Gaunt's several reports of the regent's malfeasance. To get a sense of Richard, a reader must consider both Richard's temperate words and his later wish as he sets off to see John of Gaunt after he has heard that Gaunt is dying: "Pray God we may make haste, and come too late!" His confiscation of all of Gaunt's son Bolingbroke's inherited wealth for his own use after Gaunt's death leaves little doubt that, as a monarch, Richard is not benign; he is a tyrant. From the start, Shakespeare gives us a complicated picture of Richard.

What the duel between Bolingbroke and Thomas Mowbray is about must be pieced together from remarks scattered throughout the play. Bolingbroke's first accusation against Mowbray, in a speech more than six lines long, brands him a traitor but never lists a specific charge (1.1.39ff.). When Bolingbroke finally itemizes his grievances, he saves the worst for last: the accusation of murder. For a "history" play, Shakespeare gives little account of the historical event at its root. It is only strongly hinted at in Bolingbroke's careful words, that Richard himself ordered the duke of Gloucester's murder. When John of Gaunt, Gloucester's brother, commiserates with Gloucester's widow, he argues that he has no power to execute vengeance. They must "Put [their] quarrel to the will of heaven / Who when they see the hours ripe on earth, / Will rain hot vengeance on offenders' heads," he states. "Correction lieth in those hands / Which made the fault." The sense is clear even if muffled: It is by the king's authority that the murderers of Gloucester may be punished, but it is the king who authorized the murder, and they must wait, therefore, for the justice of heaven.

When Richard interrupts the contest between Bolingbroke and Mowbray, he is not acting as heaven's representative with no investment in the outcome. He is trying to suppress a scandal implicating him. He banishes Mowbray from England forever because of their past collusion, and he banishes Bolingbroke for six years for the sake of old Gaunt and possibly out of guilt and in recognition of their shared royal blood. Richard's action violates the explicit sacred order he ought to represent in the ritual and heraldic formality that attends the trial.

Richard does not represent a strong, divinely sanctioned royal and central manifestation of power around which the state can be ordered. His self-involvement makes *him* the center of his concern. It usurps the grace of giving himself, of sacrificing himself, in his function as king, potentially placing his nation's concerns above his own. The importance, even the sanctity, of sacrificing is indicated early in the play. At 1.1.104ff., Bolingbroke compares the slain Gloucester to the biblical Abel. Gloucester's murderers

> Sluiced out his innocent soul through streams of blood:
> Which blood, like sacrificing Abel's, cries,
> Even from the tongueless caverns of the earth,
> To me for justice and rough chastisement.

"Sacrificing" is not the epithet the reader ought to expect for the murdered brother. But the line does not read, "Which blood, like sacrificed

Abel's, cries," because Bolingbroke presents Abel not as the passive victim but as actively performing the function for which he was killed. Abel was sacrificing from the best of his flock. Cain killed him because God accepted Abel's sacrifice but rejected Cain's. In Bolingbroke's allusion, sacrificing is made sacred. It is the kingly act that Richard neglects until he becomes the sacrifice when he returns from the Irish war, already in defeat. With ambivalence, he sacrifices himself to Bolingbroke. In act 3, scene 2, Richard's focus on himself becomes his proper regard and not a dereliction of responsibility. Sacrificing himself to the duties of monarchy is no longer his role or his task or in his power. Surrender to Bolingbroke is surrender to his own underlying nature; it is a grim liberation from his constituted, divinely sanctioned role. Abdication unleashes the spirit and the language of lyricism in Richard. Sacrificing himself, he excavates his inner, mortal self and becomes the pervasive personal identity of the play that challenges a historical and divinely appointed royal identity. Bolingbroke's historical victory is a lesser human accomplishment than Richard's defeat. Or is it? Might a writer argue that *Richard II* is a play that does not yield answers to primary questions of value but describes some of the defining human tensions that continuously beset our lives and judgments and require us to decide what is worthy of our allegiance?

TOPICS AND STRATEGIES

The essay that you write on *Richard II* need not and, in many instances, realistically cannot adhere solely to a discussion of such isolated or specifically defined elements as character, theme, or genre. If you choose to write about Richard's character, for example, one important way to understand it is to compare and contrast it to Bolingbroke's. If you write about the nature of Shakespeare's verse, you may be led to write about how Richard's character—or Bolingbroke's or Gaunt's—is revealed by his use of language. As you reflect on character, you may find that you are thinking about themes. How do Gaunt's words reflect the conflict between submission and assertion that runs through *Richard II*? When Gaunt refers to Richard's role in the murder of Gaunt's brother, Thomas of Woodstock, the duke of Gloucester, in words that register his resigned, avuncular wisdom, he talks of the need for patient submission to divine providence rather than rising up and redressing grievances. His advice to his son is similarly tuned, yet Bolingbroke represents the opposite philosophy. Do you see Gaunt as a weak, submissive man? Richard is often shown as submissive, yet he often is shown to be verbally and physically assertive.

When Gaunt speaks of England under Richard, he refers to betrayals of the divine trust that accompanies the divine right believed to grace a king. Richard betrays this trust and is betrayed. Betrayal suggests the use of power, and *Richard II* can be studied as a meditation on the nature of power and authority. Is it God given or human-made? Look at the brief exchange the bishop of Carlisle and Aumerle have with Richard at 3.2., starting at line 27. Whether from God or the human realm, what are the burdens and responsibilities of power? How do the various characters respond to them?

Themes

Your ideas for topics will grow out of your own reading and rereading of the text. The topic you formulate will depend on what you notice, what you feel, and how you react to what you have read. There is no right response, but as you develop your responses and the reasons for formulating them, you will be refining your responses and turning opinions into substantiated arguments.

Sample Topics:

1. **Loyalty and submission/rebellion and self-assertion:** The intertwined issues of loyalty and submission are at the heart of *Richard II* and, consequently, so are their complements: rebellion and self-assertion. In grappling with these themes, you could list all the examples you can think of from *Richard II* of instances of self-assertion, rebellion, submission, and loyalty and add patience and ambivalence to your list to expand the scope of your inquiry. Once you have your initial ideas and examples jotted down, start winnowing. Group similarities together. Perhaps you have mentioned Bolingbroke's opening challenge hurled at Mowbray (and indirectly at Richard, as you would discover through rereading); Aumerle's conspiracy; Bushy, Green, and Baggot's defiance as they are being led to execution; Gaunt's dying reproaches; Richard's prison speech; York's upbraiding of the rebels; Carlisle's dire prophecy of England's future grief; or both Bolingbroke's

and Mowbray's refusal to agree to make peace when Richard attempts to intercede.

Group your thoughts under simple headings such as "instances of rebellion" or "acts of submission." Then, freewrite about each heading. Are you finding anything that connects the ideas of loyalty and submission, something that might give rise to a thesis such as "In *Richard II* the mark of loyalty is submission to an authority outside oneself" or "In *Richard II*, acts of rebellion are motivated by self-interest and not by concern for the common good." Who, then, was Richard loyal to as a monarch, or was he, paradoxically, a rebel to his proper kingly function and thus a rebel to himself? To whom or to what is he loyal when he submits and yields to Bolingbroke? Can you construct an essay around the thesis that "Richard's surrender to Bolingbroke is actually an act of strong and stubborn assertion of his true self?"

2. **The nature and ambiguity of authority:** Can you read *Richard II* as an argument about the nature and limits of authority? Does the play suggest that there are several ways to think of authority: authority conceived under a system of divine right and authority as conceived under a system governed by political and military power?

   You can examine the textual indications and evidence of a difference in the worldview of John of Gaunt and his son Bolingbroke as regards authority. The object of loyalty is at the root of the contentions about authority that define the play. Is there a difference if the object of loyalty is God, the king, oneself, honor, order, a code of behavior, or a principal? All these possibilities are encompassed within the borders of the play. Does the text offer a unified theory of authority or conflicting views on the subject?

3. **The nature and ambiguity of loyalty and treachery:** Being loyal to one idea, ideal, or set of interests may entail betraying another notion or consideration. A given action can both serve and betray the same intended goal, as, it may be argued,

Sir Pierce of Exton's murder of Richard in the tower both serves and betrays King Henry's interests. The conflict between the duke and the duchess of York after learning of their son's involvement in a plot against Henry concerns the proper object of loyalty. The choice of loyalty is between son and king. At Bolingbroke's unauthorized return from exile in act 2, scene 3, York's allegiance is challenged. Should he be loyal to Richard's divine right or Bolingbroke's just grievance? What does the exchange between York and Bolingbroke suggest about the conflict between firm adherence to principles and a regard for human sympathies?

Loyalty and treachery are words that have shifting meanings depending on one's particular interest and the context in which these words are used. Bolingbroke and Mowbray bring charges of treason against each other. The answers to the questions of who is the traitor and who is the loyal man depend on your perspective. What is the perspective given in *Richard II*? Is there only one? How can you determine what it is? Does Shakespeare have a position on the issue?

Once you answer the question concerning conflicting loyalty, however you answer it, the next question to pose may be, does the answer to that question really matter in the world of the play? Why or why not? Even if loyalty and treason are central themes, is the play ultimately concerned with something that transcends those themes? Is Shakespeare examining how a person's identity is formed by the way he responds to conflicting authorities? Is there a particular moral lesson to be derived from the play, or is *Richard II* a literary vector diagram mapping the clash of irresolvable and perhaps inevitable tensions that come with being alive? Ultimately do we judge, esteem, or disparage Richard or Bolingbroke because they are right or wrong, or is there something else that influences how we regard them? How are they made into human figures rather than contrasting figures representing opposing forces or values?

4. **Heroism and villainy in *Richard II*:** How might you write about heroism and villainy in *Richard II*? Is there a hero or a villain? Is it Richard or Bolingbroke? Is each one an example of both?

Can you use the play to argue that the greatness and value of art resides in its capacity to, rather than offer solutions, illuminate the insolubility of certain problems and map the ways people negotiate these seemingly unresolvable issues?

5. **The idea of order in *Richard II*:** Consider the idea of order in *Richard II*? Does the play posit justice as antithetical to order?

List the number of scenes that are built around the representation of order or in which the idea of order plays some part. What role does the problem of justice play in those scenes?

6. **The formation of identity:** What does *Richard II* say about identity? How is it formed? Why is it important? What is the connection between Richard's identity and his role? Or Bolingbroke's? York's?

Character

Because the complexity and creation of character is essential to the plot of *Richard II*, the study of character involves also the examination of the dynamics of social interaction. A fruitful approach to the analysis of character in *Richard II* could involve comparing characters in the play with one another—not with the object of defining each but defining the constellation of associations they create and represent.

Sample Topics:

1. **Richard and Bolingbroke as creations of each other:** Richard and Bolingbroke are antagonists. Their differences seem obvious, but how does each illuminate or even create the other? Harold Bloom has written that "without [Bolingbroke] Richard would not be Richard, lyrical self-destroyer" (250). What values does each represent? Are there any ways in which the two men are similar? We see Richard and Bolingbroke together three times in the play, in scenes 1 and 3 of act 1 and in the deposition scene in the fourth act. You might not only compare their characters but also the way they behave to each other or the changes in the way they behave from the first to the fourth act when their positions of power are altered. Do you see any change in

these men beyond the obvious role change? If you were to argue that Richard is now "more himself than he was," what does that mean? In which passages does each character reveal himself? How do they create each other?

Ruling or deposed, how is Richard the same man despite his outward change in circumstances? Banished or returned, how is Bolingbroke the same man? Can you show how the power relationship that is explicit in the deposition scene is already implicit in the trial scenes? How much of that power relationship depends on external circumstances? How much on the characters of the two men? What does that say about the forces that move history? Your challenge always is to draw evidence from the play to support the thesis you develop.

Is it accurate to say that Bolingbroke as a character is primarily determined by his actions and Richard primarily by his feelings and that each is the motor for the creation of the other's actions and feelings? Without his social identity, would Bolingbroke be a nonentity? If he had not been stripped of his social identity, would Richard have any depth of being? Discuss how a character's words convey his or her personality. What is the implication of words left unspoken or of slips of the tongue? Is the drama of Richard's defeat the result of Bolingbroke's victory or of the words that defeat brings to Richard's mouth?

Harold Bloom calls Richard a masochist (258). That is a psychosexual classification. How would you go about demonstrating the accuracy or inaccuracy of such a designation? Bolingbroke, as he is drawn, is a lesser character than Richard in terms of his inwardness. He is not a dramatic world unto himself as Richard is, although Bolingbroke becomes the architect of the world that everyone else inhabits. What do his responses to others reveal about him? Consider his sense of humor in response to the conflicting pleas of the duke and duchess of York in regard to Aumerle as well as his skill in diplomacy. What do his responses to Richard throughout show about him, about his self-confidence?

2. **How secondary characters are brought to life:** The secondary characters in *Richard II* are defined by their responses to the

main characters, yet, often by using the intricacies and accidents of speech, Shakespeare endows them with traits that suggest that they are fully realized persons with interior lives. As the duchess of Gloucester bids farewell to John of Gaunt at 1.2.58, she begins by speaking about grief. By the fifth line, when she asks Gaunt to "commend" her to her brother, the duke of York, she is a woman speaking from within grief. Her grief affects the way she expresses her thought. There is something more she wants to say. Then she cannot remember what it is. Then she remembers: Tell him to "visit me," she says. Then, realizing her utter desolation, she changes her mind: "let him not come." This is character portraiture, not narrative. Shakespeare depicts her state of mind through her deliberately vague and imprecise use of language.

Alternately, you might choose to write about the nature of the interplay of character and speech in *Richard II*. After York learns of his sister's death at 2.2.98, speaking to the queen, he laments the fate of England under Richard. After eight eloquent lines, he makes a slip of the tongue that shows how grief for his sister's death torments him. "Come, sister," he says, "—cousin, I would say—pray, pardon me." What other instances do you find in *Richard II* in which the way a character speaks or remains quiet reveals his or her inner workings? Why is it important in this play that the personalities and the inner concerns of the characters are brought forward, that characters are not just presented as types (for example, grieving wife or tyrannical king, hero or rebel) but as individuals? Does *Richard II* enact and reflect the existential conflict between the world as it is and the world as individual characters wish it to be?

History and Context

The circumstances of Richard's reign provided the essential material for Shakespeare's play, yet Shakespeare altered, reconstructed, and simplified that history. Why did he choose to do so, and what are the implications for the play overall?

Sample Topics:

1. **Shakespeare's variations on history:** Examine the actual events of Richard's reign and compare the history with Shakespeare's play. What light does the comparison shed on *Richard II?* Consider an essay arguing that Shakespeare's interest in history is as a vehicle for presenting a drama of human character rather than of historical process. Does Shakespeare show in *Richard II* that historical process is a function of the interplay of human character?

Given the historical Richard, Shakespeare might have written a play in which Richard is presented as a far more heinous character than he appears to be in *Richard II.* Shakespeare might have constructed a drama in which the historical events are shown in far greater intricacy. One potential thesis reflecting this observation could be, "The drama of Richard's defeat is not a historically motivated event but the drama of his own personality." How do the events of act 2, scene 3 affect or alter this assertion?

2. **The double historical focus:** There are two historical contexts to consider with regard to *Richard II.* Besides the year in which the action of the play takes place, 1399, there is also the period in which *Richard II* was written, performed, and printed—the final years of the reign of Queen Elizabeth I. Shakespeare may have been using the story of Richard II obliquely, writing about Richard and the past in order to consider something in Shakespeare's present that it was not possible to refer to directly. The deposition scene, for example, was omitted from some early editions. In several important respects, Lily B. Campbell shows in *Shakespeare's Histories* (1947, *Icon*, 122ff.), the reign of Elizabeth I strongly resembled Richard's.

With some research into the events and politics of the final decade of Elizabeth's reign, you can develop an essay that offers useful insight into the role and reception of *Richard II* at that time. Although *Richard II* is concerned with the fall and rise of kings and the actions of the nobility, there are scattered references to the common people that hint at the popular rebellions that threatened Elizabeth's rule. Consider an essay about the conditions of the commoners or working class during Elizabeth's reign, their responses to these conditions, and how these incidents and concerns are reflected in *Richard II*.

Philosophy and Ideas

In a drama that intends to be true to nature and humanity and not a work of propaganda, the ideas and philosophies it conveys are contained in and dramatized by the situations and the characters it portrays.

Sample Topics:

1. **The ambiguity of identity—Richard:** The notion of identity, which becomes important to Richard II once he is stripped of his crown, is closely linked to the conflicting ideas of majesty and mortality that affect how the person of the king is regarded.

   After he is deposed, is Richard a king or a displaced, uprooted, unrooted man who lives in his imagination? If he is both, sometimes one and then the other, then he is also neither, for identity, according to the play, is unstable, without permanence, deceptive, an unrealistic constructed image, as suggested by the scene with the mirror. Consequently, if identity is fleeting, how does *Richard II* deal with the problem of how a man can know who he is? Richard grapples with this problem in his soliloquy at 5.5.81ff.

2. **The ambiguity of identity—Bolingbroke:** Who is Bolingbroke? Is he a usurper or a king? Does one role preclude the other? Is he a scheming manipulative man who uses circumstances to advance his ambition or a victim of tyranny who rightly refuses to suffer injustice and is motivated by the good of England to remove its unfit king? Considering Bolingbroke, you might hypothesize a connection between identity and the idea of majesty. With the

character of Bolingbroke, Shakespeare potentially signals the demise of the medieval idea of the divine right of kingship. In its place arises the beginning of power politics and the manipulation of public opinion as the basis of national leadership.

Once Bolingbroke secures his place as king, how comfortably and securely does that identity belong to him? His plaintive question, "Can no man tell me of my unthrifty son?" (5.3.1) may express an anxiety that goes beyond his concerns about his wayward son. His identity is not monolithic. Does he link his insecurity as a father to the "plague [that] hang[s] over us" that Carlisle predicted would result from Bolingbroke's usurpation (4.1.136ff)? As king, he is father to the English people. Does instability challenge his royal identity among his subjects, as his son challenges his paternal identity by slighting his filial duty?

The murder of Richard later fortifies Bolingbroke's identity not simply as a king but as a usurper. In addition, it amplifies the gap between the man himself and the image as a politician he works to project. It is with a view to the duplicity of his character that Shakespeare begins *1 Henry IV,* and duplicity is one of the dominant themes of that play.

3. **York:** Who is York? Richard's surrogate, Henry's subject, Rutland's father, the husband of the duchess, loyal man, traitor?

Each identity demands something of him that places him at odds with himself and his true nature. Do you agree with the assertion that York's primary identity is forged by his characteristic habit of transcending his own self-interest?

4. **England:** England itself, arguably a major "character" in the play, as John of Gaunt describes the island, suffers from an identity crisis. How is it brought about? What does that say about the inhabitants' obligation to the land they inhabit? How is this dualism or bifurcated sense of identity reflected in the play's characters? How are they affected by such an identity rift?

Form and Genre

Richard II is the only one of Shakespeare's plays written entirely in verse. Its poetry is sometimes ceremonial, seldom used to incite or inspire action, as it frequently is in *Henry V,* and usually it reflects the inner workings of individual consciousness and perception as they struggle to express and identify themselves. A writer might choose one or several of Richard's speeches and through an analysis of his poetry show how he develops and creates a sense of identity.

Sample Topics:

1. **Rhyming couplets:** In a study of the way rhyme is used in *Richard II,* a focus on rhyming couplets can lead to a discussion of how Shakespeare's use of rhyme affects the dramatic structure and mood of the play. How do such formal and structural concerns influence our feelings about a particular character?

   What do rhyming couplets accomplish that other forms of verse do not, emotionally, intellectually, and musically? How does the rhetoric of a rhyming couplet reflect on the importance of a character and the nature of what he or she is saying? Are there particular dramatic points in the play when rhyming couplets are specifically used? Rhyming couplets can also indicate ritual or illuminate interactions between characters. Examine examples of this rhetorical device and why it is so prominently featured in the play.

2. **A comic interlude:** In scenes 2 and 3 of the fifth act, "The Beggar and the King," Shakespeare inserts a comic interlude. In the introduction to the Signet edition of *Richard II,* Kenneth Muir says that "V.iii.73–134 is so bad that critics would like to believe that Shakespeare did not write it at all." He adds, after arguing that it probably is Shakespeare's, that "the situation is farcical. . . . Shakespeare must have been aware of the absurdity, but he seems to have miscalculated the effect of the scene" (pp. xxv–xxvi). Do you think this is an accurate assessment? As stated, it is a series of unsubstantiated opinions. What, if anything,

makes the section "so bad"? Muir suggests that Shakespeare "miscalculated the effect of the scene." What do you think the effect of the scene is? What does the scene accomplish? What does it mean to call the scene a farce? Is being farcical at this point in the play a failing or a tonal misstep? (It may help in your analysis if you know that the word *farce* comes from the French verb *farcir,* which means "to stuff," and that the literary genre farce owes its name to the kind of cooking that involves stuffing a mixture of ingredients into a bladderlike skin or into a vegetable, as in a sausage or a stuffed tomato.) What might be the function, within the overall design of the play, for a farcical scene inserted at this point in the play? How does it influence a reader's perception of Henry?

Muir's objection echoes an ongoing criticism of Shakespeare that was common during the eighteenth century when critics argued that Shakespeare often violated the structural unities of time, place, action, and aesthetic décor by mixing comic and tragic elements within the same work. Nineteenth-century critics such as Samuel Taylor Coleridge (1772–1834) and August Wilhelm Schlegel (1767–1845) countered that unity was not a function of following rules but grew out of a text's organic wholeness. How does this scene contribute organically to the wholeness of *Richard II*? You can argue that it helps to establish Bolingbroke's authority. Is Bolingbroke a comic figure in this scene? What is the effect of casting rebellion now as a comically melodramatic affair? Why is comedy just right at this moment in *Richard II* considering both what has gone before and what will come after?

3. **Chiasmus:** Chiasmus indicates a structural relation of parts that can be diagrammed by the letter *X*, whose Greek designation is *chi*. Each side of the letter *X* mirrors the other. The four extending arms of the letter meet at a central point. Applying this concept, you can show how in *Richard II*, as Richard falls, Bolingbroke rises and the drama simultaneously traces these upward and downward trajectories.

A good argument can also be made that as Richard falls from his royal height, he rises as a man. The opening trial scenes are inverted and repeated, mirrored in the deposition scene when the plaintiff, Bolingbroke, becomes the judge, and the judge, Richard, becomes the defendant. How would you structure and support an essay arguing that Richard's is a transcendental fall?

Language, Symbols, and Imagery

The language of *Richard II* is rich in imagery, and the action is replete with symbolism. After you have read the play through several times, a particular scene may have especially captured your attention, perhaps Gaunt's encounter with Richard, the garden scene, the deposition scene, or the scene of Richard's imprisonment in the tower. Scan a scene for its images; see how often certain images are repeated and how they are used.

Sample Topics:

1. **The preponderance of metaphors and how they function:** What does the mirror in the deposition scene reflect about Richard? What does it show the reader? The use of metaphor is evident in the very steps Richard takes to meet Bolingbroke in the deposition scene. He descends to the courtyard at the beginning of the scene and is conveyed up to the tower at the end of it. How do you connect these images with the image of a balance or scale that recurs throughout the play? How is that image of weighing relevant in the scene between the duke and duchess of York with Henry about their son's treason? How might you compare Richard's relationship with the English earth in act 3, scene 2 to the scene with the gardener's relationship to the earth in act 3, scene 4, a scene full of symbols that is itself a metaphor?

2. **The function of theater, the construction of images, and the exercise of power:** Richard's last soliloquy presents the mind as a theater—it is not the only image of the theater in the play— and consciousness as dramatization. Upon what stage is history played out? How are Richard and Bolingbroke theatrical? How do they "stage" themselves? In 5.3, Bolingbroke acknowledges the entrance of the duchess of York by saying, "Our scene is alt'red from a serious thing," deliberately using a theatrical

metaphor. The first scene of the play is theatrical as well, as is the deposition scene. Even the words describing how the people of London reacted as the deposed king, Richard, and the newly installed king, Henry, passed through the streets borrow from the language and imagery of the theater. What, if anything, does *Richard II* say about the relationship between the construction of theatrical images and the exercise of power? You might want to look at 1.2.199ff. and 3.2.36ff. in *Henry IV, Part 1* if you consider using this question as the basis for an essay.

Compare and Contrast Essays

A compare and contrast essay can focus on characters, structure, images, settings, or themes in a work that then serve to excavate something about what the work means or how it achieves meaning. Such an essay can also compare one work with another or aspects of one work with aspects of another, adducing the implications of the commonly or disparately treated elements.

Sample Topics:

1. **Richard and Bolingbroke:** A comparison of Richard and Bolingbroke is an obvious but by no means trivial subject. You can start off by showing that it is essential for the understanding of each to know and understand the other.

   Contrasting these two men, their ambitions, their responses to adversity, the way they speak, even their similarities will allow you also to consider some of the major themes such as power, identity, authority, and loyalty contained in *Richard II.*

2. **The duke and duchess of York:** Comparing the duke and duchess of York, in regard to their response to their son's incipient rebellion against Henry, allows you to consider the significance of gender difference in their respective attitudes and the value each attaches to loyalty to the sovereign or to family.

3. **Richard II and Henry V:** These two kings have often been considered as representative models of the weak introspective poet and the heroic extroverted warrior, respectively. In comparing

them, you can consider two fundamental, psychological types as well as two fundamentally different dramatic experiences.

4. ***Richard II* and Christopher Marlowe's *Edward II*:** *Edward II*, written by Christopher Marlowe (1564–93) probably around 1592, traces the events that occurred during the reign of King Edward II, who was murdered in 1327, and ends with the ascension to the throne of his son, King Edward III, who avenged the murder of his father. Edward III reigned until 1377, when, at his death, Richard II became king. There are many elements in *Edward II* that strongly suggest Shakespeare was familiar with it when he wrote *Richard II*. It is a play worth reading for itself but one that is considerably enriched by comparison with *Richard II*. An essay contrasting the two plays can compare Richard's and Edward's characters, the political machinations portrayed in each play, the psychological depths achieved in each, and the effectiveness of the poetry of each play.

Bibliography for *Richard II*

Some of the titles listed below may be helpful in stimulating your thinking about *Richard II*. Many are available on databases that you can access through your school or public library. Because *Richard II* is the first play of a tetralogy, critics have often written about it in essays that also deal with the two *Henry IV* plays and *Henry V*. Therefore, you will find other bibliographical material that discusses *Richard II* in the bibliography sections following the essays devoted to those three other individual plays.

Bloom, Harold. *Shakespeare: The Invention of the Human.* New York: Riverhead Books, 1998.

Campbell, Lilly B. "From *Shakespeare's Histories*" in *Shakespeare: Richard II.* Icon Critical Guides, Coyle, Martin, ed., pp. 122–25. Icon Books, 1998.
  (Coyle's collection of critical essays on Richard II *is a useful handbook for a student of the play, presenting important pieces of criticism from the Elizabethan period up to the end of the twentieth century. An informed narrative thread shows the coherence of that criticism and how critics responded to one another's readings.)*

Erable, Richard. "Shakespeare's *Richard II.*" *Explicator,* 61:2 (Winter 2003), pp. 73–75.

(Erable analyzes the image of Phaeton, son of the Greek sun god, Helios, that Richard uses in the deposition scene in order to argue that enlightenment comes too late to him.)

Fitter, Chris. "Historicising Shakespeare's *Richard II*: Current Events, Dating, and the Sabotage of Essex." *Early Modern Literary Studies*, 11:2 (September 2005): 1–47.

(Presents a scholarly account of 1) the events surrounding the career of the earl of Essex, a political figure under Elizabeth, who was executed for involvement in a plot to topple her and whose career and aspirations are possibly suggested by Bolingbroke; 2) strategies for dating Richard II; 3) the likely political resonances Richard II suggested to an Elizabethan audience; and 4) speculation, on the basis of Richard II, about Shakespeare's political sympathies in regard to Essex and the failed plot against Elizabeth.)

Forker, Charles R. "Unstable Identity in Shakespeare's *Richard II*" in *Renascence: Essays on Values in Literature*, 54:1 (Fall 2001): 3–21.

(Using the instability of Richard's identity, Forker examines how it reflects the change in notions of identity that characterized the Middle Ages and the Renaissance.)

Hanrahan, Michael. "Defamation as Political Contest During the Reign of Richard II." *Medium Aevum*, 72:2 (Fall 2003): 259.

(Although it does not deal directly with Shakespeare's Richard II, Hanrahan's essay is an important resource for understanding the political culture in which the play is set. It is a study of the role of slander in the political oppositions of the period. Consider in this light the opening contest between Bolingbroke and Mowbray in Richard II.)

Harmon, A. G. "Shakespeare's Carved Saints." *SEL: Studies in English Literature, 1500–1900*, 45:2 (Spring 2005): 315–31.

(Harmon sees similarities in Shakespeare's depiction of Richard and his murder to the historical figure Thomas à Becket [1118–70], who was murdered on the orders of Henry II.)

Landau, Aaron. "'I Live with Bread Like You': Forms of Inclusion in *Richard II*." *Early Modern Literary Studies: A Journal of Sixteenth- and Seventeenth-Century English Literature*, 11:1 (May 2005): 1–23.

(Presents an account of the socioeconomic situation of the common people during the last decade of Elizabeth's reign and of popular protests and how those circumstances and upheavals are reflected in Richard II.*)*

Lemon, Rebecca. "The Faulty Verdict in 'The Crown v. John Hayward.'" *SEL: Studies in English Literature, 1500–1900,* 41:1 (Winter 2001): 109–32.
(This is an essay that will be of interest to students wishing to understand and know more about the political climate in which Shakespeare wrote Richard II *and to see in Hayward's history,* The First Part of the Life and Raigne of King Henrie IIII *[1599], how the same material Shakespeare treated in* Richard II *was handled. For its alleged seditious nature, Hayward was tried and imprisoned until Elizabeth's death in 1603.)*

Schuler, Robert M. "Magic Mirrors in *Richard II.*" *Comparative Drama,* 38:2–3 (Summer-Fall 2004): 151–81.
(Schuler considers the symbolic use of the mirror and of mirror images in the deposition scene.)

Scott, William O. "Landholding, Leasing, and Inheritance in *Richard II.*" *SEL: Studies in English Literature, 1500–1900,* 42:2 (Spring 2002): 275–92.
(Beginning with Gaunt's reproach to Richard about his poor stewardship of English land, Scott discusses the conflicting rights of property and power in Elizabethan England and how an understanding of that conflict can influence a reading of the play.)

Shakespeare, William. *The Tragedy of King Richard the Second,* edited by Kenneth Muir. New York: Signet/New American Library, 1963.

HENRY IV, PART 1

READING TO WRITE

IN *HENRY IV, Part 1*, often notated as *1 Henry IV,* Shakespeare transformed the history play from a chronicle of events and an account of the machinations of historical figures into a meditation on and a critique of history itself. This shift is largely due to the presence of Falstaff in the work. In *Richard II,* Shakespeare had already reinvented the history play by presenting the inner psychology of a deposed monarch and the revelation of the man beneath the king. In *1 Henry IV,* Shakespeare established a counterforce to history in the mythic figure of Falstaff. Enmeshed as he is in the action of the play, Falstaff exists, nevertheless, outside time and the historical spectrum traced by the English kings. Everything about him serves as a critique of the very system of history that kings represent and the list of values they endorse. Hal's betrayal of Falstaff is, accordingly, a foregone conclusion: Had Hal not banished Falstaff, the nature of history would have been redefined and, fundamentally, its spirit altered, subverted, not merely challenged but turned inside out and deflated. Hal does cast out Falstaff, however, and that allows Hal to reemerge as his father's son and to become Henry V, a champion defender of history, a practitioner of uncompromising power, and a man, too, whose time will prove to be limited.

What Falstaff brings to *1 Henry IV* is a repudiation of everything that is held sacred by the others, whichever side they take in the political confrontation the play chronicles. Falstaff's wit and amorality, his lies and transgressions, make him the mirror of the other characters' vices and a parodist of what they think of as virtues. He becomes the scapegoat banished to the wilderness for displaying the faults that actually underpin the workings of the society that banishes him. *1 Henry IV* can, in this light, be seen as a profoundly allegorical drama representing the combat of guile with mischief, where guile, in the form of Henry IV and Prince Hal, represents duplicity and devious stratagems, and mischief, in the form of Falstaff, represents the powerful mockery of irreverence. Between these two poles is the impetuous, unmediated energy of impulsive ambition and impetuous aggression personified by Hotspur. Hotspur stands on the edge of history, itching to enter its course and divert it. It is an energy that impels Hal as much as it does Hotspur and Henry, but whereas Hotspur is naïve, the king and the prince are cunning. Like his father, because of his ambition and because of what he is willing to do to further it, Hal is duplicitous. Both Hotspur and Falstaff, as different from each other as they are, are alike in as much as neither is duplicitous.

Duplicity suggests the condition of being double, of showing yourself as one thing and really being something else. Hotspur is simple. He is what you see. Falstaff is complex. He keeps showing you something else, openly going through his repertoire like an actor, dancer, or acrobat showing the range of his talent. Although he is always performing, always improvising, always taking another leap, he is always recognizably himself and there is always more of him. Neither Hotspur nor Falstaff is keeping anything secret. Henry and Hal are and, consequently, they are not to be trusted. They are both politicians. Their speech and their actions are devised to mobilize obedience and support by charming and distracting others, even as the father and son fabricate public images designed to serve a private agenda that has great public consequence. Hotspur is not such a man. Impetuous, he is transparent in his ambition, in his rebellion, in his displays of anger, pride, and self-assertion. He is even honest in his secretiveness; he openly refuses to reveal his plans to his wife. Falstaff is not duplicitous. He lies openly and goes from projecting one illusion to another with grace and candor. It is no secret that he always has something up his sleeve. It is part of his identity and vocation to be as he is. He does not lie in order to deceive but to deflate and delight. He is not deceiving but playing and inviting his interlocutor into the game. Usually a comic character suffers some form of deflation and is then reintegrated into society, but Falstaff does not. Falstaff does the deflating—of everything that is taken seriously—and then he is banished from society because of it.

All these assertions, these generalizations, are conclusions derived from repeated readings of the play. You do not come to the play with them. They come to you from the play. *1 Henry IV* is a play strongly shaped by the personalities of its characters, by their dramatic confrontations and interplay. Close analysis of these structures and modes opens the play to a wealth of interpretations. Consider the play's opening speech. Henry is speaking. Where? Why? To whom? All the original stage direction says is "Enter the King, Lord John of Lancaster, Earl of Westmoreland, with others." On a first reading, we do not even know who these people are, what kind of assembly it is, and who the "others" might be, so we are reading to establish sense and clarity. At the end of the king's address, we have learned that a divisive war has ended and, although the king speaks of peace, he seems to be planning another war. That war, he says, will be a better war than the one that has just ended. It will not be fought on home territory like the last one but on foreign shores, in the Holy Land. It will not be a civil war where factions that ought to be allied are in opposition but will bring those who had opposed one another together to "march all one way" in a crusade. Henry moves from talk of war to speak of "Christ's blessèd feet / Which fourteen hundred years ago were nailed / For our advantage on the bitter cross." After all this rhetoric about peace, holy war, and Christ, after bringing a religious solemnity to the proceedings, Henry then basically states, but this is not what we are here to discuss. The war on English soil is apparently not over: Westmoreland received a report last night about a battle in which Henry's forces were massacred. The scene is set in the council chamber. Henry is addressing the court. A reader may sense that this is a political speech designed to manipulate the courtiers hearing it, to arouse religious and patriotic sentiment, to consolidate Henry's power, to rally support for his northern wars, to stave off rebellion, and to cement his legitimacy. One may suspect Henry's sincerity and question his motives and even wonder, when he speaks of Christ's death being "for our advantage," if he refers to it for his own *political* advantage. To be sure of any doubts about Henry, though, one must already have read through both parts of *Henry IV* and remember Henry's talk with Prince Hal on his deathbed. In act 4, scene 5, starting at line 202, of *2 Henry IV,* Henry reminds Hal of how insecurely the crown sat on his head. Henry tells Hal how unsure he was of the loyalty of those who had helped to make him king by toppling Richard and how he feared they might turn against him. "Which to avoid," he says,

> I cut them off; and had a purpose now
> To lead out many to the Holy Land,
> Lest rest and lying still might make them look
> Too near unto my state. (IV.v.208–12)

Recalling that, we know the motive for Henry's first words and thus understand how to read them and how to view and interpret the character of Henry IV. Henry is a self-interested man, artful in manipulating the responses of his auditors for his advantage. By the end of the first scene of *1 Henry IV,* we also know that his son Hal is absent from the council, as usual, and that Henry envies his adversary Northumberland, for his son, the valiant Hotspur, has taken prisoners in the battle but in defiance is refusing to give them to the king. Thus Henry is facing two kinds of defiance to his already shaky, because usurped, authority, in the form of political defiance from the valiant Hotspur and filial defiance from the renegade Hal.

Scene 2 shifts from Henry to Falstaff, from the father who frets over his son's absence and the challenge it implicitly signifies to his authority to the surrogate paternal figure who commands Hal's company now but who will be the one, not Henry, on whom Hal displaces the need to reject his father. These two fathers are the outward markers of Hal's duplicity. The conflict embodied in Hal is between the responsibilities he owes to his place in history, for which he is beholden to his father, and the possibility he has created to escape and transcend his duty and historical destiny in the escapism and wish fulfilment represented by Falstaff.

What might lead a reader to think of Falstaff as existing outside history? In the first words he speaks, he asks Hal the time. Hal's answer is a scolding: "What a devil hast thou to do with the time of the day? . . . I see no reason why thou shouldst be so superfluous to demand the time of the day." What interests Falstaff, Hal says, is eating, drinking, and lechery. The king is concerned with the minute before and the minute after, how he got his power and how he will guard and keep it in the future. Falstaff lives in a sensual, eternal present.

From this oppositional structure, a strong thesis can potentially then be developed: In *1 Henry IV,* Prince Hal embodies the conflict between the demands of history, expressed by the burden of duties that his historical identity as prince of Wales imposes on him, and the possibility of a life of play free of the responsibilities and constraints of history that

Falstaff offers. Once the thesis sentence has been formulated, a writer's job is to defend it, to substantiate it, to show that it is a reasonable statement to make about *1 Henry IV*, to show how Falstaff can be designated a force outside history and antithetical to its existence and demands. A close reading of each statement that Henry makes in his first speech establishes a sense of his character, the force of his personality, and the burdens and contradictions that mark his life: from his celebration of the end of war alongside his declaration of continuing hostilities; from his condemnation of civil war for its divisiveness alongside his glorification of religious war; from his call for collective, selfless involvement through allegiance to him; from his self-confidence as king to his perplexity and insecurity as a father. These juxtapositions show us Henry as a cunning Machiavelli, the model of a man who ruthlessly creates his possibilities at everybody else's expense. Henry's words also enact and dramatize one of the play's central concerns: war, power, contention, competition, and death as each a component part of the business of history.

In order to develop a full sense of the play, it is important to remember Henry's characterizations of war and Hotspur's thirst for war's glory and honor once Falstaff's contrasting attitudes and contempt for war become a subject of the play. At first, a reader might tend to condemn Falstaff's behavior as a recruiter and squadron leader. Whereas Henry, Hal, Hotspur, and all the others revere and glorify war, Falstaff holds it utterly in contempt. His method of recruitment, the men he chooses, and the way he speaks about them actually reflect negatively not on Falstaff but on war itself. Falstaff is cynical, no doubt, but he is not wrong. He understands that a soldier's ultimate job description is to be killed. For that end, he argues, his miserable specimens are as good as highly skilled and trained soldiers. The insult Falstaff levels is not to humanity but to war, in the grade of humanity he chooses to send into battle. Because war feeds on all men, why waste good ones on it, Falstaff argues. Falstaff is no more sacrificing men than is the king, who marshals thousands to die to protect his interests. Similarly, Hotspur willingly throws away his own youth and love for his wife with a cavalier and wanton bravado: "Doomsday is near. Die all, die merrily."

Observations, arguments, and comparisons come from puzzling over details the play presents. Look at 3.1, beginning at line 95. Glendower and Hotspur are arguing over how they will divide the land they have not yet won. Hotspur insists that his share is less than Glendower's and that he will, therefore, have a dam built, to divert the current, open a new channel, and enlarge his portion of rich land. What is the purpose of the scene? Clearly it highlights Hotspur's character. For the sake of his honor he will fight—"cavil," he says—over territory he has not yet even won. When read on the level of metaphor, however, the incident does more than illustrate an aspect of Hotspur's psychology. It shows his relationship to history. He wants to possess time and bend its course to his will just as he wants to alter or redirect the current of the stream.

Falstaff does not. He imagines being swept along by the current of history when Hal becomes king and enjoying himself then just as he does now. Time is nothing to him, because he inhabits a continual present and has, consequently, no direct relation to time. This was made evident at his first appearance in 1.2. At the end of 2.4, when reality intrudes on the world of the tavern, interrupting Falstaff's play, in the form of the sheriff seeking to arrest Falstaff because of the robbery he committed, Falstaff is impervious to it, "asleep behind the arras, and snorting like a horse." Nothing fazes him, not even the hostility in Hal's responses, as long as Hal continues to offer his companionship. The ambiguity of Hal's esteem essentially provides Falstaff with the prods to spur his ongoing feats of self-realization and comic dexterity.

Hal's psychological split and his struggle to determine his identity, despite his first soliloquy, are more disturbing to him than even he knows. They are clearly, even if obliquely, presented in the practical joke he induces Poins to help him play on Francis at the tavern. The scene thus emerges as more than just a passing episode of royal high jinks. Lines 1 through 98 of act 2, scene 4 present a rather mean-spirited picture of the prince, and a reader must ask what could motivate him to toy so meanly with a harmless man below him in rank who holds Hal in good esteem. Clearly, Hal's sport with Francis uses Francis as a proxy or substitute for Hal himself in order to represent and enact his own state of mind: The prince is a man of fluid identity, drawn this way and that by opposing forces. These forces threaten to paralyze him if he cannot master them. In this brief interlude, Hal tries to master them by making Francis the victim of those contradictory impulses. Moreover, Francis has actually done something to offend the prince. He has taken Hal at his word as Hal has presented himself, as a good fellow—"a good boy," as Hal tells Poins Francis and his companions have described him—and given him a packet of sugar. Through a practical joke, Hal shows Francis he is no such thing.

The kind of reading suggested here is intended to help a reader develop interpretations of *1 Henry IV* by detecting in small and seemingly minor phrases or actions clues to larger, unifying ideas. The following suggested topics present several possible directions, but you may also find that you will start to develop your own chain of insights as you forge a path through the text.

TOPICS AND STRATEGIES
Themes

The drama of *1 Henry IV* comes not just from the interplay of characters and the conflicts they generate but from the variations Shakespeare presents on a number of related themes that are introduced by and in relation to the play's characters.

Sample Topics:

1. **Instability:** Henry's first words, "So shaken as we are," refer to the instability not only of his claim to the throne and to the shaky condition of England, made unstable by the past contentions that have put Henry on the throne and by the possible threats that arise to challenge his power. Henry is also shaken by his son's wayward behavior, insecure as a father and worried about the durability of his line of succession.

   If you choose to write about the importance of instability in *1 Henry IV,* you can consider the causes of instability. How are they historical? How are they psychological? How are they the result of politics and the competition for power? You can also examine the effect of instability on each of the play's major characters. The Percy family is one cause of it. How do they benefit by it? Is it useful, for example, for Hal? How does he create and exploit instability? What is Falstaff's relation to instability? Can you show that he thrives on it? How does the theme of instability govern the drama of the play and the action of its characters?

2. **Usurpation:** Usurpation, the act of seizing and holding power without a legitimate right to do so, is a theme that offers students

a great many opportunities for essays. Not only are there many instances of usurpation and attempted usurpation in *1 Henry IV*, but the play is also replete with the problem of what determines the legitimacy of possessing power and what constitutes the proper way or ways of gaining and holding authority and control.

To begin to write about the theme of usurpation, a student can focus on each character individually and consider what each seeks, what he actually possesses, what he is legitimately entitled to, and what constitutes that legitimacy in his and in other people's minds. Is Henry a usurper or a legitimate king? Or both? Can circumstances cause usurpation to become legitimate? How is Falstaff an example of a usurper? With regard to Hal? With regard to his fantasies of wealth and power after Hal's accession to the throne? What about the rebel forces? Is war a usurper of peace? Consider Hotspur's wife and how war and ambition rob her of her husband long before his death.

3. **Deception:** Politics, one may argue with citations from *1 Henry IV*, is the practice of deception turned into a fine art. Deception not only underlines the events of the play, but it is a pivotal part of the verbal and rhetorical strategies the work features and employs.

To write about deception in *1 Henry IV*, you can focus on Henry's public rhetoric, Hal's general behavior and the strategy he outlines in his first soliloquy, Falstaff's lies, the tricks Hal and Poins play on Falstaff and Francis, the false reports delivered to Hotspur before the battle with the king's army, the soldiers dressed like the king in battle, or Falstaff's claim to have killed Hotspur. Deception clearly is a prevalent, ubiquitous presence in the work.

From Hal's first soliloquy at the end of 1.2, the reader knows that he is not what he seems. A writer can examine how the spirit of his interaction with Falstaff and Poins gives a degree of psychological authenticity to his apparent pretense of madcap rebellion. Given his high spirits and his Machiavellian disposition, a writer might argue that Hal is a highly disciplined actor who is skilled at staging himself for whatever audience he is performing to.

What is the effect of so much deception on the climate of the play? On the meaning of the play? Consider the theme of self-deception too. Can you argue that the characters who are so thoroughly practiced in the art of deception are also deceiving themselves?

4. **Honor:** Because of Falstaff's battlefield catechism, the theme of honor takes pride of place in *1 Henry IV.* It is the value that Hotspur lives and dies by, that Falstaff debunks, that Hal manipulates, that the king has ignored in his usurpation of the crown, and that Northumberland and Worcester violate by betraying their words and Hotspur's trust.

Whether Falstaff's dismissal of honor is simply an indication of his cowardice and dissipation or is a serious critique of the values presumed to be virtues by the other major characters in the play is worthy of an essay. Falstaff is a comic character, but does that mean he is not to be taken seriously? You can argue that absorbing or subsuming all the critiques—what are they specifically?—that Falstaff represents into a grotesque sort of comedy is the only way that the questioning of honor can be presented. In order to refute Falstaff's position on honor, is it necessary to show that it is a rationale for cowardice? The question of whether Falstaff is a coward has been the subject of many essays. It is also a common observation that Falstaff misleads Hal, but Falstaff repeatedly argues that Hal has corrupted him. Can you take what he says seriously and defend his assertion, arguing that the conception of honor most of the characters openly subscribe to dishonors something fundamental about each of them?

Character

Although *1 Henry IV* deals with a period of history fraught with political crisis, and despite its fierce battle scenes, it is not so much an action-driven work as a play richly endowed with characters. In terms of theatrical performance, the play offers a number of great roles for actors. Its characters are old and young, comic and heroic, subtle in their villainy and in their virtue. They are also all masters of language: Their speech, moreover, fits their characters and shows them as individuals. If you think about writing an essay on character and speech, you could begin by selecting representative passages from the speeches of the major characters and show how their attitudes are defined by the patterns of their speech and the notions and ideas their words express.

Sample Topics:

1. **Falstaff:** To write an essay about how Falstaff develops throughout the course of *1 Henry IV,* you might consider the difference between a character and a caricature. Which is Falstaff? What is it that makes him what he is? How much depth does he have? How does Shakespeare give Falstaff the depth he does attain? Look at Falstaff's speech at 2.4.466ff. when he is pretending to be Hal defending Falstaff before the king. By the end of that speech, who is Falstaff speaking as, Hal or himself? What does the speech suggest about Falstaff's need for Hal's love?

   When Falstaff says, as he does several times, that Hal has corrupted him, is he just being perverse and tauntingly twisting the reality of the situation, or is there truth in his contention? Can you argue that Falstaff is the central character in *1 Henry IV?* Or that his presence in the play is essential for the definition of Henry, Hal, Hotspur, and the key issues that define the play? Without Falstaff, the idea of honor would exist in *1 Henry IV* as a conventional attitude with hardly any dramatic significance.

   How interesting a character or how complex would Hal be or seem without the presence of Falstaff? Look at *The Famous Victories of Henry V,* an anonymous chronicle play written before 1588. The same riotous and dissolute figure of the young prince appears, but without Falstaff. Is Falstaff immoral or beyond morality?

2. **Hal:** Considering how thoroughly the course of Hal's life has been mapped out—as shown by his first soliloquy in act 1, scene 2, his four-word answer to Falstaff's plea not to banish him in the play Hal and Falstaff stage in the tavern, and his avowals to his father in act 3, scene 2—does Hal develop as a character? If so, how?

What kind of figure is Hal, heroic or tragic? Is he a man who realizes himself or who ultimately betrays and alienates himself when he banishes Falstaff? Does the nature of his character suggest that, in order to own and control one's own sense of identity, a literal or figurative self-betrayal or self-banishment is necessary? For this essay, a writer would need to be familiar with the second part of *Henry IV* and with *Henry V*. A good place to start is with an analysis of the opening lines of Hal's first soliloquy: "I know you all and will awhile uphold / The unyoked humor of your idleness." Hal is addressing himself in order for Shakespeare to convey his thoughts to the spectators and readers, but to whom is he speaking in his imagination, to his tavern companions or to himself? To whom do the words *you* and *your* refer? The word *all* can mean "all of you." Then Hal is saying, "I know what all of you are about—idleness." But *all* can also mean "entirely." Then Hal is actually addressing himself, as if he were his own parent. "I know all about you, and I will permit you to have your disreputable fun for a little while longer until I say you have to get serious." In that case, Hal is both the sun and the clouds that he goes on to describe. How do these different readings of "you" and "your" affect an understanding of Hal's character?

What does Hal's treatment of Falstaff reveal about Hal? Discuss how, rather than treating Falstaff like a man whom he could have chosen to befriend or leave alone, Hal has taken his cohort as a kind of demon, a repository for aspects of himself that he wants to exorcise. Is there overt cruelty in Hal's treatment and manipulation of Falstaff? It is not the only instance of how he uses people. Hal tells Henry at 3.2.147, "Percy is but my factor." Write about the scene with Francis and its implications for Hal's character.

3. **Henry:** An essay might attempt to show that Henry continuously asserts a power that is ever threatened. He is a usurper and never sure of the firmness of the grip he has on power. He is highly skilled in rhetoric, and his speech seems always to be intent on manipulating the emotions of his hearers, whether in public or in private.

Consider an essay about reproach as a rhetorical strategy of Henry and in relation to him. Do Hal and the Percy family have good reasons to reproach Henry? Notice how often reproach creeps into Henry's speech. Is he defending against possible reproaches to himself for his past crimes by taking the authority to reproach others before they can do so to him? Despite his allusions to Jesus and to his Christian duty, Henry essentially is an atheist. He is a self-made man whose fealty is to his own power.

4. **Hotspur:** An essay that describes the reasons for Hotspur's rise and fall can show how the same qualities that serve to lift Hotspur above other men are responsible for his downfall.

How does Shakespeare reveal Hotspur's character to the reader or audience? Discuss Hotspur's attitude toward women and the traits he possesses that are stereotypically considered feminine. Consider his speech to Henry about his encounter with a courtier on the battlefield just after a skirmish. Consider his exchanges with his wife. What is Kate like? How does Shakespeare show her strengths and her weaknesses? Does her husband appreciate her? How can you tell? What indications in the text describe the kind of marriage they have? Look at how they talk to each other and act when they are together. Can you argue that Hotspur is driven by a cult of masculinity? Is he a tragic or a comic figure? Is he heroic or impulsive? How does Hotspur's reaction to Owen Glendower contribute to our understanding of Hotspur's character?

History and Context

Not surprisingly, history is writ large in Shakespeare's English dramas and forms the centrepiece of *1 Henry IV,* both the history of that king and his era and the distortions, variations, and embroidering of that history that Shakespeare fashioned or refashioned in order to create his play. There is also the literary context for the play, the work seen as a precursor to Shakespeare's version, *The Famous Victories of Henry V.*

Sample Topics:

1. **Sir John Oldcastle:** When Shakespeare wrote *Henry IV,* Falstaff was first called Sir John Oldcastle, as was the character from whom he was derived in *The Famous Victories of Henry V.* There was an actual, identifiable Sir John Oldcastle in English history. His date of birth has not been established, but the date of his death is known, as he was executed on December 14, 1417. Who was the historical Sir John Oldcastle, and why did Shakespeare fictionalize his name as Falstaff? Is there any resemblance between the two figures? What about significant differences?

   Ellen M. Caldwell's essay "'Banish all the wor(l)d': Falstaff's Iconoclastic Threat to Kingship in *1 Henry I*" offers historical background and ideas about Oldcastle's influence on Shakespeare's play and is a good place for a writer interested in the period in which *Henry IV* takes place and the period in which it was performed to start.

2. ***The Famous Victories of Henry V:*** The existence of this play suggests a good comparison and contrast essay as well as an essay detailing the context of *1 Henry IV.* A writer may show how Shakespeare derived *1 Henry IV* from the earlier play as well as theorize about how Shakespeare worked, how he altered and amplified the earlier play to place history inside the context of humanity through the creation of complex characters and concepts, rather than merely reproducing common historical caricatures and legends.

Philosophy and Ideas

Like Falstaff's assertion that he is not only witty but the cause of wit in others, *1 Henry IV* is not only replete with ideas but the progenitor of ideas in others.

Sample Topics:

1. **Moral hollowness:** Grace Tiffany argues that "Falstaff's moral hollowness . . . is balanced by his exposure to the hollowness of royal claims to authority." There are two arguable assertions in

this sentence: that Falstaff is morally hollow and that Henry's claims are as well.

A writer who wishes to defend these assertions is obliged to show that they can be substantiated. What arguments can you make, drawn from your reading of *1 Henry IV* and of *Richard II*, to show that Henry has no authority to kingship? How can you show Falstaff to be morally hollow? Can you make the opposite argument? What exactly is moral hollowness in the context of *1 Henry IV* and *Richard II?*

2. **Cowardice:** Just as heroism and honor are key concepts presented in the play, so, too, is the idea of cowardice. It is usually introduced in a debate about whether Falstaff is or is not a coward.

A writer entering into that debate, after scanning the critical literature, can draw examples of Falstaff's behavior from the text to justify her position on the issue. Perhaps a distinction can be drawn between discretion and cowardice, just as one might be drawn between hotheaded impulsiveness and heroism. Can you see the play as a challenge to or reconsideration of the accepted idea of cowardice?

Form and Genre

A thoughtful consideration of form and genre can help shape an understanding and appreciation of a work of literature. A work like *1 Henry IV*, moreover, may straddle categories or be seen as deliberately ambiguous as to which genre it most closely aligns with. Shakespeare's history plays may absorb the realism and details of a given period or moment, but are there elements of comedy, tragedy, or romance present as well?

Sample Topics:

1. *1 Henry IV* **as a comedy:** A writer might argue that a play that includes the character of Falstaff cannot be exclusively or traditionally seen as a history when it features its comic aspects so prominently.

Especially telling is that both Falstaff and Hal cross over from the tavern to the battlefield. Can you argue that *1 Henry IV* is a play that uses historical events as a vehicle for psychological or philosophical purposes, rather than a mere presentation of the life and times of a group of individuals?

2. **Mirroring:** In order to examine the significance of mirroring to the drama of *1 Henry IV*, a writer can begin by cataloguing the instances and varieties of mirroring present in the play. How do events and characters in the play reflect, echo, or mirror one another? What dramatic effect is achieved with the play within the play, much less that it is presented in and arises from the world of the tavern? Is there a contrast to be made between the realm of acting and performance (or "playing") and the realm of history? Notice, too, how each of the major characters works to dramatize himself and to stage his own concerns. Characters like Hal and Hotspur both mirror each other and present variations on each other. Consider the significance of the fact that three of the leading characters have the same name.

3. *Miles gloriosus:* Falstaff's origins and the origin of his characteristics can be traced to the comic trope or type, the *miles gloriosus* or boastful soldier, a figure that has been prevalent in the theater since the comedy of the Roman playwright Plautus.

A writer can assemble an account of the type, the history of its use and development, before discussing how Falstaff reflects, continues, or enlarges the figure. What does the presence of the embodiment or a variation of the boastful soldier contribute to the play?

Language, Symbols, and Imagery

Although military might is the guarantor of power and the primary means of attaining and securing it, in *1 Henry IV*, power is formulated, exercised, defined, and asserted through the use of language.

Sample Topics:

1. **The use of language to assume or assert power:** There are a number of strategies a writer may use in arguing that the acquisition of power is a function of rhetoric. An analysis of the king's first speech reveals words being used as a means of asserting his power as authentic and manipulating his position in relation to the rest of England. Prince Hal's first soliloquy is likewise a disquisition on linguistic strategy. Hotspur bears a complex relation to language as a stutterer. A reader may also consider that his revenge against Henry includes the fantasy of having him hounded by the name *Mortimer,* which he refuses to hear. In addition, Hotspur's conflict with Owen Glendower is an argument over the language of nature.

   Falstaff himself can serve as a model for the importance of language in the construction of reality. Examine the way he defines the world by the words he uses or imposes his image of himself less through his enormous physical presence than by the words he uses to represent himself. A writer can consider the embellishing of the number of assailants he fought off at Gad's Hill as a paradigm for the use of language as the assertive tool of power and see Falstaff's boasting as a mockery of the other characters' manipulative assertions.

2. **The symbolic significance of setting:** Locations that have an objectively nonsymbolic function in the play, that serve as places where actions are set, can also be seen as having symbolic significance, particularly when examined in relation to one another.

   How do the scenes set respectively at court and at the tavern express opposing values and opposing aspects of Hal's personality and choices? Consider how they become intermixed in the mock encounter between Hal and his father when Falstaff plays the king in the tavern. A writer may also think about the two battles that appear in the play, the one on Gad's Hill during the robbery and the one on the battlefield of Shrewsbury when the king's forces confront Percy's. A writer may exam-

ine the effect of Falstaff's presence at both events or how the
second event shows the evolution of Hal's character and the
degree to which it has changed.

Compare and Contrast Essays

One of the ways of framing a work of literature and seeing its overarching elements is by comparing and contrasting elements within it. Doing
so helps a writer see the patterns and constellations of ideas, events, circumstances, characters, or locations that give it its shape and its unity.

Sample Topics:

1. **Father and son relationships:** There are a number of significant father-son relationships depicted in *1 Henry IV.* Not all of
them are blood relationships, but they do partake of the dynamics that form and are associated with the parent-child relationship. Examining the relationship in its recurring manifestations
can lead to an understanding of the major themes and issues
presented in the play.

A writer may notice that it is Henry himself who first implicitly compares Harry Percy's relationship with his father to the
Prince's relation to him. The comparison, which is to his disadvantage, indicates one of Henry's primary moods. He is forever
unsatisfied, always fearful, always lacking something. A writer
can show how his relationship with his son mirrors his relationship with England and with his own unstable sense of accomplishment. Securing the kingship has not been an existential
blessing for him. Hal's relationship with Falstaff is a father-son
relationship that can be compared with the relationship Hal has
with Henry. Alternately, a writer may consider just what elements of filiality Hal has displaced onto Falstaff and what the
significance of this displacement is for his development.

2. **Attitudes about honor:** *1 Henry IV* seems an ideal work for
comparing and contrasting the various attitudes it expresses in
regard to honor. So much is said or implied about honor in the
play, and each of the characters seems to have to define himself
through his response to the demands of honor.

Merely listing each character's concept and appropriation of honor will not accomplish much for you in the development of a thoughtful essay or in gaining insight into the possible meanings the play presents. Move beyond an urge to merely list to consider the implications of Shakespeare introducing honor in various guises. What do the several responses to the call of honor tell about the idea of honor itself and about the characters involved?

3. **The Falstaff of** *1 Henry IV* **and the Falstaff of** *The Merry Wives of Windsor:* Harold Bloom calls the manifestation of Falstaff that appears in *The Merry Wives of Windsor* an anti-Falstaff. To consider why, a writer can undertake a comparison of the character as represented in each of the plays. Show how they differ from each other. Or, if you disagree, demonstrate how the portrayals are consistent and mutually supportive. Look at the two Falstaffs' use of language, at their attitudes and dispositions, at the degree of their activity or passivity as agents of mirth.

How would you define the anti-Falstaff's behavior and character? What would be the effect on *1 Henry IV* if Falstaff had been the anti-Falstaff? How would the Falstaff of *1 Henry IV* fare in the world of *The Merry Wives of Windsor?*

Bibliography and Online Resources for *Henry IV, Part 1*

Caldwell, Ellen M. "'Banish all the wor(l)d': Falstaff's Iconoclastic Threat to Kingship in *1 Henry IV*." *Renascence: Essays on Values in Literature,* 59:4 (Summer 2007): 219–46.

(*Caldwell discusses the case of Sir John Oldcastle, who was executed as a Protestant martyr for his iconoclasm, as she argues that Oldcastle is the source for Falstaff and that Falstaff continues to represent Oldcastle's Protestant iconoclasm in his comic subversion of the images and abstractions that are promoted to elevate the idea of monarchs, in this case Henry IV and Prince Hal, to figures seeking to be regarded as greater than common men.*)

Council, Norman. "Prince Hal: Mirror of Success." *Shakespeare Studies* 7 (1974): 125–46.

(Council discusses the way Hotspur, Falstaff, and Hal treat the code of honor as it was defined in Elizabethan England, emphasizing Hal's indifference to honor as a principle and his use of it as a means of advancement.)

Forker Charles R. "The Idea of Time in Shakespeare's Second Historical Tetralogy." *Upstart Crow* 5 (Fall 1984): 20–34.
(Forker discusses the ideas of time and history as they shape the actions and confrontations in the four plays of the second tetralogy, Richard II, 1 *and* 2 Henry IV, *and* Henry V.*)*

Grossman, Marshall. "Recovering the Terror of Trifles." *Shakespeare Studies* 27 (1999): 51–64.
(This is a rather complicated essay that brings together the psychoanalytic thought of Jacques Lacan and theories of how readers' relationships to texts turn bundles of words into characters with personalities. Its central argument is that the weight of Hal's future identity as Henry V influences his present assertion and quest for identity in 1 Henry IV.*)*

Heims, Neil, ed. *Henry IV, Part I* Bloom's Shakespeare Through the Ages. New York: Chelsea House, 2008.
(This is an essential collection of critical and interpretative essays on 1 Henry IV *from the sixteenth century to the present day.)*

Kastan, David Scott. "'Killed with Hard Opinions': Oldcastle, Falstaff, and the Reformed Text of *1 Henry IV.*" *Textual Formations and Reformations,* edited by Laurie E. Maguire and Thomas L. Berger, pp. 211–27. Newark: University of Delaware Press, 1998.
(Kastan rejects recent editorial decisions to replace the name Falstaff with Shakespeare's original name Oldcastle and describes the religious and political acts for which the historical Oldcastle was executed; it also discusses how they are relevant, in Kastan's opinion, to 1 Henry IV.*)*

Kern, Edith. "Falstaff—A Trickster Figure." *Upstart Crow* 5 (Fall 1984): 135–42.
(Referring to the archetypal categories devised by the psychoanalyst Carl Jung, Kern reads Falstaff as a trickster figure and compares him with the figure of Molière's Scapin in Scapin the Trickster, *arguing that Shakespeare gave the archetype unusual depth and complexity.)*

Krieger, Elliot. "'To Demand the Time of Day': Prince Hal." *William Shakespeare's Henry IV, Part 1,* edited by Harold Bloom, pp. 101–08. New York: Chelsea House Publishers, 1987.

(Krieger distinguishes between Hal's approach and relationship to time and Falstaff's, showing how these divergences define their characters and their social roles.)

Krims, Marvin B. "Hotspur's Antifeminine Prejudice in Shakespeare's *1 Henry IV*." *Literature and Psychology* 4, nos. 1–2 (1994): 118–32.

(A psychoanalytic interpretation of Hotspur's character relying on close textual readings and arguing that his masculinity is an expression of an aversion, resulting from fear, to what are regarded as feminine characteristics.)

Quinones, Ricardo J. "The Growth of Hal." *William Shakespeare's Henry IV, Part 1,* edited by Harold Bloom, pp. 71–95. New York: Chelsea House Publishers, 1987.

(Quinones traces the development of Hal's character and his alienation from Falstaff and its significance through the two Henry IV *plays.)*

Tiffany, Grace. "Puritanism in Comic History: Exposing Royalty in the Henry Plays." *Shakespeare Studies* 26 (1998): 256–87.

(Tiffany explores the religious and political climate of Elizabethan England in the 1590s, focusing on attitudes about Puritanism, theatricalism, the image of royalty, and the means by which monarchs created a sense of legitimacy.)

English Lollardy and Sir John Oldcastle
http://history.wisc.edu/sommerville/123/123%20173%20Lollards.htm

HENRY IV, PART 2

READING TO WRITE

ALTHOUGH EACH of the four plays that together make up the tetral-ogy consisting of *Richard II; Henry IV, Part 1; Henry IV, Part 2;* and *Henry V* is, ostensibly, a complete and independent work in itself, *Henry IV, Part 2* nevertheless seems least able to stand on its own. The play is concerned with what happens after *1 Henry IV* and before *Henry V.* A reader approaching it without knowledge of those plays may feel at an interpretive loss. Each of the plays, after all, is a part of a greater whole and is best read in conjunction with the others. If a reader is to fathom each play's depths and intricacies, or to absorb and appreciate their humorous aspects, familiarity with the other plays is essential. You are reading more deeply, for example, when you examine Henry IV's open-ing address in *Part 1* in light of his dying words to Prince Hal in *Part 2.* You will miss the joke in *Part 2,* 2.4, when Hal and Poins shout "Anon, Anon" together if you do not recall the trick they played on Francis in 2.4 of *Part 1.* Still, these lapses or potential gaps of information do not limit or qualify the integrity or wholeness of either play.

In the well-known Aristotelian formulation, a play must have a beginning, middle, and end. *2 Henry IV,* however, seems to be all mid-dle. What constitutes the completeness of a drama, however, is not the span of its narrative arc but the integrity of its action. In *Richard II* the action involves the fall of one monarch and the rise of another. In *1 Henry IV,* the action traces the coming of age of Prince Hal, set within the context of his contention with and triumph over his two shadow figures. Hal must prove himself more worthy of regard and admiration than the heroic Hotspur, and he must renounce the substantial allure

133

of the sensuous idleness and boisterous mischief of Falstaff. In *Henry V,* the action concerns the wartime king forging his credentials and his right to rule as a hero-king. In *2 Henry IV,* which covers the final defeat of the rebellion, the death of Henry IV, and Hal's succession to the throne, the central action is the tragic fall of Falstaff. When what seems to be the main plot, the history of England, as conveyed through an account of the lives of its kings, is relegated to a subplot, and what seems like the subplot, the adventures and the fate of Falstaff, is taken to constitute the main plot, the integrity of the play becomes apparent.

The fall of Falstaff, the central preoccupation of *2 Henry IV,* is a result of the death of Henry IV and signifies the rise of Henry V. With the old king's death, Falstaff is no longer necessary as an object on which Hal can displace his resentment of his father and act it out. With Falstaff's banishment, Hal stabilizes his identity as Henry V. Symbolically, Falstaff is the overthrown king, like Richard II, whose fall allowed Hal's father to ascend to the throne. Equally as symbolic, Falstaff is the father who is rejected, or symbolically murdered, so that the son can free himself from his influence and achieve and occupy his own conception of manhood. Because Shakespeare made Falstaff the despised father instead of Henry and because Falstaff's place as a social outlaw makes it seem appropriate and even virtuous for Hal to reject him, Henry IV can be cast as the worthy father Hal may someday become. Hal's exchange with the chief justice in act 5, scene 2, lines 92–112 makes clear this evaluation of Henry and Hal's identification with this image of his father.

Like *Part 1, Henry IV, Part 2* is only nominally a history play. The word *history* does not appear in its complete title, *The Second Part of Henry IV.* As if underlining the point, *2 Henry IV* begins with a figure so far removed from a historical personage as not even to have a temporal existence. Rumor, "painted full of tongues," is the allegorical figure that opens *2 Henry IV* with a direct address to the audience. Rumor's most obvious function is to serve as a narrator linking the two parts of *Henry IV* and thereby establishing their separateness. Rumor quickly recapitulates what happened in *Part 1*—"in a bloody field by Shrewsbury / [Henry IV's army] Hath beaten down young Hotspur and his troops, / Quenching the flame of bold rebellion." Then Rumor announces how *Part 2* will begin, commencing with a wry self-reproach for "speak[ing] so true at first." Rumor explains that he has released a set of lies about the outcome of the battle, telling us what we will see in the first scene of *2 Henry IV*. Consequently, when that scene commences, immediately following Rumor's exit, we are not concentrating on narrative or on irony. The vicissitudes of perception, the foolishness of certainty, and the consequences of character, not history, are the main concerns of the scene. We know what happened; we know what is going to happen; and we know that what Northumberland first hears is a mistaken account of the outcome of the battle.

Our focus is on the vacuousness of Lord Bardolph, on the character of Northumberland, and on the themes of a father's betrayal of his son and the unreliability of words. As Northumberland responds to news of his son's death, he vows to mobilize his forces in a renewed assault on the king. "Now let not Nature's hand / Keep the wild flood confined" (1.1.153ff), he rants in the manner of the dead Hotspur. However, when the time comes, in 2.3, for him to lead his troops to the field of battle and supplement the other rebel forces, he withholds this promised support from his partners in rebellion, as he had before from his son, and flees to safety in Scotland. What Northumberland says and what he does remain at odds. He is all talk. Consider an essay discussing the proposition that just as Northumberland is the object of rumors, he is the agent of hypocrisy and hypocrisy is a variety of treachery. For the full extent of his treacherous character, you will want to review his role in the deposition of Richard II.

Although act 1, scene 2 moves from Northumberland to Falstaff, the theme of rumor, of the promiscuous nature of gossip and unsubstantiated language, is extended. Among Falstaff's first words are his concern for his reputation and the extent to which he is the subject of other people's talk. Falstaff embodies the liberation of language from fact. Like rumor, language for Falstaff is an aesthetic feat, signifying nothing but itself, the pleasure of its own performance, and the effects it allows a speaker to create. Language severed from veracity or factuality is not exclusive to Falstaff or to the sort of accidental misinformation that comes to Northumberland: It is an art practiced in several scenes of *2 Henry IV* by the king, the prince, and his brother, John of Lancaster. Were you to write about this aspect of the use of language, you would need to choose a number of examples to show that language determines our perception of reality sometimes more than our perception determines our words. How does the play treat language as a tool of deception, as a means to be used for achieving power, and as an instrument of power?

Rumor not only introduces the play, by means of that introduction, but it establishes a formal boundary separating *1* and *2 Henry IV*. Rumor also taunts the audience for its curiosity and alerts the audience to the folly of trusting what it hears and is told. The liability and the lability of language, its capacity to suffer transmutations and, consequently, to deceive and betray, through lies, equivocation, and the distortions of memory or desire, constitute the themes that dominate the play and shape its events and the actions of its characters. *2 Henry IV*, then, because it is made formally independent by means of an allegorical introduction, because the dominant themes include the vicissitudes of language and the ambiguities of power and personality, and because it has a single unifying action to which the other actions of the play attach themselves, is an independent, self-contained work of literature.

Like all of the plays in the tetralogy and like the complete body of Shakespeare's work, *2 Henry IV* gains in meaning, depth, and resonance when it is read with its companion pieces in mind even when it can stand as a unified work by itself. Without the character of Falstaff, however, *2 Henry IV* would be a page in a textbook recounting a failed rebellion and the resulting, with Hal's ascension to the throne, consolidation of Lancastrian power. Viewed, alternately, as the fall of Falstaff, *2 Henry IV* becomes, in part, a tragedy. The dramatic conflicts and tensions that Henry and Hal endure separately and in relation to each other are catalyzed by Falstaff. You might consider developing an essay to show how the fact of Falstaff as a character in the play affects the historical characters and events that exist apparently outside the boundaries of Falstaff's tragedy.

Before Falstaff can be properly understood as a tragic figure and as the central figure of the play, he must be seen as a problematic figure. For a reader hoping to write about Falstaff's role in *2 Henry IV*, the challenge is not in succumbing to a reductive or overly simplistic view of the character and seeing his primary function as comic relief intended to distract attention from the serious business of British history. A reader must detail everything about Falstaff that makes him nuanced, multidimensional, and potentially difficult to understand and locate within the world of the play. An examination of each of his scenes should yield a sizable catalog of problems. The question is what sort of constellation these problems form and what generalizations about Falstaff can be drawn from thinking about them. Perhaps the first response a reader can have after considering Falstaff in the aggregate is ambivalence. Can you argue that the ambivalence that attaches to Falstaff also ought to character-ize the way we regard Henry, Hal, and John? Is the defining difference between them and Falstaff that their rank and power legitimize actions in them that we can see as grotesque and deplorable in him, a representa-tive of a lower social class and order?

While the Falstaff of *1 Henry IV* is charming despite what many may see as his incorrigibility, the Falstaff of the second part is far more grat-ing. As a recruiter for the army and as a conman who takes advantage of Shallow, for example, he seemingly stands in opposition to any sense of decency. Whereas Falstaff in *Part 1* may be seen as a corrective, deflating the sins of ambition and power, the Falstaff featured in the second part seems to be a sinner in those very realms himself. Yet he is not, like the ersatz Falstaff of *The Merry Wives of Windsor,* a different person altogether from the character presented in the first part. He is still himself, yet, if possible, he is inflated. In *1 Henry IV,* he had Prince Hal for an audience and as a corrective who served as the essential "other" to whom he could offer his comic persona for their mutual gratification. In *2 Henry IV,* fre-quently lacking Hal, Falstaff recoils in the lack of a confidant, protégé, or sidekick. He becomes full of himself and overconfident, intoxicated by his own comic power to charm. He lacks the discipline of Hal's adversarial affection to contain his expansiveness. He pushes beyond the boundaries of himself and treats the world as if it were contained within him. It is a form of hubris and, in his case, a comic tragic flaw.

If you were to pursue this argument in an essay, you would want to check the classical understanding of tragedy, reacquaint yourself with the idea of hubris and the ironic ambiguity that defines a tragic flaw, and examine Falstaff's scenes to see his flaws and show how, metaphorically, Falstaff defies the gods by assuming their stature and falls because of the very greatness and elevated position he achieves. Oddly enough, in that way he represents a humanity that the king and the prince do not share.

TOPICS AND STRATEGIES

The reason we write essays, beyond to fulfill a requirement or to success-fully complete a course, is to say something important to us that we want other people to know in a way that engages them. Writing about a play of Shakespeare's often presents the challenge that we are more than 400 years removed from the world he was writing in and about and that he wrote in an

English that, although modern, unlike Chaucer's or Edmund Spenser's, is yet not quite the English that we use today. Some of the excitement derived from reading Shakespeare comes from realizing that he writes about us, in a language that is ours, and that more than distance and difference, there is proximity, interrelation, and a similarity of experience presented in the work. As readers, then, we must be patient and careful and bring ourselves to bear on the act of reading. The American philosopher John Dewey (1859–1952) argued, in *Art as Experience,* that art is not something out there that we passively look at, watch, read, or listen to but rather is an experience that happens in the space created midway between the work of art and the person encountering it. For the work of art to exist, it is just as important that we bring something to it as that it brings something to us.

When you read, for example, the scenes with Northumberland, you think of what it feels like to be betrayed or to have betrayed someone else. When his widowed daughter-in-law, Kate, Lady Percy, speaks to him in act 2, scene 3, about his honor, she is not reciting speeches but reminding Northumberland, while controlling her anger, that he betrayed his son, the husband she loved and still loves, and let him die in a battle during which Northumberland feigned sickness in order to avoid fighting. When you read the exchanges between Henry IV and Hal, remember that they are a father and his son: a father complaining that his son does not love him, does not behave as he would like him to; a son torn between his duty to his father and his powerful ambition to be on his own, torn between indulgence and responsibility. Although you will not be writing about your own biographical experiences, your own experiences will give dimension to what you have read and inform the argument you formulate about Lady Percy's character, or Falstaff's bravado, or Northumberland's capacity for rationalization, or Henry IV's unsettling sense of his own hollowness.

Themes

Finding the themes in *2 Henry IV* involves examining the text closely for ideas, situations, and even words that recur. Consider writing about the importance of any of the following themes: betrayal, time, rumor, deception, rebellion, violence, disease, retribution, nostalgia, sleep, and weariness. With these topics in mind, return to the play to see if having one or several of these topics in mind helps you focus on what a scene is about or on how several apparently diverse scenes have common elements.

Sample Topics:

1. **Disease:** References to disease and sickness and allusions to illness occur throughout *2 Henry IV*, beginning with Rumor's mention of Northumberland as being "crafty-sick." Falstaff's first words are an inquiry about his own health. There is something to do with sickness in nearly every scene thereafter. Henry IV suffers from a recurring illness that finally kills him, and his realm is sick with strife.

   Examine the number of instances and references to illness and the types of illness presented. Consider the way Shakespeare uses disease and sickness dramatically and as metaphor. From your survey, develop a thesis about the role and significance of illness and disease in the play.

2. **History:** How is history itself a theme in the play?

   The scenes with Justice Shallow are a good place to start in order to develop a thesis about the vision of history presented in the play. Shallow continually refers to the past with a nostalgia that suggests that his memory and his disposition have distorted the past. Falstaff confirms this in his remarks about Shallow. Rumor also challenges the authority and unassailable veracity of history. Time, as Henry V's response to his own actions as Prince Hal suggests, can alter, if not the facts of history, then an understanding of those facts.
   Using examples from the text, you can argue that the play shows the unreliability of history and how history is subject to distortion because of human frailty, vanity, and mutability. This internal critique of history affects the way we view and interpret the events we are reading in this history play.

3. **Betrayal, deception, and rebellion:** Should you choose to write about the theme of betrayal, you will need to do more than list instances of it in the play despite how numerous they are. One of the first things you might consider and demonstrate is that betrayal, deception, and rebellion are actually versions of the

same thing and each potentially supports, encourages, or bleeds into the other.

You will want to consider what constitutes betrayal, deception, and rebellion, how betrayal is a function of point of view, how deception is a fault or a strategy, and how rebellion is a term each side can apply to the other. Henry's faction considers Northumberland's as betrayers of the monarchy, while Northumberland's camp believes Henry betrayed his initial promise when he stood against Richard.

You can also discuss what effect betrayal has on individual characters, both on the betrayed and the betrayers, how it shapes the social order. What might Shakespeare be saying about the role of betrayal in the acquisition and consolidation of power, or about the relation of expectation to the actual outcomes in the play of historical events and their effects on people. In Shakespeare's history plays, is history itself fundamentally a chronicle of one betrayal or deception after another?

4. **Sleep:** What is the role of sleep in *2 Henry IV?* How is sleep portrayed, and how do the characters in the play speak of sleep? The king complains of not being able to sleep although his poorest subjects can. What does this say about monarchy? Or does it say less about monarchy and more about the way Henry got the crown and the trouble he had in keeping it because of external rebellion and his own sense of guilt? Are there textual indications that Henry feels guilt for deposing Richard? What happens when Henry is finally able to fall asleep in act 4?

Hal, upon becoming king, says he has awakened from a sleep in which he dreamed of Falstaff. What does that indicate about Hal's sense of the humanity of others, how he sees their existence in relation to his? If you have read *Henry V,* what does it presage about his reign, his war, and his use of others in the play? How does sleep contribute to the way a reader thinks about various characters in the play and the nature of their roles? What relationship does Shakespeare draw between sleep and power? Is the price of power constant wakefulness? What does that say about power?

5. **Rumor:** How can you evaluate the role of language in the play? A writer can start with Rumor's prologue. What is the relationship between the use of language and the wielding of power? Are there instances of action that show a difference between rumor and speech? Consider the bond between rumor and deception as forms of speech and the importance of deception, whether John's, Falstaff's, or Hal's.

What is the relationship between truth and the spoken word in *2 Henry IV*? Again, look at how Falstaff, Northumberland, Hal, Henry, Shallow, the chief justice, Prince John, Pistol, and Mistress Quickly speak, what their relationship to truth is, and what truth means to them. How does their speech assemble or construct their presence as characters? Are they reliable speakers? Is it coincidental that in a play introduced by Rumor there is also a character named Silence? How reliable are speech and language in the pursuit of truth in *2 Henry IV?* If language is unreliable, is the truth of history absolute or only an authorized version of codified rumors? How does the presence of Falstaff affect your view of the truth of history? You might review events from his perspective as well as from the official perspective.

Character

Essays focusing on issues of character development can look at a character's speech patterns. What makes one character sound different from another? What, for example, characterizes Henry's speech? What are the means of characterization Shakespeare uses to make us know a character? How does an audience learn about a character from what he or she says about him- or herself or from what others say about him or her? Does a character change as the play proceeds? Does Falstaff presume himself increasingly invincible as the play proceeds? How can we tell? Are there indications of a buildup to Hal's rejection of Falstaff? How does Shakespeare create the illusion that a character is an individual?

Sample Topics:

1. **Falstaff's character development:** To write about Falstaff's development in *2 Henry IV* it is useful to go back to *Part 1*. How has Falstaff changed from the first to the second part, if at all? If he has changed, is he the cause or are there other circumstances, like changes in Hal or the historical agenda, that are responsible? How do his changes affect the nature of the play itself in comparison to *Part 1?*

   Following his actions in *Part 2*, do you see Falstaff developing? Discuss what events indicate that change and propel it in turn through the play. Is there a difference between robbing the carriers in *1 Henry IV* and fleecing Shallow in *Part 2?* Does Falstaff become increasingly covetous and self-aggrandizing? Does the nature of his covetousness change? Consider comparing the role of playfulness in his character and motivation in each play. How important is his distance from Hal in *Part 2* for his development?

2. **Hal's character development:** How does the portrayal of Hal differ in *2 Henry IV* from his portrayal in *Part 1?* What is the significance of his diminished contact with Falstaff? Of his exchanges with Poins? How does Shakespeare show the audience what Hal is like? How is Hal different from how he appears in the court scenes as opposed to the tavern scenes? When he appears in act 4 with his father and in act 5 with the chief justice and then with Falstaff, is Hal recognizably himself, or has he become an entirely different person from the one he had been? Consider the degree of his own self-awareness, by reviewing his utterances throughout the two plays, as a unifying factor in Shakespeare's portrayal of him.

   When Henry accuses the prince of wishing his father's death, does Hal's response reflect something he has learned from Falstaff? Notice how Shakespeare shows both what Hal says as he takes the crown and when he addresses it while Henry sleeps and what Hal tells Henry he said. How much has he integrated deception and rumor into his rhetorical arsenal? How does Hal, as the new king, dramatically exploit the tense expectations in regard to his opinion of the chief justice? What does his sense of his own dramatic possibility foreshadow for *Henry V?*

3. **Lady Percy as a character:** Excepting Mistress Quickly, the tavern keeper, and Doll Tearsheet, the prostitute, Lady Percy is the only major female character in the play. Lady Northumberland, her mother-in-law, speaks all of five lines.

What kind of figure is Hotspur's widow? She appears in only one scene, yet she bears a great deal of moral weight in the play because of a strong sense of the basic humanity that attaches to her. How does Shakespeare convey her humanity? A writer would need to examine her own tributes to Hotspur and her responses to her father-in-law and the way she speaks to him to show how Shakespeare portrays how she mingles anger and love for (or is it duty to?) Northumberland, how she reproaches and shows concern for him, all in the context of her living grief for her dead husband. How does her presence affect a reader's judgment of the other characters in the play, if at all?

4. **Henry IV and Falstaff:** How are these characters presented in the play? Are they complementary figures, or do they represent significantly different kinds of people?

This essay would need to describe and evaluate both characters, their relation to Hal, and their relation to each other, which does exist, despite the fact that they never exchange a word and Falstaff is only once in Henry's presence in *Part 1.* Their relationship is a function of Hal's relation to each of them. Are there qualities or characteristics that they share? If so, what does that signify for the play? How does each regard the other? How does each regard Hal? How does Hal's behavior to them and his opinion of them influence ours? How do we know what Hal's opinions are?

5. **The character of Prince John:** Depending on your point of view, Prince John is either a brilliant strategist or a knave with no sense of honor. Can this ambiguity be resolved? Or is the presence of this seeming duality an important insight into human conflict?

Although he is not a major character, Prince John is important as a leader of the king's army against the rebels, and he is particularly potent as a contrast to Prince Hal, especially because in *Part 2* there are moments of interaction between him and Falstaff. You might begin to consider his character by looking at Falstaff's remarks about Prince John. His performance at the battle of Gaultree Forest, a skirmish that does not take place, is central to understanding him. Any discussion of John ought to begin with the concept of equivocation.

6. **Falstaff:** Just about everyone has something to say about Falstaff, including Falstaff himself, and a majority of the characters, from the women in the tavern to the princes of the realm to the newly crowed king, interact with him. How does Falstaff serve to reveal the characters of others in *2 Henry IV?*

History and Context

As in *1 Henry IV,* both the history of Henry and his era and the historical distortions, variations, and embellishments that Shakespeare fashioned or refashioned in writing the play emerge as central concerns. Meditations on kingship and nationalism are also at the heart of these plays. A writer could use these works to evaluate the authority generally afforded to history as a force for governing our values and ideals.

Sample Topics:

1. **Politics in the play:** The kind of politics called Machiavellian is implicit throughout the four plays that constitute the second tetralogy. Both Henry and Hal are adept Machiavellians. Falstaff represents the opposite of Machiavellianism, although he has no compunction about telling lies.

Writers interested in the history of the evolution of government and power in Shakespeare's time can look at Nicolo

Machiavelli's *The Prince* (1513, published 1532) and discuss Machiavelli's philosophy of governing and its relevance to understanding the politics of *2 Henry IV* and the psychology of its major characters. Although the word *Machiavellian* is usually used in a pejorative sense, can you argue that Hal— you would be arguing from Hal's point of view—is a positive embodiment of the typically vilified Machiavellian figure?

2. **Puritanism:** Falstaff was originally named Oldcastle and was thought to be based on Sir John Oldcastle. Oldcastle was a Protestant martyr executed for sedition in 1417 for having plotted against Henry V. Because there was strong anti-Puritan sentiment in the England of the 1590s, some scholars have seen Falstaff as a caricature of Puritanical values.

Writers interested in studying the influence that Puritan attitudes and attitudes about Puritanism may have exerted on Shakespeare's play should examine the history of Lollardy (a Protestant sect founded in England, in 1330, by John Wycliffe), the life of Sir John Oldcastle, and the activities of the Puritans and the popular response to them in the 1590s.

Philosophy and Ideas

History is more than an accumulation of facts, and it is not a record of objective truth. Facts themselves are not unalterable and universally agreed on. History, it can be argued, is an interpretation of facts, written to promote one set of ideas or to exclude another; it can be seen as a kind of interpretive argument or a form of philosophy. The *Henry IV* plays, while they can be read as versions of history because of their ambiguity and because of Falstaff's presence in them, can also be seen as challenges to history, as deliberate subversions of history's authority.

Sample Topics:

1. **Order versus mirth:** The undisciplined and idle mirth that Falstaff represents and the controlling order and eventual Lancastrian power that Hal pursues and ultimately stands for are opposing characteristics that seem to provoke and justify

each other. Falstaff's unchecked license suggests the need for restraints that the state can impose. The rigidity and heartlessness of a state's power suggests the defiance, disorder, and disregard that Falstaff brings.

To pursue this topic in depth, you might consider drawing material from the play that shows this position to be true and demonstrate how each provokes and demands the existence of the other. You might begin by showing what the Falstaffian vision of life is, what the monarchical vision is, and how they interact.

2. **Individuality and conformity or the struggle between self and society:** The struggle between the individual and society, between conformity to the rules of the established order and a defiant spirit of individualism, still an important issue today, seems to be at the root of the troubled relationship that exists between Hal and Falstaff. It also seems to be at the heart of the tensions that trouble Hal's relationship with his father.

To construct an essay examining how this tension governs Hal's character and behavior, or Falstaff's, draw on material from the play that shows how the conflict tests and defines the characters and their relationships. What is the significance of the way or ways in which the conflict between individual desires and social responsibilities is or fails to be resolved in the play? You can argue that Hal's dissipation, although overtly a strategy devoted to developing a bright royal image for him, can also be seen as his attempt to be a private person. You can also argue that the public sphere keeps intruding on Falstaff's privacy. Can you contend that in his fantasy of his own good fortune, after Hal becomes king, that Falstaff is imposing private matter in the public realm and that Hal's disengagement from him is a rebuke of the public realm?

3. **Virtue:** Although the word appears all of three times in the play, twice to mean "power," a reader can still pursue a fruitful discussion of what *2 Henry IV* has to say about the idea of virtue.

Does the play give a sense of what constitutes virtue and what constitutes vice? Or is the play ambivalent when it comes to these subjects? Consider Hal's renunciation of Falstaff in this regard. Is it a virtuous assumption of responsibility or a vicious betrayal of a deep friendship? In either case, how can you tell?

Form and Genre

Form and genre provide helpful ways of thinking about and describing literary works. In the case of *2 Henry IV,* the form is drama, but what exactly is the genre? Ostensibly, it is history, but is that a completely accurate assessment? Certainly all the scenes with Falstaff, although they occur (some quite tangentially) within the context of historical events, are not concerned with history. Given Falstaff's frequent designation as a buffoon, are they comic instead? Comedy is a genre that relies on a happy ending, usually the marriage of lovers, and on the deflation of the comic figure who stands outside the social order and threatens it until the end of the play, when he is deflated, reduced in his own self-regard, rendered harmless, and integrated into the community, just as the lovers are through marriage and the force of passion tamed by that social institution. *The Merry Wives of Windsor* is a textbook example of such a comedy, and the ersatz Falstaff of that play is a comic character who threatens the social order and is then deflated and reintegrated. *2 Henry IV,* however, does not follow this pattern. While Hal's coronation might be regarded as a kind of marriage, a ceremony making him the husband of the English people (remembering that a husband is a manager, coming from the verb *to husband,* which means "to manage prudently like a good steward"), is Falstaff deflated at play's end? He is crushed, decommissioned, and expelled from the community, but can you make a case that that rejection endows him with greater stature in our eyes than he had acquired before, that it is Hal who is deflated? Could you argue that Falstaff's part in the play is a kind of tragedy, representing the fall of a great man who in the pride of his self-regard overreaches the boundaries of mortality and in consequence loses his exalted place if not his life, as it will be reported in *Henry V* that Falstaff does? Or can you argue that *2 Henry IV* is a generic hybrid enclosing comedy and tragedy inside the envelope of history? Is Hal's ascension as a king, paradoxically, a fall as a man?

Sample Topics:

1. **History as comedy/comedy as tragedy:** If history is more than facts and, at the very least, represents a particular arrangement of facts and a supposition or reconstruction of motives, how does your perspective concerning *2 Henry IV* affect the meaning and experience of the play?

   What happens if you read Falstaff as a comic figure? As a tragic figure? Or if you read King Henry as a comic figure, endlessly harping on his son? Alternately, is he a tragic figure, diseased by his own ambition? Can you read Hal as a tragic figure whose coronation represents the death of a dream, a dream that his rank, responsibilities, and social circumstances prevent him from pursuing?

2. *2 Henry IV* **as drama:** *2 Henry IV,* like all of Shakespeare's plays, was written for the stage, not for the classroom or for personal reading, which is where and how most of us often encounter it. It is, after all, a play intended to be performed before an audience for entertainment and enjoyment, and it had to keep the spectators' voluntary attention.

   Discuss the elements of *2 Henry IV* that make it exciting as drama, as comedy, and as a depiction of human experiences. Are there things about it that tend, in your view, to weaken it? Are there parts that you find tedious or extraneous? Describe them and, closely citing the text, discuss why and how they seem to fail. Refer to the language of the play, the stage directions and conventions, the action, the emotions aroused or not aroused, and the tensions created or the interactions that fall flat.

Language, Symbols, and Imagery

Language is in itself symbolic because it represents abstract meaning through the use of words. Words themselves are actions, not just in the theater, but in and of themselves. When Hal, now Henry V, repudiates Falstaff, it is a dramatic gesture accomplished by language. Falstaff's response, also spoken, to himself can be seen as symbolic also. He makes the excuses he does not only for Hal but in order to hide a broken heart. The pathos of his bluster symbolically recalls when this sort of sparring between them, when Hal's continuous repudiation of him, was a game that was the outward indicator of their closeness.

Sample Topics:

1. **Disease:** The way that the use of imagery contributes to theme may be considered through Shakespeare's use of disease imagery. Disease is a significant theme in *2 Henry IV*. Among the numerous images of disease in the play, one of the most interesting comes in 1.2.246 ff. Falstaff begins by speaking of "this consumption of the purse" and concludes with the resolution to "turn diseases to commodity."

   You might begin by considering the meaning of the word *commodity* as Shakespeare used it in the Bastard Faulconbridge's soliloquy beginning "Mad world! Mad kings" at line 561 of act 2, scene 1 of *King John*. From there, you might consider how the idea of "wasting away" functions throughout *2 Henry IV*. The king, Henry IV, who began as such a figure of strength in *Richard II* and throughout the course of *2 Henry IV*, has been wasting away. Hal, on the other hand, has used the strategy of turning liabilities to assets as a strategy for success. Can you show by an analysis of his speech that, in his mind, he has emerged from a diseased association?

2. **Key images:** Sometimes one image can serve as a key to an entire work. Consider this passage, beginning at line 119 of act 1, scene 1:

   > And as the thing that's heavy in itself,
   > Upon enforcement flies with greatest speed,
   > So did our men, heavy in Hotspur's loss,
   > Lend to this weight such lightness with their fear
   > That arrows fled not swifter toward their aim
   > Than did our soldiers, aiming at their safety,
   > Fly from the field.

Pay particular attention to the implicit comparison of soldiers to arrows. Men are being imagined as things. From that image one might begin to argue that the worldview promulgated in *2 Henry IV* denies men a multidimensional definition of humanity and determines them to be instruments intended for a specific end. This view can apply to the king as well as to the lowest soldier. Inside a world so determined, how is Falstaff, who also uses men as things and is used as a thing himself, not an inevitable presence? What other images in *2 Henry IV* can you find that can penetrate one of the work's fundamental meanings?

Compare and Contrast Essays

The value of a paper comparing and contrasting two works or several elements within a particular work is that it can illuminate the works or the elements—characters, attitudes, ideas, mannerisms, ways of speaking, codes of behavior or of ethics—by means of showing the significance and implications of the similarities and/or of the differences you discover. Comparing Prince Hal and Prince John and discussing whether John becomes more like Hal or Hal becomes more like John not only tells you something about each of them but presents an insight into the view of power and honor that guides the House of Lancaster. That can help you formulate an argument about your opinion of Henry IV and Prince Hal.

Sample Topics:

1. **Hal, appearance versus reality:** The problem in distinguishing between appearance and actuality runs through Shakespeare's work, and it plays an important part in the construction of Hal's character. Hal repeatedly thwarts or fails to fulfill other characters' expectations, from his father to Falstaff. In the scene with the chief justice, Hal reveals himself in an unanticipated way. He often defines himself not only by the way he addresses himself but by the way he addresses others, revealing himself and surprising them, whether it is his father, Poins, his brother, or the other tavern folk. You can begin an essay in comparison by examining a number of his speeches and utterances.

   The contrast between what he says as he takes the crown from his father's pillow, for example, and what he later says he said when he explains to his father why he took the crown reveals things about his character in regard to his thoughts about himself and about the way he invents himself. Ultimately, these considerations suggest the kind of king he will become and the strategies he will use as a ruler.

2. **Comparing the two parts of Henry IV:** *Part 2* continues to tell the story of English monarchical history, but *Part 2* is not a recycling of *Part 1*, although there are structural similarities. Many of the same characters inhabit both parts, and although they remain recognizably themselves, they are not the same in *Part 2* as in *Part 1*. They develop and change over time. You might say they become more themselves or one aspect becomes predominant. There are also characters introduced in the Falstaff sections who were not present in *1 Henry IV*.

   Discuss what effect these new characters have on the differences you find in the plays and what they contribute to the play's themes. Are they simply replacements for characters like Hal, whose time is not devoted any longer to Falstaff, or do they bring something new to Falstaff and to the play? The tone, feeling, and spirit of the two parts are different, as well as the structure, although the first part sometimes anticipates the second, and the second part sometimes recalls elements and aspects of the first. Comparing and contrasting the two parts can help you develop a thesis about the view of history, or character, or narrative propounded by the plays and/or about the vision the plays present in regard to the relation between the individual and society or about attitudes toward responsibility.

3. **Comparing and contrasting what Falstaff says about himself and what others say about him:** A character whose opinion of himself is so at odds with everyone else's view of him must be deluded. Yet, that term hardly applies to Falstaff. Or does it? Is he deluded about Hal? Or is he venturesome despite an inevitability he senses? How does Falstaff's idea of himself compare to other characters' notions and opinions of him? Is he deflated by other characters' observations about him, or is his peculiar

greatness actually reinforced by their attitudes and statements and by his reactions to them? Is he diminished or enhanced by his final, great rejection? There is a great deal in the text available to use in support of this topic.

Because Falstaff speaks copiously about himself, as do many other characters, a writer can find many approaches to drawing conclusions about Falstaff that derive from within and from outside himself and meditate on the power of perspective in producing reality.

Bibliography for *Henry IV, Part 2*

Black, James. "Discourse of Occasion in Henry IV." *Cahiers Elisabethains*, no. 37, April, 1990, pp. 27–42.
(*Focusing on both parts of Henry IV, Black separates the comic and historic strands of the play and discusses the influence of each on the other, contending that the historic section involves "redeeming time" and the comic section concerns avoiding conclusive action.*)

Crawford, Nicholas. "The Discourse of Dilution in 2 Henry IV." *Renaissance Papers*, 2002, pp. 61–76.
(*Crawford explores the nature of speech as presented in* 2 Henry IV, *concentrating on its power to falsify, obstruct, delay, and sabotage historical progress.*)

Davis, Jo Ann. "Henry IV: From Satirist to Satiric Butt." *Aeolian Harps: Essays in Literature in Honor of Maurice Browning Cramer,* edited by Donna G. Fricke and Douglas C. Fricke, pp. 81–93. Bowling Green, Ohio: Bowling Green University Press, 1976.
(*Davis traces Henry's development from* Richard II, *where she sees him as a satirist of Richard's authority and a figure who dominates the action, to an object of derision in the two plays named for him, in which he is not the dominant figure but the butt of Falstaff's mockery and superceded in paternal authority by the chief justice.*)

Goddard, Harold. *"Henry IV."* In *Modern Critical Views: William Shakespeare: Histories and Poems,* edited by Harold Bloom, pp. 57–110. New York: Chelsea House Books, 1986.

(Goddard is one of the great twentieth-century Shakespeare critics. Among many brilliant insights is his character analysis of Henry and his description of the duality of Hal's personality and its expression in the alternating scenes of tavern and court.)

Grady, Hugh. "Falstaff: Subjectivity between the Carnival and the Aesthetic." *The Modern Language Review*, vol. 96, no. 3, July 1, 2001.
(In an essay sometimes weighed down by academic jargon, Grady presents a picture of Falstaff as a freeing libidinal force countering the governing forces of Machiavellian power.)

Hawkins, Sherman H. "Virtue and Kingship in Shakespeare's Henry IV." English Literary Renaissance, vol. 5, no. 3, Autumn 1975, pp. 313–43.
(Hawkins interprets the subject of both parts of Henry IV *to be Hal's education for kingship, which consists of his learning the four "kingly virtues," "temperance and fortitude," in Part 1, by overcoming Falstaff and Hotspur and "justice and wisdom" in Part 2 by learning to govern himself and rule others.)*

Taylor, Mark. *"Henry IV* and Proleptic Mimesis." *Shakespeare's Imitations*, pp. 66–106. Newark: University of Delaware Press, 2002.
(In addition to discussing the resemblance of the four plays that constitute what some critics call the Henriad to the Aeneid, *Taylor focuses primarily on scenes that are plays within the four plays in order to show how "later moments [in the plays] always condition and reconfigure earlier ones." As part of this discussion, he analyzes the importance of "The Beggar and the King" interlude in* Richard II.)

Weiss, Theodore. "Now of All Humours: *Henry VI, Parts I and II.*" *The Breath of Clowns and Kings: Shakespeare's Early Comedies and Histories*, pp. 260–97. New York: Atheneum, 1971.
(Weiss argues that the plays represent the rich diversity of the culture of the English Renaissance as opposed to the narrow medievalism represented by the figure of Richard II and that such rich diversity is brought together in an acceptable order by Hal when he becomes Henry V.)

HENRY V

READING TO WRITE

THE ALLURE of *Henry V* (1598–99) is not necessarily found in its brisk action, the grand events it recounts, or its range of colorful characters. It is a consequence of the self-conscious theatricality with which those elements are presented and of the way its royal hero is able to dramatize himself and his will. The structure of the play deliberately calls attention to the fact that it is a play. Each act is preceded by the Chorus, who calls attention to the structure and construction of the play, to the fact that it is a work of dramatic writing being acted in a theater, to the limits of representation, as well as to events that are only narrated or are about to be shown. The Chorus, additionally, identifies the audience as such and asks it to play its role as spectators and "piece out our imperfections with your thoughts."

Within the context of this overt theatricality, the figure of Henry performs himself not just for the audience members but for the characters in the drama, investing himself with his role as king. By turning everyone, whether onstage or in the audience, into spectators, he secures their consent to his authority. In this way, Henry V does the same thing that his father, Henry IV, had done throughout his career and that he himself has done in his youth in the two parts of *Henry IV.* The difference is that, in *Henry V,* the fact that the king is a theatrical figure who uses theater to advance and sometimes to mask his projects is not just part of the plot but becomes the central theme and the essential action of the play. Henry IV and Prince Hal, in the two parts of *Henry IV,* must keep the fact that they are acting hidden. Look at Hal's act 1, scene 2 soliloquy in *1 Henry IV* as an example. Henry V, however, differs because of the transparent way he openly performs for us and for everybody in the play—his soldiers, his adversaries, the woman he woos, even himself. Consider how you would develop a thesis centering on this key observation: In *Henry V,* acting is not a sign of insincerity, as it is in the two parts of *Henry IV. Henry V* makes acting the way sincerity asserts itself.

Henry's success is the result of his bravura use of language. Whether he is speaking as a man deeply burdened by care in his "Upon the king" speech or praying in "O God of battles," even when alone, Henry plays a role. It is as if he is reassuring himself, as well as everyone else, that he is the royal personage he portrays and not the boisterous follower of Falstaff, the role he has rejected, nor an heir to the throne with only a precarious claim. Henry's theatricality, not his heroism, makes him a great character. By means of his theatricality, because he is so good at it, Henry becomes heroic because he can create the impression that he is heroic. The persona that he projects reflects the idea that what he accomplishes is at once heroic and the will of God. In the fifth act prologue, the Chorus describes his theatrical renunciation of theatrical pride when Henry refuses "his lords['] desire" to bear "his bruised helmet and his bended sword / Before him through the city / Being free from vainness and self-glorious pride / Giving full" credit for the victory "to God."

No matter what we may think of Henry's motives for war, or of Henry as a politician or conqueror, his dramatic eloquence—which is essential to his capacity for self-reflexively dramatizing each of his actions, gestures, and ventures—charms and impresses us, as it wins over nearly everyone in the play, excepting the ludicrous Dauphin. Henry's cunning wit and his resourcefulness at playing the kind of tricks that defined Hal's behavior in the two parts of *Henry IV* have not disappeared with his ascension to the throne and his rejection of Falstaff. They have been translated into another realm or mode, revived in the way he responds to the Dauphin's gift of tennis balls; in the way he works up to the execution of Scroop, Cambridge, and Grey in act 2, scene 2; in his nocturnal visits in disguise with his soldiers in act 4, scene 1; in his staging a quarrel between Williams and Fluellen in act 4, scene 7; and in his wooing of Katherine in act 5, scene 2. Every time Henry speaks, he is staging himself, always in order to present himself as a humble, heroic figure doing God's work with God's help. Henry's courage is beyond intimidation by any circumstances, no matter how

daunting they may seem, yet he is never foolhardy because the rhetorical and dramatic resources of humility, good nature, and heroic majesty seem inexhaustible within him.

His campaign begins in France outside the gates of Harfleur with
one of Shakespeare's most powerful set pieces, the great clarion cry to
battle, "Once more unto the breach, dear friends." These 35 lines illuminate Henry's character, showcase his rhetorical skill, and demonstrate
the sensibility of the drama that contains him. Analysis of the speech
must combine discussion of its content with dissection of its individual
words, of assonance and consonance and of the metrics that bring heroic
music to the long utterance. The force of *Henry V,* like the moodiness of
Richard II, resides in its poetry. Henry is as much a poet as Richard, but
it is not Richard's self-exposing, introspective lyricism of inquiry that
he commands but an epic martial verse of pageantry and exhortation. A
discussion of *Henry V* that does not account for its music cannot comprehend the play any more than a discussion of Verdi's *Traviata* or Wag-
ner's *Tristan* can comprehend the opera by treating only its libretto.

An essay focusing on the defining importance of "Once more unto
the breach, dear friends" would shed light on how Shakespeare's verse
works to instill life into Henry's character and to reveal his vital spirit.
Line-by-line analysis can show how Shakespeare weds sound (music) and
content. The speech, as it begins, with the rhyme created between "once"
and "unto" propels the audience and the troops into battle, casting them
and us forward. The word *breach,* which finishes the command before
the rhetorical reiteration and closure of "dear friends, once more," is a
word that receives a powerful final stress, anticipating the attitude of
body and breath the king will command starting in line 15. "Now set
the teeth, and stretch the nostrils wide / Hold hard the breath, and bend
up every spirit / To his full height" is not only martial music, but it is
choreography too. By his words, Henry is constructing a fierce posture
of anger, aggression, and soldiership. Aggression is generated in the
repeated use of *t* and *d* and *th.* The stubborn rigidity of anger is mimed
in the phrase "Hold hard." The word *breath* draws attention to the words
themselves and the very act of speaking. Line by line, the speech yields to
this sort of close analysis. An essay deconstructing the speech does not
lessen its intensity. It shows how Shakespeare creates the kinetic force
that powers and propels the play. The powerful rallying cry can also show

one of the ways, Henry's way, that war, the essential theme of *Henry V,* is made seductively exciting and physically alluring.

A play not only about war but in which war is staged by actors playing at war the way children sometimes do, *Henry V* has great battle scenes. Or, at least it has the potential for great battle scenes; their full depiction had to wait for the twentieth century when Laurence Olivier, in 1944, and Kenneth Branagh, in 1989, made film versions of *Henry V.* The presentation of battle on the Elizabethan stage, no matter how creative, had to rely primarily on its representation through language. The conflict in arms between the English and the French that is at the heart of *Henry V,* therefore, is often sublimated into a conflict in rhetoric. For an example of this rhetorical competition, writers may compare scenes 2 and 3 of act 4. In each scene, Shakespeare presents the leaders of the troops addressing their forces before the start of battle. Since the French king is old and a figurehead and the Dauphin, his son, is a vain fool, it falls to the constable of France and to Grandpré, a French lord, to rally the forces. In the following scene, Henry rallies his army. Henry wins the battle before it begins by the stirring force of his speech as well as the forceful humility of his character, which is opposed to the foppish grandiosity of the French.

Writing an essay about this implicit rhetorical battle and how it shapes our responses to the opposing camps, the student writer could look, as in an analysis of "Once more unto the breach, dear friends, once more," at the content and purpose of the speeches that are made in both camps and at the mechanics of their language. The beginning of the French constable's speech, "To horse, you gallant Princes! Straight to horse," reduces the first words of Henry's "Once more unto the breach, dear friends, once more." The echo of that speech (even in the whisper of "more" in "horse") reverberates for the reader and creates anticipation as to what Henry will say in the next scene. Notice that an awareness of verbal resonance and reverberation relies on repeated readings of the play. The French orations lack the propulsive drive of Henry's first call to arms because of their inferior poetry. In addition, the content shows the difference in the degree of magnanimity that distinguishes the two camps from each other. While King Harry rallies his troops with praise for them and for the parents who sired them and calls on their blood for the sake of England and God, the ungracious argument of the constable's oration emerges as a pathetic, inferior version of Henry's rousing oration. Incorporated into the Frenchman's speech is the cocksure arrogance that has characterized the conversation of the Dauphin and his coterie. The constable's rhetoric is uninspiring, and Shakespeare mocks him by embedding vague echoes of phrases from Henry's earlier speech that show the weakness of the constable's verbal abilities and strategy. Henry's description of his soldiers' forebears who fought "like so many Alexanders . . . / And sheathed their swords for lack of argument," for example, is transmuted into the boast, "That our French gallants shall today draw out" their weapons and, finding so few among the scrawny forces of the enemy, will have to "sheathe [them again] for lack of sport." Compare the sound as well as meaning in the words *sport* and *argument*. When Granpré takes up the second part of the oration with the feeble mock rebuke, "Why do you stay so long," nearly all his speech, more colorful than the constable's, is yet devoted to unchivalric berating of the English as "carrions, desperate of their bones," who sit on broken horses that have rheum running from their "pale-dead eyes."

A writer can compare how Granpré's overweening pride is dramatized, in contrast to the way Harry's humble and heroic determination is presented, and then speculate what the effect on their respective armies must be, as well as on the audience and its expectations of the outcome of the battle. The constable's verse, a writer can show by examining a few of its colorless lines and the unimaginative singsong rhythm, reflects the weakness of the French military effort against the English. An analysis comparing the wordy involutions of the verse spoken by the French with the brilliant immediacy of Henry's exhortation—"This day is called the Feast of Crispian"—can show how Shakespeare worked, how he created the effects necessary to make Henry the hero of his story. It can also demonstrate Henry's theatrical flair. Even in this speech, Henry stages an imaginary play. Each of his soldiers becomes the center of a drama with "Harry the King" and his generals as characters and familiars. In years to come, each soldier will tell the story of the battle that they are about to fight to an audience of his townsmen who were not there, just as *Henry V* is recounting the story to an audience of spectators who were not there.

Henry's role and rhetoric and the contest with the French are not all there is to *Henry V.* Just as Shakespeare highlights Henry's valor and England's greatness by juxtaposing scenes of the decadent French with portrayals of the valiant English, so he subverts the glory of war by a series of contrasts. The scenes that idealize war by showing the gallantry of

English determination and heroism are challenged by scenes of the brutality and heartlessness that war can also inspire. The wily ambiguity of the play is represented through the immediate juxtaposition of the scene that immediately follows Henry's "Once more unto the breach" oration. Bardolph enters, shouting a wild parody of the king's words. Pistol's bluster is as much the rhetoric of war as Henry's grand bombast, and so is Captain Macmorris's reproach that there is no time for talk when "there is throats to be cut" (3.2.112). The disputations over the principles of war that sporadically engage Fluellen, Gower, and Macmorris are absurd exercises in distraction when set beside the grim accounts of battlefield casualties. The English revelling in the number of French dead undercuts the Christian humility the king affects. When Henry finishes a recitation of the names of the nobles fallen in battle by saying, "None else of name; and of all other men / But five and twenty," he shows himself a man who promises brotherhood to his soldiers before battle and leaves them as nameless numbers once they are dead. Henry's rhetoric is at times laced with sadism. Outside the gates of Harfleur, Henry describes for the people within the consequences of holding out against him.

> as I am a soldier,
>
> . . .
>
> I will not leave the half-achieved Harfleur
> Till in her ashes she lie buried.
> The gates of mercy shall be all shut up,
> And the flesh'd soldier, rough and hard of heart,
> In liberty of bloody hand shall range
> With conscience wide as hell, mowing like grass
> Your fresh-fair virgins and your flowering infants.
> What is it then to me, if impious war,
> Array'd in flames like to the prince of fiends,
> Do, with his smirch'd complexion, all fell feats
> Enlink'd to waste and desolation?
> What is't to me, when you yourselves are cause,
> If your pure maidens fall into the hand
> Of hot and forcing violation?
> What rein can hold licentious wickedness
> When down the hill he holds his fierce career?
> We may as bootless spend our vain command

Upon the enraged soldiers in their spoil
As send precepts to the leviathan
To come ashore. (3.3.5, 7–26)

The king who is in control of everything suddenly proclaims he is help-less before his soldiers' riotousness. Here is "Once more unto the breach" as it is spoken on the other side of the looking glass. The rhetoric is still magnificent and deliberate, but there is terror in the words, not glory. That Shakespeare places it immediately after the discussion of "the dis-ciplines of war" adds irony to it, and the careful reader will see that the character of the four disputants Henry most nearly resembles is Mac-morris, whose idea of war is to "cut off [the] head" of his foe, whom he does not acknowledge to be "so good a man as myself."

Is Henry V "the mirror of all Christian kings," as the prologue to act 2 proclaims him? Or is his professed "Christianity" less a reflection of him than a convenient and necessary aspect of the image he wishes to project? Christianity is not at issue in *Henry V*; theatricality—the stag-ing of Christianity and humility along with war—is. The skull of war revealed beneath the skin of theater in *Henry V,* a writer may argue, is the central lesson of the play: Theatricality is proper for a play or dra-matic spectacle but is worthy of suspicion in the world of actuality. It can be a ruse of power, summoned to compromise or alter judgment and, therefore, is best confined to the theater where it can be taken for what it is and not mistaken for reality. *Henry V,* by means of its glorious and heroic pageantry, a reader may also choose to argue, shows that war as an arousing game and war itself are considerations quite differ-ent from each other.

TOPICS AND STRATEGIES
Themes

Henry V has one central theme, war, which it portrays with an ambigu-ity that befits a subject that stirs a disparate array of conflicting passions when people think about or discuss it. If you choose to write about war and how war is portrayed in the play, it is important that you stay close to the text, no matter what your argument is, and that you remain aware of the ambiguities of the text despite the nature of your conclusions. Stay-ing close to the text, in this case, means noting the subtle shifts in attitudes the text may project depending on which section of the text you choose to make your focus. Does the play show war as noble or brutal, as worth the cost, or is it portrayed as a vain and sickening endeavour?

Is *Henry V* a play about national integrity, or is it a play about how propaganda works? Is Henry a great king or a great fake, a man sincerely dedicated to England or only to himself, a statesman or a manipulator of his subjects? Is Shakespeare suggesting there is no difference? If there is no real difference between the two, what does that indicate about the nature and order of our social and political arrangements? Is Henry's greatness as a king contingent on his greatness as an actor? Is greatness the same thing as goodness, as in goodness raised to its highest level, or is greatness something entirely separate from goodness?

Sample Topics:

1. **Order:** Consider how *Henry V* treats the importance of order and the roles that order imposes on members of society. How is the theme of order implicit in the prologue? You can demonstrate that the Chorus divides the tasks necessary for the presentation of a play between the audience, the author, and the actors and provides a neatly ordered dramatic surface for the play by its appearance at the beginning of each act. The theme of order predominates, too, when the archbishop of Canterbury expresses concern for preserving the traditional order that has ensured the power of the church. In addition, he presents a model of human society based on the order of the beehive. Henry's nighttime conversation with his soldiers before the battle is also a debate about order.

How does the vision of order presented in *Henry V* affect the way one thinks of individuality and humanity? How does it affect the drama and the tone of *Henry V*? How does it influence the way we look at the characters in the play? Is the idea of order in *Henry V* an idealization of power? The play offers that proposition as a serious thesis for an essay. Consider that Henry becomes angry with Williams and initiates the duel between Williams and Fluellen when Williams questions the power of ordinary men to influence the king's decisions. Think of Williams's remarks in relation to the archbishop's. If the idea of order depends on a hierarchical society, like the beehive that the archbishop of Canterbury describes, how is that hierarchy determined? By whom? Consider the king's Crispin's Day speech as a starting point. In it, he refers to several models of order and imagines an order that is both fraternal and bound together by obedience to his will. Evaluate that system using the play as an example of how the system functions. What is the relationship between obedience and order? What are its implications for individual freedom? Obedience seems to be the foundation on which order is built. How does *Henry V* describe and resolve, if it does, the tension between the individual and society? What does the text say in regard to how much society ought to be shaped to accommodate people and how much people must conform to the order of society? Consider the absence of Falstaff with regard to how the play treats this question. If the king represents the center of order and if the way order is facilitated is through obedience, examine Henry's own development in both parts of *Henry IV* and in *Henry V* to help you show how Henry himself is a model of the way abstract roles take precedence over concrete human appetites.

2. **Confidence and overconfidence:** The themes of confidence and overconfidence inform an understanding of *Henry V.* They are overtly referred to by the Chorus in a prologue. An essay can argue that, by the way Shakespeare plays the two emotional states off each other, he directs our sympathies away from the French and to the English.

How are confidence and overconfidence represented in *Henry V?* How are they presented so that they can be distinguished from each other? Look for instances of Shakespeare's use of comedy and caricature when portraying the French commanders' attitudes. Focusing on Henry and on the Dauphin will show the contrast sharply. Consider the difference between Henry's anger at being belittled and the Dauphin's vanity with respect to his own self-regard. Also look at secondary characters such as Fluellen, Gower, Jamy, and Macmorris in their arguments about the art of war. How does Pistol's characterization contribute to our insight into the nature of confidence? How does Pistol's bluster affect our appreciation of the king's rhetoric?

3. **Responsibility:** If you have read both parts of *Henry IV,* you know that Henry V, when prince of Wales, was the model of irresponsibility. As Henry V, "the mirror of all Christian kings," he endeavors to establish himself as a highly responsible ruler and warrior. He meditates in the soliloquy that starts "Upon the king" that he is burdened by his role as ruler with relentless responsibilities that common people never bear. Responsibility suggests a person, a power, or a principle to which one is responsible.

What is Henry responsible for? What connection does *Henry V* suggest exists between responsibility and order? How does the king think of responsibility and the duties of his role?

Character

You may want to consider the difference between a character and a role when you think of the persons portrayed in *Henry V.* Character indicates who a person is. Role indicates the part a person plays, a socialized function perhaps. The concept of an actor—whether that term is applied to someone working in the theater or an individual interacting with the day-to-day world—is absorbed into the heart of the play, influencing all Shakespeare presents.

Sample Topics:

1. **Henry:** A writer may consider Henry as an actor filling a role in the drama of kingship and discuss the quality of his performance, examining how he invests the role with character. For him, how does playing a powerful role by extension make him a powerful monarch?

Great as Henry's battle cry "Once more unto the breach, dear friends" is, a writer can argue that it can foster both distrust and admiration for Henry because of the theatricality of its rhetoric. Can you show that Henry never acts without an ulterior motive and without a fundamental disregard for anyone but himself? In examining Henry's conversation with his soldiers, when his identity is obscured by darkness and he is cloaked in Thomas Erpingham's cape, a writer may consider whether he is a compassionate leader or a moral bully. An analysis of this scene could entail a rigorous review of the points that both Williams and the king make in the discourse as well as an analysis of Henry's rhetorical strategy. How does he avoid directly dealing with the question of the justice of the war and his responsibility in it, turning the focus instead to his soldiers' previous moral rectitude so that he may disclaim any responsibility for the state of their souls should they die in battle?

What does it say about the king that he has two names, Henry and Harry and that both are used? What are the implications of the fact that his third name, Hal, which is primarily used in the two parts of *Henry IV,* is never used in the play?

Most of Shakespeare's history plays are marked by the instability they dramatize. Despite the fact that most of the action of *Henry V* occurs on battlefields, the play is characterized by stability, not by instability. A good argument can be made that this stability is a reflection of Henry's character, that it is the result of the kind of man and leader Henry is. Drawing on Henry's words and using what others say of him, discuss the king's character as a stabilizing force in the play. Does he change throughout the course of the drama? If he does, how? If he does not, is it a weakness of the play? Does he grow in stature as a man as he increases his reach as a monarch? Evaluate Henry's character as a ruler and a politician in light of the play's epilogue. The Chorus announces that what Henry won will all be lost, and he explains why. Henry VI "lost France" because "so many had the managing" of the state. Henry V gained his authority through the display of his power and his control. Trace the various ways in which he amassed and expressed this power.

In addition to being heroic, Henry seems to be self-effacing. Is he really? In what ways? Discuss how being self-effacing contributes to his charisma and to the drama of the play. Contrast him with Henry VI, who is genuinely self-effacing and gains nothing as a ruler from being so.

2. **Fluellen:** What sort of man is Fluellen? How does Shakespeare make him a recognizable character? Look at the way he speaks, the things he says, Henry's feelings about him, his relationship with Pistol, and his attitude about war, loyalty, and honor.

Why is the continual emphasis on Fluellen being a Welshman important? How do characters like Fluellen, Jamy, and Macmorris affect the definition of English nationalism?

3. **The Dauphin:** When writing about the character of the Dauphin, one strategy might be to show how he is a foil to Henry, how he contrasts with the king, and how his presence can serve as a reminder to the reader that Henry is not like the Dauphin even though, in his youth, it seemed like he might be.

In discussing the character of the Dauphin, you can examine how he speaks, the things he speaks about, how he uses words to represent himself—which he does frequently—and how others, his fellow soldiers and his father, the French king, speak about him and treat him.

4. **Pistol:** What is Pistol's role in *Henry V?* Can you analyze it in terms of the absence of Falstaff? How does he differ from Falstaff?

A writer concerned with how Shakespeare develops our perception of Pistol can examine the first 90 lines of act 3, scene 6. In this scene, Shakespeare dramatizes how Pistol appears at first glance and the sort of character he actually is through his interaction with Fluellen and his fellow officers. Fluellen finds him entirely disreputable. Is Pistol without redeeming qualities? His first encounter with Fluellen reveals Pistol to be all talk and no action as he pretends to heroic soldiership.

Their exchange is followed by Henry's encounter with Montjoy, the French envoy. How is the first section of the scene important to the second? How does seeing Pistol affect the way we see Henry in this scene? How does Pistol's sense of moral obligation differ from Henry's consideration of the contradictory responses to Bardolph's execution for pillaging? Is Pistol a replacement Falstaff or an indication that Falstaff is irreplaceable? What is missing in *Henry V* without Falstaff?

5. **The boy:** Although nameless, the character the boy, a member of Henry's army, is one of the most engaging actors in the play, particularly because he speaks, like the Chorus, directly to the audience. Still, as a character in the play, he is affected by the action it presents and contains. Like the Chorus, he comments on what transpires and expresses a moral point of view about the action both in his direct address and when, as in the scenes where he acts as translator for Pistol, he is a participant in the action.

What kind of person is he? How does he develop throughout the play? Is it significant that he is nameless? How significant is it that he is the only character in a play about a war between the English and the French who is shown to be proficient in both languages?

History and Context

Henry V covers the period between 1415 and 1429, one of the last phases of the Hundred Years' War (1337–1453), the century-long power struggle between England and France for territorial domination. Looking at Shakespeare's source, Ralph Holinshead's *Chronicles of England, Scotland, and Ireland* (1587), and consulting nonfiction works such as Christopher Allmand's *The Hundred Years War: England and France at War, c.1300–c.1450* (Cambridge University Press, 1988) and Anne Curry's *The Hundred Years War* (Macmillan Press, 1993) can help you discuss the way Shakespeare used his source in fashioning his drama and how faithful he was to historical fact. How did Shakespeare's account deviate from the historical record, and what are the implications of this creative license he takes?

Sample Topics:

1. **Religious context:** An alliance between the church and the state is at the heart of Henry's war. The nature of the alliance is spelled out in the opening conversation between the archbishop of Canterbury and the bishop of Ely. It is omitted in the 1600 Quarto.

What effect does Shakespeare's presentation of this alliance have on how we read Henry's many references to divine aid in battle? Does it provide depth or irony? What is the effect on the play when the conversation between Canterbury and Ely is omitted? Is *Henry V,* in the First Folio text, a grim satire of the kind of heroic, nationalist play it seems to be? Does the imprimatur of the church, considering the motives that direct the archbishop of Canterbury and the bishop of Ely to sanction the war, give weight to the war, or does it serves only to discredit Henry's project? How do Canterbury and Ely affect the way a spectator thinks about the power of the church? Can you argue that a commentary about the Elizabethan church is embedded in the play?

2. **The Irish War:** In March 1599, the year *Henry V* was first performed, Queen Elizabeth appointed Robert Deveraux, the second earl of Essex, to be the lord lieutenant of Ireland. In the fifth act prologue, the Chorus mentions Essex's expedition leading a force of approximately 17,000 to Ireland as part of an ongoing war between the English monarchy and rebellious Irish factions.

After doing research on England's war with Ireland, Essex's campaign, and the popular and political responses to the war and his campaign—the members of the audience were like the "gentlemen in England, now abed," whom Henry belittles in his St. Crispin speech—consider discussing *Henry V* as a play performed in the time of war. In such a discussion, you might also consider a modern instance of the play being filmed in a time of war: Laurence Olivier's *Henry V,* which appeared in 1944.

Philosophy and Ideas

How Shakespeare thought about war and its connection to nationalism and patriotism can prove a fruitful topic for writers exploring *Henry V.* One thesis a writer can pursue is that, in *Henry V,* Shakespeare shows the corrupt nature of Henry's endeavor but that he did it so carefully, because of the political danger of undermining royal authority, that his subtle, muted condemnation may evade spectators and readers.

Sample Topics:

1. **The ambiguous presentation of war:** The prologue to the first act of *Henry V* is a breathtaking burst of martial verse. Initiating a pattern that will reappear throughout the play, Shakespeare follows the heroic idealism of the Chorus with a scene of cynicism and corruption. Rather than seeing "horses printing their proud hooves in the receiving earth," we are presented with the archbishop of Canterbury and the bishop of Ely closing their tight fists around the nation's wealth, conspiring to ensure that the church is not stripped of a major portion of its capital and property by financing and supporting a war in France more liberally than the clergy ever had before.

   Can you argue that the alliance between the clergy and the king—who needs a foreign war, as his father had noted, in *2 Henry IV*, in order to divert his subjects' minds from the question of his legitimacy as monarch—can be regarded as a thieves' bargain? How does the alliance come to bear, as a point of moral reference, on Henry having Bardolph and Peto hanged for pillaging?

   Alternately, the opposite position may also provide a strong thesis: Despite the fact that Henry's idealism is a contrivance and can be seen as manipulative, cynical, and staged in order to maintain his power, and despite the material interest of the heads of the English church, Henry's war is beneficial to the state because it establishes a strong central figure who, because of his power, provides order and stability. The exploits of Pistol, Bardolph, Peto, and Nym can be cited as the kind of corruption men are subject to without an overwhelming external authority.

2. **The relationship between war and theater:** Considering how much attention Henry puts into performing his role as king and dramatizing his military undertaking, and considering the overt theatricality Shakespeare marshals in constructing the play's narrative, what, according to the play, seems to be the relationship between war and theater?

Form and Genre

Henry V dramatizes one great action, how Henry defeats the French at the battle of Agincourt, but it is a play of diverse and varying episodes. Reading those episodes within the context of the entire narrative arc of the play gives the work depth and breadth and makes it more than a pageant celebrating a moment of English history.

Such a reading does not compare and contrast one scene with another but considers a scene in light of other episodes. How does the work resolve the tensions that its various scenes produce when they are viewed in the context of the play as a whole? What happens, for example, when you juxtapose Pistol and the Dauphin or when you think of Mistress Quickly's report of Falstaff's death during the scene in which Hal woos Katherine? What are the implications of Henry ordering the death of Bardolph, the character we remember from both parts of *Henry IV* as Falstaff's man and one of Hal's own gang? How does it affect a reading of the play when you notice that the scene following the choral description of the enthusiastic preparations for war is a scene of rowdy bickering between Pistol and Nym over possession of Mistress Quickly? Imagining how removing any one scene from the play might affect the play overall is a strategy for thinking about how a scene functions in the play. You might look at the 1600 Quarto text of *Henry V* to see what seems like the complete play but is actually a heavily edited version of the much fuller and more complex text we know from the First Folio. They are two different plays, but what exactly is the difference?

Sample Topics:

1. **Illusion:** Shakespeare often mapped the obscure and intangible dimension hidden in the murky division separating illusion from reality. Although *Henry V* achieves neither the psychic terror of *Othello* nor the aesthetic refinement of *The Tempest,* nor the romantic mystery of *Twelfth Night,* and is presented as a hyperrealistic history of the circumstances and results of battle, *Henry V* is a play as much about creating illusions that mask as reality as it is about showing the circumstances surrounding the battle of Agincourt. Shakespeare creates the illusions of national and military grandeur and, at the same time, subverts them by showing how he creates illusion. This is not accomplished by the story that

is told but by the way it is told, by the dramatic structure of the play and the way the plot is organized, by means of choral prologues and the dramatic juxtapositions of events, characters, words, and imagery that affect the speeches in which they are used.

In order to discuss how Shakespeare creates illusion, much less the awareness of the existence of illusion in qualifying and altering reality, examine the structure of the scenes of the play, the kinds of juxtapositions he creates, his use of language and characterization. What is the point of making the conscious creation of illusion a primary subject of the play? Thinking about this problem, you might consider the difference between the illusions Henry creates and the illusions the Dauphin is exposed to and suffers.

2. **Juxtaposition:** The first act concludes with Henry's humorous response to the Dauphin's taunting gift of tennis balls, a serious declaration of war against the French that is staged as the graceful return of an insolent serve. What purpose—or purposes—does introducing comedy to the play at that particular moment advance? How does the scene serve to illuminate how juxtaposition is one of the structural strategies of the play?

Spectators and readers may be apt to find most of the scene preceding the French ambassador's entrance with the trunk of tennis balls, from lines 33 through 233, difficult to follow as the archbishop of Canterbury and the bishop of Ely weave a complex legal argument, interlaced with theology and substantiated by analogies to the discipline displayed by bees, to defend Henry's right to the French throne and the expediency of pursuing it. A writer can argue that the comic interlude that follows, involving the tennis balls, is a dramatic necessity. Shakespeare potentially resorts to a comic mode in order to recapture and refocus the audience's attention that had potentially shifted during the clerical dissertation of genealogical rights and homeland defense. The comedy helps to cut through the bureaucratic and tortuous ecclesiastical justifications to a direct acceptance of Henry's motive for war.

Language, Symbols, and Imagery

Pageantry is often conceived of in terms of spectacle, but the pageantry in *Henry V* often involves spectacular rhetorical performances by the king and, in the host of comic scenes, by comic characters who speak a variety of dialects or, as when Pistol captures a Frenchman, do not speak English at all. Much of the linguistic pageantry on display in the work belongs to the king, a master poet.

Sample Topics:

1. **The poetry of exhortation:** Usually when we think of poetry we think of a way of narrating adventure (as in an epic), of giving external voice to the complexities of inner life and the subtleties of perception (as in a lyric), of conveying the complexities of interpersonal relations (as in dramatic monologues), or of celebrating or decrying personal or social occasions (as in an ode or lament). From the start, the poetry employed in *Henry V* reflects a mood different from any of these functions or modes.

   The verse of the prologue repeatedly instructs the spectators how to view and perceive the play and, in particular, Henry's speeches: whether to his troops, to himself, to his enemies, or to Katherine. Examining this mode and functionality of the language, a writer may demonstrate that the verse of the play is a poetry of exhortation and consider how such a poetics is particularly appropriate to a work of this nature. What do aspects of the poetic contribute to the play as a spectacle?

2. **The symbolism of the commonplace:** A writer analyzing symbolism in *Henry V* will not need to go beneath the surface of the words or the events but rather should observe how common objects, phenomena, and activities are given symbolic value. As a result, how are the dimensionality and complexity of the play enhanced?

   How is the church used as symbol of moral authority? How much force lies in the symbol of the beehive as a model community? Is the symbol here more potent than true? Whose interest does it serve? You could examine how Shakespeare uses tennis balls as symbols of blind arrogance or greyhounds as symbols of soldiers and what the effect of such representation is on our acceptance of Henry's agenda. Horsemanship, for the French, is a symbol of virility and male potency. What effect does this have on our esteem for the French in the play? Leeks are a symbol of national potency. Is there a strategy, a writer may consider, in using such an earthy symbol to stand for an abstract concept? A writer may also develop a connection between marriage and national confederation. What is the power of making marriage symbolize the joining of governmental realms? A writer may show how the wholesale use of symbolism prepares the spectators to accept the king himself as a symbol of the state and the lion as a symbol of the king.

An essay that develops a unified sense of the symbolism of *Henry V* will show what symbols recur throughout the play in various forms and what underlies and informs the inclusion of the varying symbols, latent or manifest in the play. An anatomy and analysis of symbols can show how Shakespeare deepened the meaning and extended the narrative range of the play as well as how he achieved a sense of the national unity so dear to Henry, and so important in his own era, in introducing a unified network of symbols. How does Shakespeare turn what is actually only a construct—nationalism—into something that seems like a divine inevitability?

Compare and Contrast Essays

Literature is self-contained, but it exists not only within its own historical context but within ours as well. It is possible, therefore, to seek an understanding of a work by comparing it to our own experiences and to deepen our understanding of our experiences by comparing them to a work of literature.

Sample Topics:

1. **Then and now:** Stories of war and warlike exploits have always been popular and have often served as the basis for literature and popular entertainment. In the twentieth century, war was the subject of countless movies and television shows.

Now, technology has become so sophisticated and the dissemination of information and viewpoint so continuous and pervasive that ongoing wars have become part of daily life and an awareness of the state of the world. Consequently, the line dividing war and theater has become as fine in our time as it is in *Henry V.* Compare the way Shakespeare presents war—and the various characters' responses to it—to the way present, ongoing wars are packaged, presented, and perceived. One focus may be on how Shakespeare's way of representing the ways war is popularly presented can affect our responses to present wars. How is Shakespeare's mode of representing war similar to the presentation of conflicts in the present day? How do contemporary or modern wars recapitulate similar themes, events, and actions of the war Henry wages?

2. **Comparing various characters' attitudes about war:** While it may be impossible to determine what Shakespeare's attitudes about war might be from *Henry V,* it is possible to see the play as an anatomy of possible attitudes. An interesting way to approach this topic could be in comparing various characters' attitudes toward war, attending not only to what they actually say but also to how they act and interact with one another.

Consider what light a comparison of Pistol and Fluellen can cast on the exploration of Shakespeare's sense of war. What about a comparison of Henry and the Dauphin as regards issues of leadership or of characters such as Bardolph and Peto to the archbishop of Canterbury and the bishop of Ely? A closer look at how attitude and opinion are indicated or made manifest can help reshape one's vision of the play.

Bibliography for *Henry V*

Banerjee, Rita. "The Common Good and the Necessity of War: Emergent Republican Ideals in Shakespeare's *Henry V* and *Coriolanus.*" *Comparative Drama,* Spring 2006, vol. 40, issue 1, pp. 29–50.
(Argues that in Henry V *Shakespeare showed that he favored "a republican vision of history" and attempted to "break through the facade of the official*

ideology and historiography [that war was good for the common interest and the common people] to which Henry V . . . *only nominally subscribes.")*

Crunelle-Vanrigh, Anny. "*Henry V* as a Royal Entry." *Studies in English Literature, 1500–1900,* Spring 2007, vol. 47, no. 2, pp. 355–78.
(Argues that the choral prologues in Henry V *form a "triumphal arch" for a play that essentially presents a king's progress, as in a coronation procession, to legitimacy as a monarch as the result of theatricality and the use of theatrical devices. This conjunction leads to Crunelle-Vanrigh's thesis that "if power wishes to enter into a transaction with the stage, it must then be subjected to the rule of the audience," since, in the words of the Chorus, "'tis your thoughts that now must deck our kings.")*

Harrington, Maura Grace. "The Disappearance of MacMorris: Shakespeare's Doomed Attempt at Portraying British Unity." *Shakespeare Newsletter,* Winter 2005, vol. 55, no. 4, pp. 99–101.
(Harrington focuses on the significance of the arguments that spring up among the Irish Macmorris, the Welsh Fluellen, the Scottish Jamy, and the English Gower, as she discusses these characters' importance as regional figures in the nationalizing agenda of Henry V. *She speculates about how the common English conception of the Irish influenced Shakespeare's handling of these four characters.)*

Kahan, Jeffrey. "Bardolph and 'Carry Coals': A New Reading for *Henry V,* 3.2.45." *ANQ: A Quarterly Journal of Short Articles, Notes, and Reviews,* Summer 2001, vol. 14, no. 3, pp. 14–15.
(Kahan argues that the expression "carry coals" and the images associated with it establish a contrast between Bardolph and Henry and promote the portrait of Henry as a virtuous ruler.)

Mahon, John W. "Considering Shakespeare's Second Historical Tetralogy: Some Christian Features." *Shakespeare Newsletter,* Winter 2005–2006, vol. 55, no. 4, 2005–2006, Winter, pp. 93–94.
(This is a bibliographical essay carefully summarizing a number of scholarly essays that appear in Beatrice Batson's critical anthology Shakespeare's Second Historical Tetralogy: Some Christian Features, *Locust Hill Literary Studies 35, West Cornwall, Conn.: Locust Hill Press, 2004.)*

Martin, Tony. "Updating History: Shakespeare's *Henry V.*" *The English Review,* February 2007, vol. 17, no. 3, pp. 35–39.
(Martin discusses the way the staging of Henry V *was influenced by historical circumstances at the time it was first produced, during World War II, and at the beginning of the twenty-first century.)*

Meyers, Walter E. "Hal: The Mirror of All Christian Kings." *A Fair Day in the Affections: Literary Essays in Honor of Robert B. White, Jr.,* edited by Jack D. Durant and M. Thomas Hester, pp. 67–77. Raleigh, N.C.: The Winston Press, 1980.
(Meyers traces Hal's character and its development through both parts of Henry IV *and* Henry V, *debunking criticism that sees him as a noble and heroic figure.)*

Roberts, Brian. "Shakespeare's *Henry V.*" *The Explicator,* Winter 2002, vol. 60, no. 2, pp. 58–60.
(Roberts analyzes the nature of the puns that arise from Fluellen's pronunciation of the letter b as p in words such as bridge and brave as a means of determining the quality of the marriage between Henry and Katherine, which he calls a symbolic bridge joining the two countries.)

Shaheen, Naseeb. "*Henry V* and its Quartos." *Shakespeare Newsletter,* Fall 2007, vol. 57, no. 2, pp. 43–47.
(In an essay essentially devoted to arguing that the Quartos of Henry V, *which are far shorter than the Folio text, and from which much material that might be politically or ecclesiastically sensitive is missing, were simply bad reconstructions and not deliberately sanitized editions, Shaheen presents a reading of the political and social mood of Elizabethan England at the time of the play's initial productions and a sense of what the text of* Henry V *would be like without the prologues, the dialogue between the archbishop of Canterbury and the bishop of Ely, and several of Henry's grand exhortative speeches.)*

Slights, Camille Wells. "The Conscience of the King: *Henry V* and the Reformed Conscience." *Philological Quarterly,* Winter 2001, vol. 80, no. 1, pp. 37–56.
("By focusing on conscience in William Perkins's Discourse of Conscience, James VI and I's Basilicon Doron, and Shakespeare's history plays, particu-

larly Henry V," *Slights explains, "I hope to illuminate tensions between individual judgment and obligations to authority within the concept of conscience that give us more precise understanding of religious and national identity in early modern England." She argues that Henry as a man and a king is continually beset by guilt at his father's usurpation and seeks to justify his act of going to war and his policies while fighting with the authority of moral and religious sanction.)*

Taunton, Nina. "Camp Scenes and Generals: Shakespeare's *Henry V* and the State of the Art of War." *Shakespeare in Southern Africa: Journal of the Shakespeare Society of Southern Africa,* 13 (2001), pp. 41–52.
(Taunton's essay is of particular interest to readers concerned with historical, political, and military events occurring near the time of the composition of the play. She attempts to demonstrate how the play addresses military threats that England faced in the last decade of the sixteenth century and how the play represented varying responses to them and suggested several strategies for the establishment of military camps and operations.)

Womersley, David. "France in Shakespeare's *Henry V.*" *Renaissance Studies* 9, no. 4 (December 1995): 442–59.
(Womersley discuss the topicality of Henry V *in its own time with regard to the politics of succession in England during the last years of Elizabeth's reign and with regard to English attitudes about the French.)*

HENRY VI, PART 1

READING TO WRITE

*T*HE *FIRST Part of Henry VI* (1591–92) or *Henry VI, Part 1* or *1 Henry VI*, as it is also often called, begins Shakespeare's account of the great tantrum of English history, the War of the Roses, a series of conflicts between two royal British factions, the House of Lancaster, represented by a red rose, and the House of York, represented by a white rose. Although the fifth play, chronologically, in the series of eight that trace the tumultuous course of English history from the reign of Richard II through the reign of Richard III, *1 Henry VI* is the earliest of the history plays that Shakespeare wrote, or nearly so. Some scholars think Shakespeare wrote it after the second and third parts of *Henry VI*, written around 1590–91. Whatever the actual order of composition, when read after *Richard II*, both parts of *Henry IV,* and *Henry V, 1 Henry VI* may not seem the equal of the other works. It is certainly not the lyrical masterpiece that *Richard II* is, nor the complex meditation on history, character, psychology, and existential ambiguity that is engaged through comic and tragic dramaturgy in the two parts of *Henry IV;* nor is it the epic exploration of theatrical heroism, mesmerizing rhetoric, and self-representation that we see in *Henry V.* It is crowded with characters and episodic in nature, propelled by the unstable whirligig of history itself.

Scanning its list of characters reveals the teeming, almost epical, quality the work aspires to. In addition to King Henry, there is his uncle, the duke of Gloucester, who is the lord protector, because the king is a child and has ascended to the throne after Henry V's, his father's, death. Henry VI's other uncle, the duke of Bedford, is the regent of France, that nation having been subsumed into England after the victories recounted in *Henry V.* The young English king has several great uncles, too: Thomas Beaufort, duke of Exeter, and Henry Beaufort, who is the bishop of Winchester and later appointed cardinal. Winchester opposes Gloucester's authority as protector and wants the power that Gloucester wields for himself. In addition, two other characters factor into the drama. John Beaufort, the earl of Somerset, becomes the duke of Somerset, and Richard Plantagenet is granted the title duke of York. (He is not Richard III but Richard III's father.)

York and Somerset are enemies. Their rivalry causes Somerset to delay sending troops to help Talbot in his battle with the French at Bordeaux, leading to the English rout and the death of Talbot and his son. Readers must sort through the earls of Warwick, Salisbury, and Suffolk, as well as the play's hero, Lord Talbot, who becomes the earl of Shrewsbury, and his son, John Talbot. Also present are the earl of March, Edmund Mortimer, and Sir William Lucy, Sir William Glansdale, and Sir Thomas Gargrave among the English. Among all these, Talbot is the most memorable because he is the most individualized and identifiable. He is not presented as one of the contending cohort of rival nobles. He is shown in actual dramatic situations, whether matching wits with the countess of Auvergne or meeting his death in battle, with his son, as the two of them forge a warrior's bond of self-sacrificial courage and loyalty.

Among the French, in addition to Charles, the Dauphin, who becomes king, are the duke of Burgundy, who switches his allegiance from the English to the French when Joan of Arc (who Shakespeare portrays as a witch) persuades him to, and Reignier, the duke of Anjou and the titular king of Naples. Reignier's daughter, Margaret, becomes Henry's queen as part of Lord Suffolk's scheme to rule England from behind the scenes. Ostensibly wooing Margaret by proxy for Henry, Suffolk secures her support for himself, not for Henry and forms a clandestine liaison with her. Rounding out the French participants are Alençon and the countess of Auvergne. She stands out in a play dominated by male figures and because she is presented as a character in what is like an interpolated tale. The story of contrivance to ambush Talbot is her castle and how he foils her attempt and wins her friendship is dropped in as a seeming interruption of the main action the play presents.

With such a potentially dizzying array of people represented on the stage, the task for a student writer is to bring forward the features that make the work a compelling historical narrative and melodrama. Accomplishing that may actually depend on recognizing that the play's episodic density and the petty, egotistic contentions that propel the plot development are just what the play is about: the chaos of history and the vanity of men who vie, with immense and labyrinthine futility, for power over one another.

The challenge a reader faces is to untangle the threads of the play while realizing that the tangle itself is essentially what the play is about. The tangle of the plot arguably reflects the mismanagement and ineptitude of a king unable to control his realm. In other words, the problem and substance of the play are identical. *1 Henry VI* shows the effect of monarchical weakness, showing both the incompetent ruler and the far-reaching effects and results of his incompetence.

In *1 Henry VI*, the action of the play is propelled by the rivalries among the English nobility to seize the English throne (controlled by the passive boy-king) and how the rivalries betray the English effort to keep military and, therefore, political control over France. Advancing this action and arising from it are the episodes and events that constitute the several subplots contained in the play. Chief among these is Talbot's effort to hold back the French and secure and legitimize Henry V's victories, which are being threatened by the weakness of Henry VI and the strife among his governing nobility.

1 Henry VI is composed of several dramatic episodes that collectively form the play and yet are not necessarily organically interrelated. Not every one of the play's various narrative threads is essential to the work as a whole. The fact, thus, that the play is episodic provides a strategy for writing about it. Since the play is made up of individual pieces that are fit together, a writer can examine these individual segments of the play and attempt to see how they fit together. Perhaps the most useful way of analyzing the play is also the most elementary: Begin by making lists in an attempt to define and clarify the historical events and their chronology and to distinguish among the various characters, their identities, allegiances, and interconnections. Many of the characters do not stand out vividly as individuals. Consequently, it is a good strategy to keep a notebook or a computer file open beside you as you read, so you can list each character and, each time that character appears, note what you know about him or her based on what he or she has just said or done, and from anything said about him or her. In this way you can increase your familiarity with and develop a profile for each character. Once you have done this, it will be useful for you to outline the action of the play briefly scene by scene in order to provide an overview and to clarify the action and the characters involved. For example:

1.1 1. Henry V's funeral.
2. Bickering between Winchester (representing the church) and Gloucester, the lord protector (representing the state).
3. News that France is in revolt against English rule.
4. Heroic Talbot introduced through news of his capture in battle by the French.

1.2 1. French court
2. French are rejoicing at their victories against England.
3. The French then suffer a defeat in battle.
4. Joan of Arc, disparagingly called La Pucelle in the play, suggesting "the whore," is brought before the Dauphin, convincing him of her supernatural power.
5. Reignited with hope, the French resume their battle against the English.

1.3 1. Before the Tower of London.
2. Skirmish between Gloucester's forces in blue coats and Winchester's forces in tawny coats when Winchester's forces prevent Gloucester from entering the tower.
3. Mayor of London enters with his officers and quells the disorder.

1.4 1. Orleans, a French city.
2. The master gunner and his son, defending Orleans, spy the English on the walls of the city.
3. On the walls, John Talbot tells Salisbury and Gargrave of his ransom, how the French mistreated him, and how he refused to be traded for a prisoner of lesser rank than he.

4. As Talbot, Salisbury, and Gargrave are discussing the best way to enter and take the city, the master gunner's son fires at Salisbury and Gargrave, killing them.
5. A messenger informs Talbot that the French army is advancing.

1.5 1. At Orleans, Talbot and Joan fight.
2. It is a draw, and Joan leaves Talbot with a taunt.
3. Talbot rallies the English to fight or face shame.

1.6 1. Joan recaptures Orleans.
2. The Dauphin celebrates her victory with banqueting.

That is a brief outline of the first act. Briefly it shows 1) the structure of the play, how the scenes ricochet between England and France; 2) the threefold dramatic action of the plot: a) the strife between English factions over who wields power, b) the war between the English and the French for control of France, and c) how the English strife will hinder the English in their struggle against the French; 3) several themes of the play: a) rivalry, b) the nature of heroism, c) the dread of shame, d) the role of women, e) the mutability of fortune, f) the weakness of the king's authority, g) the role of rank and class pride, h) the transition from chivalric war to war fought with gunpowder; and 4) a number of important persons and the roles they play.

This outline is not an essay in itself, but it does provide a writer with a host of possible ideas for essays. One approach could be to consider the significance of juxtaposing the funeral of Henry V with the bickering between Winchester and Gloucester. The connection between the loss of a strong central monarchy and the emergence of destructive factionalism, which is a central theme of the play, is introduced. Similarly, the resurgence of French power is yoked to English weakness. The way Talbot is introduced indicates the role he will perform in *1 Henry VI*. He is a hero in a play in which he is, nevertheless, not the central figure. There is no central figure, though, hero or villain in *1 Henry VI*, which presents another strong potential avenue for discussion and argumentation. Alternately, a writer might show how the first scene is like an overture in which all the themes that will be developed in *1 Henry VI* are presented. In view of the scene's construction, the first impression a reader may have of the disorder of *1 Henry VI* can be shown to be something like a Shakespearean trick. The order of a play that seems to lack order is being laid out and established at the beginning.

The second scene introduces Joan of Arc. Does Joan develop as a character? How is she presented at first? How is her character revealed? The reader cannot have a complete sense of her psychology until her final appearances at the end of the play. Why does Shakespeare reserve that information until the end? What dramatic or thematic purpose does it serve to hold it back? Even when Joan is fully revealed in her final appearances, is she an unambiguous character?

TOPICS AND STRATEGIES
Themes

An episodic chronicle play, like *1 Henry VI*, which delivers only a segment of a longer narrative arc and whose numerous characters are generally defined by their historical role rather than by the complexity of their personalities, relies on its themes to give the work dramatic unity and import. Thus a writer choosing to discuss one of the themes of *1 Henry VI* needs to find a common element running throughout the play that gives the work its particular identity.

Sample Topics:

1. **The weak king:** The paradox of Henry VI is that he is a good person and a bad king. What makes him a good person and a bad king is one and the same attribute, his weakness as a Machiavellian, that is, his inability to press others to his will. Rather, he is a model of resignation, a gentle soul who accepts the tribulations of life believing that what he suffers is God's dispensation and that his duty is to bow before it. His failure as a king is directly related to his virtue as a person, if indeed such passivity is virtue in a world that is defined as needing the exercise of active and strong assertive power. The paradox is that even such power reaps death, just as weakness does.

Consider comparing the consequences of Henry V's strength and Henry VI's weakness. In terms of human suffering, is there a difference? Unlike his father and grandfather—Henry V and Henry IV, respectively—Henry VI is not a cunning Machiavellian who can secure men's obedience with his invincible persona. Consequently, his government has no strength or center. Instead a host of those surrounding him vie with one another for control of the realm and thus endanger its health and security. *1 Henry VI* essentially is dedicated to describing the form that the crippled English monarchy takes. It shows the fragments of government and the contending centers of power. The consequences of the crippling of the English monarchy becomes the matter for the second and third parts of *Henry VI.*

A writer wishing to discuss the importance of a weak king to the plot of *1 Henry VI* must note all the instances of Henry's weakness that are shown in the play by referring to his speech, action, and attitudes and to the speech, action, and attitudes of those around him. Such a strategy draws together a host of characters from Gloucester and Winchester, to York and Somerset, to Suffolk and Margaret.

Henry's weakness also precipitates the French resurgence, but the French, too, are led by a weak monarch. Charles, the Dauphin, is not quite the fool he is in *Henry V* nor the petulant and fearful mongrel George Bernard Shaw makes him in *Saint Joan,* but, like Henry, he is a weak king who owes his nation's newly rekindled military might to Joan of Arc's intervention. Thus the two kingdoms that are contending with each other are both fragmented authorities haphazardly governed by incompetent monarchs who neither enjoy divine authority nor are skilled at practicing a practical form of politics. By showing such dangerously powerful engines of human destiny to be such ill-conceived, ill-assembled, and ill-driven enterprises, a writer may argue, Shakespeare suggests that history, rather than being the chronicle of heroism and national triumphs or defeats, can be a record of discord and inhumanity in which human virtue and honor are, ultimately, as meaningless as vice and wickedness.

2. **The relationship of shame to honor:** Can you show that avoiding shame, the consequence of ignoble behavior, more than pursuing honor defines a hero like Talbot? Look not only at his scenes with his son but at his account of why he refused to be ransomed. Honor, a positive quality in *1 Henry VI*, is, nevertheless, defined in the play in terms of its opposite. Honor comes as the result of behaving in such a way as not to bring dishonor or shame on oneself.

   A writer interested in describing the dynamics of shame and honor in *1 Henry VI* and the context in which these two antithetical ideals are discussed might best start by going to a Web site such as http://shakespeare.mit.edu/History/1kinghenryvi/full.html and using the "Find" function (under "Edit") in order to examine each passage—there are nearly 150 of them—in which the words or some variant of *shame* and *honor* (appearing as *honour*) occur. The problem of honor, however, in *1 Henry VI* is not an issue of its existential worth but of its historical and political value.

3. **Hypocrisy:** Without the operation of hypocrisy, the plot of *1 Henry VI* could not progress. A writer may argue that it is the pervasive operation of hypocrisy that makes a scene like the one between Talbot and his son stand out as exceptional because they are each free of hypocrisy.

   Hypocrisy is one of the strategies that ambitious but powerless individuals employ in the pursuit of power. Joan is an example of devilish hypocrisy. Is Henry an example of the danger of being unable to be a hypocrite?

4. **Rivalry and alliances:** The account of rivalries and alliances serves as the dramatic fuel for the plot, the source of the action, and the subject of the narrative in *1 Henry VI*. As with hypocrisy, which is a strategy employed within the context of

rivalry, the pervasive nature of rivalry gives dramatic intensity to a scene like the one between Talbot and his son, where they compete with each other in being most loyal to their mutual bond.

You might argue, citing examples from the play, that in a world of rivalries, alliances are not antithetical to rivalries but the form rivalries take. The drama of *1 Henry VI* comes largely from the clashes of figures like Winchester and Gloucester and from the scheming of figures like York and Suffolk.

Character

Once a reader sorts out the wealth of characters who appear in the play, the key figures and strongest characterizations begin to emerge. In a play so heavily weighted with male characters and determined by stereotypically masculine pursuits such as war and governance, the three female characters in *1 Henry VI* are particularly vivid.

When drawing up a list of characters, it would be wise to begin with Joan, the Countess, and Margaret. Not only do they stand out themselves, but they help define other characters. Thinking about Joan leads a reader to think about Charles, Burgundy, Talbot, and York. Their association with her sharpens their definition as characters. Margaret gives dimension to Suffolk, and Shakespeare uses Talbot's interaction with the Countess to help develop his character.

Just as these three women help the reader to focus on other characters, so Talbot aids the reader in individualizing York and Somerset, whose quarrel with each other contributes to Talbot's defeat. In other words, one of the ways of grasping the complicated interrelationships of not very differentiated characters in *1 Henry VI* is to trace the webs of tensions that connect them.

Many of the characters—the exceptions are the French, who are relegated to the background after *Part 1*—who are introduced in *1 Henry VI* and who seem underdeveloped return in *2* and *3 Henry VI*, where they are more thoroughly developed. It is, therefore, advisable for a writer to absorb all three parts of *Henry VI* before attempting a discussion of a character in *Part 1* who participates in the action of the later plays, even when the focus is on how that character is presented, developed, and dramatically employed in *Part 1*.

Sample Topics:

1. **Joan La Pucelle:** What makes Joan perhaps the most interesting figure in the entire play? She is obviously a controversial figure whose stature depends on who is evaluating her, the English or the French.

   To analyze how she is presented in the play, look at the way Shakespeare introduces her, develops her character through her actions, and presents her at the conclusion of the play before her last battle and after her capture. Examine the way she speaks and exerts her influence and how others speak of her and regard her. Has Shakespeare prepared us for either the scene with the spirits or her desecration of her bond with her father or her own reputation? If not, what is the dramatic effect of the way Shakespeare allows Joan's character to unfold?

2. **The Countess of Auvergne:** Although she appears in only one scene, the Countess is a strong and memorable character in the play. What makes her so? What is her role?

   Analyze how her scene with Talbot can affect the way we read the rest of *1 Henry VI.* What does it reveal about all the contentious men whose ambition directs the course of the action? What attribute does she have that they lack? What is the price of their wanting her qualities? What does the scene with her reveal about Talbot; how does it affect his characterization and the way we respond to him?

3. **Margaret:** Margaret is introduced in *1 Henry VI* and will become a much more fully developed character in the later plays. It is essential to read the second and third parts of *Henry VI* and then *Richard III* to write about her.

   However, a writer may choose to analyze how Shakespeare introduces characters he will develop in later plays, and in this case, Margaret is a strong choice for such an essay. Henry, Gloucester, York, Winchester, and Suffolk all might be considered as well. Are there glimmers or indications, in *Part 1,* of who they will become or how their characters will develop in the other two plays?

4. **John Talbot:** If *1 Henry VI* has a hero, a good argument can be made that it is Talbot. What makes him a hero? What are his skills? What sets him apart from everyone else?

A writer will want to know how Shakespeare develops Talbot's character and shows his humanity. An important strategy can be to look at his interactions with others as well as what others say about him. Consider that two key scenes devoted to him, Talbot with the Countess of Auvergne and Talbot with his son, might be removed from the play without affecting the overall action. However, the scenes' removal would radically reshape the play and strip it of an essential dimension. What would be lost without those two scenes? Does Talbot provide or represent an antithetical vision that challenges the dominant attitude of the play? Does Talbot introduce a capacity for surrender, cooperation, and reconciliation that emerges as the opposite of the combativeness that drives the play? Consider the significance of the fact that the supposed hero of *1 Henry VI* is not the central character of the play and dies in the fourth act. In addition, although war is the ostensible action of the play, war is really secondary to the drama of the play.

5. **Henry VI:** Although this is the first of three plays to bear his name, Henry is the dominating presence more by the absence he represents than by the magisterial presence that invested his three predecessors, whether weak, like Richard II, insecure like Henry IV, or flamboyant like his father, Henry V.

A writer may choose to show how Shakespeare develops the character of Henry's monarchical absence in *Part 1*. Discuss how others talk about him, how he behaves, and how he handles strife and division. What does a comparison between him and the mayor of London, as brief as the mayor's appearance is, reveal? A thorough discussion of Henry's character and the tension between the person he is and the role that he is forced to play requires a familiarity with all three parts of *Henry VI*. Nevertheless, the essential problem of his reign, his character or lack thereof, is presented in *1 Henry VI* in scenes such as 3.1, starting at line 107, where rather than commanding, Henry laments and supplicates. Rather than having the strength to be the embodiment of the kingly ideal, he succumbs to the weakness of the flesh and betrays the duty of his office when Suffolk tells him of Margaret's desirability.

6. **Humphrey, duke of Gloucester:** Gloucester is one of Henry V's brothers, Henry VI's uncle, and as the lord protector of the realm (while Henry VI, who is nine months old at his coronation, is too young to rule), the enemy of the power-hungry churchman, Winchester. Gloucester's character is far more interestingly and dramatically developed in *2 Henry VI* than in the first part, so an essay about him that limits what we know of him to only the first part would most likely not do him justice.

With that in mind, after reading *2 Henry VI*, you might want to compare how Gloucester comes across in the first part and how he appears in the second, considering, too, how Shakespeare prepares the reader for his role in the second part. Looking at the first two parts of *Henry VI*, you might want to discuss the kind of man Gloucester is and how he responds to the world into which he has been thrust and how Gloucester's fate helps to define the nature of that world.

7. **Charles, the Dauphin:** In *Henry V*, the Dauphin is portrayed as a vain, conceited, and incompetent fool. In *1 Henry VI*, he is more complicated than that. How does Shakespeare portray Charles? What techniques does he use to reveal Charles's character and to shape our responses? Is he an unsympathetic character? What are his qualities? How does Shakespeare show them?

You could begin by examining Charles's first appearance in act 1, scene 2, where rhetoric and action are counterpoised in the space of four lines, from lines 20 to 24. Look at the way

Charles behaves with regard to Joan and how she treats him. Is his faith in Joan the act of a fool? Does Charles grow over the course of the play? Contrast his final appearance in act 5, scene 4 with his earlier appearances.

8. **Henry Beaufort, bishop of Winchester:** Winchester is one of those characters who reappears in *2 Henry VI* in all the fullness of his personality. Nonetheless, in *1 Henry VI,* the reader can get a rather good sense of the sort of man he is.

Describe him and his character. How does Shakespeare reveal and develop his character? How, particularly, does his clerical identity affect a reader's response to him? Shakespeare openly conveys Winchester's venality at the end of act 5, scene 1.

History and Context

The fact that the plays about the War of the Roses were the first that Shakespeare wrote sets them in a literary context that can be of particular interest. What is there about writing history plays—does it involve a particular discipline?—that might be particularly appealing to a young playwright? Might you argue that, develop as he did into a writer of other genres, Shakespeare often wrote history plays, even when the plays went wide of the historical mark or were actually fictional? Consider, to name a few, *Macbeth, King Lear, Hamlet, Julius Caesar, Antony and Cleopatra, Cymbeline, The Winter's Tale,* and *The Tempest.*

Sample Topics:

1. **Alterations to and deviations from history in *1 Henry VI*:** Shakespeare is interested in the psychology and the drama of history more than in the exactitude of historical reporting. Establishing that as a thesis for an essay on *1 Henry VI* requires some serious research on the part of a writer intent on showing in how many ways Shakespeare altered the actual historical record of Henry VI's reign and the chronology of events.

An interesting problem a writer might confront, in tackling this topic, is whether Shakespeare's deviations are nonetheless faithful to the spirit of the historical record and illuminate the actual conflicts being appropriated. Can one argue that Shakespeare sacrificed certain particulars in order to capture an essence of the historical periods, events, and forces he uses? Or can you make a case that *1 Henry VI* is an interpretation of history?

2. *1 Henry VI* **as allusion to the anxiety of Elizabeth's childlessness:** Queen Elizabeth was around 60 when the *Henry VI* plays were presented, and there was no direct heir to the throne.

While Elizabeth may be seen as a Henry V figure who exercised a defining and unifying power over England through the force of her personality and the accomplishments of her policies, the lack of a successor to the throne, in the 1590s, might have suggested the historical figure of Henry VI. In that regard, you might consider writing an essay that *1 Henry VI* reflected the anxiety of the age over the future of England by examining an era of division from its past. Are there any historical accounts of anxiety over the succession and what problems were anticipated?

Philosophy and Ideas

The central philosophical problem presented in the history plays is what constitutes legitimacy in a monarch and what kind of person ought a monarch to be. Richard was weak and corrupt. Henry IV was a man who seized the crown and withstood rebels who would seize it from him through his Machiavellian brilliance. His son, Henry V, just as brilliant a Machiavellian, also attained the heroic stature of a victorious soldier who avoided domestic unrest through foreign war and conquered France. Each was a strong monarch, and each can provide writers with opportunities for inquiring about their virtues and their faults. Unlike his predecessors, in whom we might consider how the nature of the man shapes the monarch, Henry VI raises the specter of a monarch who does not really reign and whose character is unsuited for the role he finds himself fulfilling. The play that bears his name sets the idea of the man and the monarch against each other.

Sample Topics:

1. **The consequences of the monarch's character:** Is the argument of *1 Henry VI* that gentleness and godliness in a monarch are harmful to a realm? A writer pursuing this topic should examine Henry's character. Is he gentle and godly or simply weak? Are there indications in the play? Are there differing opinions among the differing characters in regard to his attributes? How do the scenes of Talbot and his son reflect on the play's attitude about virtue?

   If Henry is genuine, does the play argue that gentleness and godliness in a monarch are akin to weakness and that spiritual virtues equal political vices? Is Henry's goodness, if he is good, the root of social evil? Is the play arguing that Machiavellianism is necessary?

2. **Authority and ambition:** What does *1 Henry VI* have to say about authority? Can you see in the play any connection between the idea of authority and ambition? Are there variations in the nature of authority and ambition?

   Does the play argue for the need for a strong central authority, or does it criticize human vice and argue that without virtue even strong central authority will fail because there is no binding idea that allows for commerce between people and nations or binds ambition to a common virtue? Or does the play actually take no stand on the issues but simply present a drama of conflicting ambitions? If so, do you sense a position that Shakespeare articulates in regard to ambition itself?

Language, Symbols, and Imagery

The use of language and symbols in the pursuit or the exercise of power plays a major role in *1 Henry VI*. Power itself, the play seems to assert, relies on establishing symbols that can draw individuals to unite, and language can construct abstractions that command people's allegiance.

Sample Topics:

1. **The variety of roles that language plays in** *1 Henry VI:* A drama of war, *1 Henry VI* shows the use of language as a weapon. A writer can show how it is used to define hostilities and to forge factionalism. Joan uses it as a tool of war when she conquers Suffolk with words. Henry lacks the language of authority and is, in consequence, devoid of power. Can you show that he often speaks as a supplicant rather than as a commander?

   A writer may consider constructing an essay that shows how the characters in *1 Henry VI* use language to project the self-images they are intent on creating and as a tool of aggression. How often does language fail to persuade? Under which circumstances does it succeed? Talbot, for example, overcomes the Countess of Auvergne's strategy with a language trick. They can be seen as engaged in a battle.

2. **Transforming the familiar into the symbolic:** By the use of ordinary objects and actions, Shakespeare symbolically represents the theme of rivalry in *1 Henry VI.* Although the rose was long a symbol of love and of the Virgin Mary, Shakespeare did not transform it into a symbol of warlike factionalism. Historically, the opposing factions did that themselves, but Shakespeare does devote a long scene to investing the white and red roses with their symbolic values.

   Other symbols in *1 Henry VI,* like the rose, are drawn from the ordinary world and invested with meaning by the way they are used. A writer can show that walls, boundaries, and the acts of entering and of preventing entrance also take on symbolic value and give form and substance to the idea of rivalry by establishing concrete symbols of rivalry.

   A writer can look at other transformations of the ordinary as well. What does Shakespeare's use of animal imagery contribute to *1 Henry VI?* How does Shakespeare make social rank into a symbol of human worth? Even gunpowder, in the context of the play, becomes symbolic. How so?

Form and Genre

1 Henry VI is a history play whose narrative is broken into episodic fragments, suggesting the fragmented centers of authority the play recounts.
In scope, the play is epic, particularly when seen as the first part of a tril-
ogy that traces the long arc of history and shuttles between geographical
and social realms, even invoking hell.

Sample Topics:

1. **Spectacle and pageantry:** A writer can examine the performance history of *1 Henry VI* to see the degree to which spectacle and pageantry were involved in the play's presentation.
The opening of the play can be staged as a mighty display of
spectacle and pageantry.

Alternately, a writer may consider that spectacle and pageant
perform an ironic function in the play considering the divisions and animosity that spectacle and pageant actually hide.
What ought to suggest a binding unity is actually the prologue
to an epic chronicle of division. How wide, does Shakespeare
suggest, is the gulf between reality and spectacle?

2. **The use of witchcraft as a way of representing a psychological condition:** Joan of Arc is shown conjuring infernal spirits
and conversing with them. The spirits are also shown deserting
her. This is odd because *1 Henry VI* represents social and political events in a naturalistic way. Psychology must be inferred
from speech and action and is not, except for the scenes with
Joan, concretely represented in allegorical figures. When
Shakespeare brings Joan's infernal spirits onstage, he is not, as
in *Julius Caesar* or *Richard III*, showing a sleeper's dream but
treating a supernatural event as if it were a natural one.

Is this confusion of genres jarring? Or may a writer assert that,
by means of supernatural representation in a naturalistic context, Shakespeare interprets aspects of a historical account
(Joan was guided by voices) psychologically, showing the woman
as deranged by presenting onstage what is actually occurring

inside her head? In her encounter with her father, Joan seems imbalanced or insane. A writer may argue that, using the figure of Joan of Arc, Shakespeare shows mental instability to be a consequence of the experienced discrepancy between who a person thinks she is and who the world takes her to be. If this is so, has Shakespeare, in the figure of Joan, expressed a common phenomenon that women have historically had to cope with, being represented other than as they are? Or is he, you might argue, in the figure of Joan, mocking the pretensions of all the aspirants in the play who feel called upon to rise to power?

Compare and Contrast Essays

In a play devoted to rivalries, compare and contrast essays can be particularly illuminating, helping to show what real differences separate characters and issues from each other or, ironically, that few real differences exist between rivals beyond their commitment to rivalry. Comparisons and contrasts may also show how people on the same side, nevertheless, approach their oppositional tasks in varying ways.

Sample Topics:

1. **The Countess of Auvergne and La Pucelle:** The Countess of Auvergne and Joan of Arc both dedicate themselves to a French victory. Is that their only point of resemblance? Joan is defamed as an immoral woman. Does the Countess flirt with such an image in order to trap Talbot? What about her character differentiates her from Joan?

   A comparison of the two not only reveals the differences in their characters but also the range of representation that Shakespeare has undertaken in the play.

2. **The king and Suffolk:** The Duke of Suffolk becomes an important figure in the last act and makes an important speech that serves not only to advance the plot of the play but also to reveal the nature of his character.

   By a comparison between Suffolk and the king, a writer can show how their differences reveal not only the fundamental nature of each character but also two alternative ways of operating in the world.

3. **The king and the Dauphin:** Henry and the Dauphin are both weak rulers, but their weakness as rulers may be the only thing they have in common.

How are they each weak in ways that are different from each other, and how do those differences affect the way we regard them?

4. **Comparing *1 Henry VI* and *Richard III*:** Although a writer may argue that *1 Henry VI* demonstrates that a strong central authority is essential for a well-run kingdom, in a comparison between *1 Henry VI* and *Richard III* a writer can challenge the validity of that assertion.

How is each play affected when read in the light of the other? Can you make the argument that a comparative reading of the two plays suggests that a ruler must be, what seems like an oxymoron, a virtuous Machiavellian? Or that each play completes the other? *1 Henry VI* demonstrates the danger threatened by the lack of a strong central political authority; *Richard III* demonstrates the danger threatened by the lack of a strong, central, personal morality in the ruler. What conclusions can be drawn from juxtaposing these two potentially flawed models of power?

Bibliography for *Henry VI, Part 1*

Bevington, David M. "The Domineering Female in *1 Henry VI*." *Shakespeare Studies* II (1966): 51–58.

(Bevington argues that the three female figures in 1 Henry VI *[the Countess of Auvergne, Joan of Burgundy, and Margaret of Henry] "resemble one another in their desire for mastery over the male and in the enchanting spells they use to ensnare the intended victim," that "[t]he theme of feminine supremacy echoes the larger theme of discord and division throughout* 1 Henry VI," *that each woman acts as a temptress, and that these temptation scenes, "often thought to be structurally intrusive, added belatedly to pro-*

vide comic digression or to link 1 Henry VI *with succeeding plays," actually enhance the unity of the play.)*

Burckhardt, Sigurd. "'I Am but Shadow of Myself': Ceremony and Design in *1 Henry VI.*" *Modern Language Quarterly* 28, no. 2 (June 1967): 139–58.
(Beginning with the significance of the encounter between Talbot and the Countess of Auvergne, Burckhardt argues that "Shakespeare has discovered that there is a perfect analogy between the verbal and the social order," that the nature of that order in 1 Henry VI *is "combat," but the truer order suggested by this interlude is defined by kindness and generosity.)*

Burns, Edward. "Introduction: Puzzling at Joan." *King Henry VI, Part 1.* 3rd Series. Ed. Edward Burns, pp. 23–48. London: Arden Shakespeare, 2000.
(In his introduction to the Arden Shakespeare edition of 1 Henry VI, *Burns discusses Shakespeare's alterations of historical chronology in his presentation of Joan, the significance of the way her encounter with her demons is staged, and how she is a figure for a historically European conception of women and witchcraft.)*

Dickson, Lisa. "No Rainbow Without the Sun: Visibility and Embodiment in *1 Henry VI.*" *Modern Language Studies,* 30 (Spring 2000): 137–56.
(Dickson argues that by means of the imagery of 1 Henry VI, *Joan of Arc is presented as the actual successor, in terms of her authority, presence, and military power, to Henry V, rather than his son, Henry VI, but that Joan is ultimately shown to be a corrupted representation rather than an authentic one and that this fact indicates the loss of a historical era and the end of a vision of hierarchical order.)*

Hunt, Maurice. "The Politics of Vision in Shakespeare's *1 Henry VI.*" *South Central Review,* 19 (Spring 2002): 76–101.
(Hunt studies the use and the significance in 1 Henry VI *of imagery derived from the act of gazing, looking, and surveilling.)*

Jackson, Gabriele Bernhard. "Topical Ideology: Witches, Amazons, and Shakespeare's Joan of Arc." *English Literary Renaissance* 18, no. 1 (Winter 1988): 40–65.

(Without concluding anything specific about the character of Joan herself in 1 Henry VI, Jackson examines the allusions to the goddess of justice and to heroic warrior women surrounding her, allusions often attached to Queen Elizabeth, as well as allusions to witches, reflecting the ambiguity, Jackson argues, with which Elizabethan men regarded women.)

Pearlman, E. "Shakespeare at Work: The Two Talbots." *Philological Quarterly,* vol. 75, no. 1, Winter 1996, pp. 1–22.

(Pearlman considers the possibility that act 4, scene 6, in which Talbot and his son John prepare for death in battle after each refuses to abandon the other, is an earlier version of the preceding scene 5 and was mistakenly printed in the First Folio. He also discusses the Talbots as an early representation of the trope of father and son as comrades in battle that recurs throughout the plays of Shakespeare.)

Stapleton, M. L. "'Shine it like a comet of revenge': Seneca, John Studley, and Shakespeare's Joan la Pucelle." *Comparative Literature Studies* 31 (1994): 229–50.

(Stapleton argues that Seneca's Medea is the source for Shakespeare's Joan and that both represent figures of female vengeance against male authority.)

Vincent, Paul J. "Structuring and Revision in *1 Henry VI.*" *Philological Quarterly,* Fall 2005, vol. 84, no. 4, pp. 377–403.

(Vincent considers the problems of multiple authorship, dating, and revision in regard to 1 Henry VI *through textual analysis.)*

HENRY VI, PART 2

READING TO WRITE

THE ANIMOSITY that flares up among the nobility in *1 Henry VI*, when they begin to compete for power after the death of Henry V and the coronation of his infant son, blazes out of control in *Henry VI, Part 2* (1590–91). *Part 1*, initially, may challenge a reader as it is episodic and requires familiarity with a multitude of characters, their shifting loyalties, obscure rivalries, overt actions, covert ambitions, and secret intentions. *Part 2* is unified not only by the sequence of its events but by Shakespeare's underlying interest in the influence of individual psychology and national history on each other. The drama of its plot comes from the development of substantial characters of psychological depth.

A writer who begins with that assertion as a thesis has a range of characters to study. Her primary task will be to show how the circumstances of history and the way that characters respond to those circumstances interact—whether the characters attempt to shape those circumstances or to conform themselves to events that seem driven by historical or divine inevitability. Characters such as Henry, Margaret, Suffolk, Winchester, York, Gloucester, and Gloucester's wife, Eleanor, all are endowed with an individuality that is conveyed not only by their actions and reactions but by those bits of themselves that are revealed in their speeches and their gestures. Characters have moments of confrontation with themselves as well as with their enemies. The king, the queen, Suffolk, Gloucester, Winchester, and Eleanor all are worthy subjects for an analysis of how characters confront and reveal themselves. Look, for example, at the way Suffolk behaves when parting from Margaret and at the hour of his death. Gloucester and Winchester, too, reveal who they are as men by the way they die. Even minor, transitory characters, such as one of Gloucester's murderers, confront themselves, as he does, when he wishes he had not killed Gloucester.

2 Henry VI is also rich in ancillary characters drawn from the populace—workers, masters, apprentices, wives, townsfolk, and a country squire. Set within the plots and politics of the nobility are the plots and politics of a mob of Englishmen in revolt against royal and aristocratic authority. A reader of *2 Henry VI* might consider writing about how all the scenes describing the common people—the ones preceding the scenes of uprising, the scenes with Simpcox and his wife and with Horner and Peter, as well as the scenes in the street—relate to the central actions and themes concerning the nobility, their personalities, ambitions, and actions. A writer may notice that Gloucester's wife, Eleanor, the duchess, and Simpcox's wife are both ambitious, that Cade is York's agent and no less peremptory than his "betters," that Winchester is as brutal as Cade even if more sophisticated. Likewise, it is potentially necessary to note, in an analysis of the scenes of the populace in revolt, bamboozled by Jack Cade, their offstage appearance after they learn of Gloucester's death. They are represented by Salisbury in his report to the king, at 3.2.242ff. Their sense of court intrigue and danger is right, and their loyalty to the king is clear. Similarly, their street commentary on Cade is accurate.

Shakespeare's strategy for creating a sense of depth in his characters and of drama in the presentation of events is linguistic. *2 Henry VI* can be seen as an anatomy of lying. Characters in the play can be categorized as liars or as honest, irrespective of their social class. Margaret, Suffolk, Winchester, and York, for example, are liars but each in a particular way. Henry, Gloucester, Peter, and Alexander Iden are not. There are many passages in the text that a writer may cite to show that Henry, in fact, is honest and clearsighted, that he is saintly in his resignation, seeing history as the unravelling of God's will even when performed by duplicitous men and women; but those are not qualities, a writer can show, that make him an effective monarch or even a man able to benefit others. Gloucester's haughty and ambitious wife is not a liar, either, despite her dabbling in witchcraft, yet that does not make her honorable. Sir John Hum, who betrays her, is a liar. Jack Cade, Saunder Simpcox, Simpcox's wife, and Thomas Horner, the armorer, among the common people, also are liars. What does the emphasis on lying suggest about the truth and nature of history?

The populace in revolt in the streets, despite being portrayed as fickle, are not liars. They are shown to be honest but bad at reasoning, as if to suggest that their uprising is not wrong in itself but wrong in its expression because of the illogical nature or weak faculties of its practitioners. A writer wishing to pursue this line of argument could begin by examining the passage in act 4, scene 2, beginning at line 138, for an example of the operation of a logical non sequitur.

The effect of the interplay of liars and honest people is to establish a fundamental theme of the play and a fundamental conflict: the contention between lies and truth as well as the dramatic contrast between power and ineptitude. The bleak conclusion that prevails in 2 Henry VI suggests that truth does not necessarily vanquish falsehood in what seem to be endless skirmishes between the two. In pursuing this thesis, though, a writer must remember that 2 Henry VI is the second part of a narrative tetralogy. A structural problem for a writer to unravel is how the play exists in relation to the other works with which it forms a series. In other words, the play, while being a complete work unto itself, at the same time exists in the midpoint of the overarching tetralogy of which it is part.

Unlike its immediate predecessor, 2 Henry VI is a good story. It traces the interplay of violence, conspiracy, social classes, gore, mob justice, and the emergence of clearly defined rival power centers in brutal and bloody contention with one another. Whether 2 Henry VI was actually written before or after 1 Henry VI, readers ought to take them in their historical order. If you have read 1 Henry VI, the large number of titled characters in the second part, who must be distinguished from one another as they rearrange their allegiances and challenge each other's right to govern, or even to live, ought to be less daunting. Some figures will have grown familiar and, because of the strength of the plot, many will be recognizable. If you have not read 1 Henry VI, you ought to go back to it after reading 2 Henry VI in order to understand what is happening in Part 2. Similarly, after you have read Part 2, Part 1 will be viewed in a somewhat different light. You will have a sense of the characters then, and you have the privilege of knowing what they are going to do later. You can enjoy the aesthetic pleasure of recognition. Characters in 1 Henry VI who seemed, the first time around, to be nondescript appear in greater definition and resolution because you know where they are heading.

Rereading closely related or interrelated works not only sorts out characters and plotlines, but it also guides a reader to other problems and pleasures. It is only after several readings, for example, that it becomes clear that the earl of Cambridge, whom Henry V executed in act 2, scene 2 of *Henry V,* was the father of the duke of York. Although a detail not of overwhelming significance, it does give a sense of historical depth to the character of York and a motive for his animosity. Once a reader attains familiarity with *2 Henry VI,* small details emerge that add texture and nuance. In Margaret's first speech in *2 Henry VI,* as she introduces herself to Henry, after Suffolk has brought her back to England from France (and she has already begun an affair with Suffolk, fueled by their mutual love of power), she uses the word *alderliefest,* in regard to Henry, calling him her "alderliefest sovereign" (1.1.28). The word *liefest* recurs at 3.1.164, after Suffolk arrests Gloucester on trumped-up charges of treason. Addressing each of his false accusers, when Gloucester comes to Margaret, he says, "you, my sovereign lady . . . / Causeless have laid disgraces on my head / And with your best endeavor have stirred up / My *liefest* liege to be mine enemy" (emphasis added). The echo of Margaret's earlier "alderliefest" in Gloucester's "liefest" does more than add aural resonance and complexity to the play. By this simple repetition, Shakespeare is underscoring the difference between the duplicitous Margaret, who used the word falsely—Henry is not her best loved—and the true Gloucester, whose honest use of the word underscores Margaret's falseness. In addition, the echo of the word reinforces the lesson of history that *2 Henry VI* delivers: The good are often brought to grief not by any evil of their own but by the evil work of others. This is a proposition for a writer to investigate using passages from the play that either substantiate or challenge it. A related problem a writer may choose to examine is what can be derived from *2 Henry VI* in regard to the problem of what makes the good good. Is Henry's virtue real virtue when he is powerless with regard to Gloucester's well-being, if all it allows him to do is either to supplicate men whom he ought to command by right of his rank or to resign himself to human evil that he sees as the will of heaven?

In *2 Henry VI* Shakespeare presents a more colorful and varied canvas than he did in *1 Henry VI.* The play takes the reader through the environs of the courts peopled with aristocracy, onto the fields of battle and siege, as well as into the streets of London, teeming with a mob in rebellion against the aristocracy and following a leadership, in the person of Jack

Cade, with a program and a rhetoric presaging with terrible accuracy the tyrannical, revolutionary regimes stretching from the French Revolution to those of Stalin, Hitler, Mao Zedong, Pol Pot, Augusto Pinochet, and the junta of Myanmar. A reader could decide to look at Shakespeare as a political writer who does not limit himself to anatomizing court intrigues. In *2 Henry VI*, Shakespeare looks at the effects of a corrupt political system on the spirit of the common people. He is an anatomist, not a partisan.

The great theme of *2 Henry VI* is revenge, one of the major dramatic contrivances and motives to be presented on the Elizabethan stage. Mixing the genres of gory revenge tragedy with chronicle history puts the story of the kings of England and their struggles for power into a perspective that subverts and questions the purity of their nobility and the nobility of their actions. Revenge hinges on a dramatic structure that highlights factional feuds and the acts of violence and brutality that such feuds generate. Factional conflict makes for powerful drama not only because it often leads to actual violence in the form of riots and battles but because it brings to the surface the dark and usually hidden aspects of incensed human nature.

Revenge is played out in the social as well as the individual realm in *2 Henry VI*. The popular rebellion can be seen as an expression of revenge by the people for the wrongs they suffered from the nobility, often through the exercise or defiance of the law, as is apparent in the scene where Suffolk rips up a petition mistakenly presented to him that names him as defendant in a suit intended for presentation to Gloucester.

Conflict elicits cruelty and misrepresentations of the truth, the lying that is the fundamental linguistic preoccupation of *2 Henry VI*. Watching conflict represented onstage, or following it on the page, by necessity, imposes the need for the spectator or reader to develop the complexity of understanding that comes from having a dual or even multiple perspective, of becoming aware of the undermining power of irony, of developing the intellectual finesse that looking at all the sides of a conflict or any situation enforces. The representation of conflict gives rise to dramatic irony and dramatic confrontations. Speech and action become performance and are used as vehicles for self-assertion, mastery, and deception. Naïve comments by third parties become grim indications of the opposite of what the speaker intended, as for example, at line 37 of act 1, scene 1, when Henry's courtiers kneel and cry, "Long live Queen Margaret, England's happiness." The reader already knows from the last scenes of *1 Henry VI* what this and succeeding plays will reveal, that Margaret is not and will never become "England's happiness."

TOPICS AND STRATEGIES
Themes

Many of the themes that will reappear throughout Shakespeare's career are present in this early work. Such themes as war, rivalry, revenge, violence, family, loyalty, ambition, duplicitous wives, and the relationship between the populace and the aristocracy—all serious concerns throughout Shakespeare's work—are important elements in *2 Henry VI*. Writers approaching the play can begin by identifying a central theme they see as important and then decide what it is that the play is saying about that theme and what that theme contributes to the play. To identify a theme, a writer may look for ideas, words, or even images that recur in the play. As you examine the play with a particular theme in mind, what do you think the play is saying about that theme? What effect does the way the theme is presented have on you? Does it elicit, for example, your sympathy or animosity?

Sample Topics:

1. **Violence:** How does *2 Henry VI* define violence, and how does Shakespeare represent and evaluate the use of violence? How does the play show the consequences of violence?

   To write an essay centering on this topic, a student can begin by identifying the moments when the play presents acts of violence, discusses violence, or shows the effects of violence. What, in the context of *2 Henry VI*, constitutes a violent act? Look to see if characters discuss the morality or consequences of violence or if the action of the play supplies a commentary on the acts of violence performed in the play. From this, a thesis can be developed about the role of violence in the play or its efficacy as a force of history. What do you think Shakespeare's moral stance is in the play, in regard to violence?

2. **Family/marriage:** What is the purpose or the function of marriage in *2 Henry VI*? How does the play portray the marriage between Henry and Margaret and the marriage between

Gloucester and Eleanor? Compare the two. In what way or ways are they similar as partnerships, and in what way are the various partners like one another? Do Margaret and Eleanor or Henry and Gloucester share any characteristics as wives or husbands? How does the marriage of Saunder Simpcox and his wife compare to the marriage of these two couples? Look at the adulterous relationship between Margaret and Suffolk as well. Do they seem to have more in common in terms of passions and personalities than the members of the play's sanctioned marriages do?

Such an essay would need to look at the scenes in which Henry and Margaret, Margaret and Suffolk, Gloucester and Eleanor, and Simpcox and his wife are onstage together as well as moments when they are apart but talk about one another.

3. **Ambition:** Ambition is a driving force for many of the characters in *2 Henry VI*. Although it does not appear to be so for the king himself, does Henry show any traces of ambition? Consider his "deal" with York when he makes York his heir. How does the play depict the effects of ambition on individual characters and on the world they live in?

An essay on this topic might choose to focus on one character, showing how the theme of ambition affects his or her development and affects the tenor of the play. Alternately, an essay could focus on a number of ambitious characters, uncovering the nature and quality of ambition, its effects on personality, on interpersonal relations, and on the health of the polity. Is it ambition that impels the peasant revolt? What indications are there in the text in regard to their motives? How must a writer distinguish between the populace and its leader?

4. **Power:** The pursuit of power is a theme that binds nearly all the characters and events of the play. In demonstrating this, a writer may begin with any instance of the desire for or exercise of power, compare it to others and show the effect of the pursuit of power on individuals and on the social system as a whole.

5. **Allegiance or loyalty:** The problem of loyalty is a recurring theme in the play, whether the focus is on the loyalty husbands and wives owe each other, subjects owe to the king, the king owes to his office, or individuals owe to one another as an obligation of their humanity.

What does the play seem to be saying about loyalty? Are there both virtuous and evil forms of loyalty? Look at Winchester, for example. By being loyal to himself, the cardinal, in his death throes, is shown to have betrayed his own humanity. Or consider how by being loyal to her overweening ambition, the duchess of Gloucester betrays not only her husband's office but her own pride.

6. **Hypocrisy/duplicity:** A writer may choose to write about lying as an important theme in *2 Henry VI* or as one of the principal techniques of its dramaturgy. The struggles for power within the realm turns speech into a mechanism of the speaker's will. In *2 Henry VI*, is lying essential in the pursuit of domination? Can you show that in the play loyalty to one's word or to another person is often harmful to one's immediate interest?

A writer might show how most of Margaret's tirades are lies, that courtiers lie to the king and break vows, and that *2 Henry VI* often confronts the question of what makes vows legitimate. An essay might consider the effect of lying on the characters and events of the play.

Character

Essays that focus on questions of character development are essentially investigating what makes a particular character the person he or she is and what distinguishes him or her from other characters. Additionally, a focus on a character may lead a writer to consider that character's effect on the development of plot. In addition to leading to an examination of actions, the question, "How does Shakespeare influence our perception of a particular character?" directs readers to an analysis of the language of the character, the imagery associated with that character, how his or her language reveals character, what others say about that character, and how reliable what they say is given their own demonstrated characters.

Sample Topics:

1. **King Henry's character development:** How does Shakespeare give us a sense of Henry's personality? Is he monolithic in his character? What are Henry's conflicts? Consider the contrast between his complaints about being king and his bargain with York to remain king and how he twice asserts his right to the crown, once against York and once against Edward.

   How does Henry grow or change (or does he grow or change) over the course of the play? What causes these changes to occur (or prevents the king from growing or changing)? What is the effect of Henry's character on other people in the play and on its essential action?

2. **The representation of character:** A writer may focus on quite a few characters besides the king in *2 Henry VI*. Margaret, Suffolk, Gloucester, Eleanor, York, and Cade may prove to be of particular interest.

   How does Shakespeare show the kinds of people they are? How do they speak? How does their way of speaking reveal what they are like? How does their speech vary as their situations change? If it does change, is that change caused by something in their character? How does Shakespeare show them reacting to triumph or adversity? How does he develop any of these characters' personalities by showing how they are in their interactions with other characters or in the face of historical circumstances? How do these characters help to determine the actions of other characters or the movement of history? Consider, for example, writing about how Jack Cade's death is an indication of the inefficacy of his character and not of his political position.

3. **Character and history:** A general essay, less interested in anatomizing a particular character, could focus on the way Shakespeare develops a relationship between a person's character and history in *2 Henry VI*. The essay should demonstrate how history (collective and individual history) can determine a person's character or how a person's character can influence the course of history.

History and Context

A useful approach to *2 Henry VI* is to consider the period in which it was first performed. What significance did historical events and characters drawn from the late fourteenth century and from the middle of the fifteenth century have in the late sixteenth century? Of what importance could a weak king like Henry VI be to a strong monarch like Elizabeth I? In order to answer, it is necessary to discover what the last decades of Elizabeth's era were like with regard to political intrigue and the threats of war and invasion.

Sample Topics:

1. **Witchcraft:** In *1 Henry VI*, Joan of Arc is portrayed as a witch. In *2 Henry VI*, Gloucester's wife, Eleanor, dabbles in witchcraft and employs the service of a witch, Margaret Jourdain.

   How prominent were witches, the belief in witches, the fear of witches, the persecution of witches, and the literary employment of witches at the time Shakespeare wrote the Henry VI plays? Did writers of the time write about witches? If they did, what did they write?

2. **Politics in the play:** *2 Henry VI* is, in essence, a political play. It concerns itself with questions of good and bad government, tyranny, succession, usurpation, and popular uprisings. What kind of commentary on these political issues does the play present?

   This is a broad topic, and the writer would need to focus on several defined elements and evaluate the play's position on them. Techniques might include a close reading of characters talking about kingship, succession, the commoners, or lineage and rights, for example. Or a writer could analyze the complaints of the people in light of prior events in the play. It might also be useful to consider the period tradition of giving advice to monarchs represented by a work such as *Mirror for Magistrates*, which is a series of admonitory stories of past rulers.

3. **Social instability, threats to order, and government spy networks in Elizabeth's England:** Writers with a particular inter-

est in history may wonder how much Shakespeare used the events of Henry VI's era to reflect on events of his own.

Research into social instability under Elizabeth, into religious disputes, into the effect of large segments of the population unmoored (such as the veterans returning from the wars against Spain), and into the spy and torture networks employed by the crown can put the play as well as the time into perspective and show how Shakespeare might have indirectly touched on subjects he otherwise could not directly address.

Philosophy and Ideas

Exploring the philosophical ideas that circulate in *2 Henry VI* can serve as an extension of or give support to the thematic approaches already presented. Engaging a play's philosophical aspects or the abstract ideas it presents and grapples with can universalize your vision of the play and broaden the scope and resonance of your essay.

Sample Topics:

1. **The active versus the contemplative life:** Shakespeare was writing at a time when the question, "Which is more worthy of emulation, the active or the contemplative life?" had been posed and considered by such figures as Italian poet Petrarch (Francesco Petrarca) and French essayist Michel de Montaigne. How does *2 Henry VI* contribute to that conversation?

   Look at passages that reflect both attitudes and examine their tone. Can you argue that Shakespeare does not come down on either side of the issue but seeks a compromise? The problem is not one that Shakespeare finishes with in this play. He is still concerned with the debate in the last play he wrote in its entirety, *The Tempest.*

2. **The conflict between mercy and vengeance:** The conflict between vengeance and mercy, one of the principal concerns of *2 Henry VI*, is a problem that absorbs Shakespeare on the profoundest level throughout his career. How does Shakespeare present the problem of these opposite modes in *2 Henry VI?*

What conclusion about these opposite concepts does he seem to come to? How can you substantiate your conclusion? Your conclusion will become your introduction, your thesis. The essay, as it develops, will make the case for your thesis by taking instances from the text that speak conclusively to your position.

You may also attempt to see how Shakespeare regards and defines these opposites by exploring how he treats the conflict between justice and mercy or between revenge and reconciliation in other plays. *The Merchant of Venice, Hamlet, King Lear,* or *The Tempest* are a few of the plays deeply concerned with the problems of vengeance (or justice) and mercy.

3. **The role of a king or leader:** A great many of the characters in *2 Henry VI* want to be rulers. They want to be at the head of England and of France too. As far as you can tell from the play, what are their motives: to promote the common good; to make right prevail; to do the will of God, as they understand it; to exert and enjoy the experience of raw power; to flatter their vanity; or to continue on the path that their forebears set them on?

Analyze what characters say about their own ambitions or how they say nothing about either ambitions or motives. Then examine how they act to further their ambitions. How does the nature of their action in the pursuit of power serve as a commentary on their ambition or a reflection of their character? What evidence does the play offer suggesting what Shakespeare thinks about power and leadership?

4. **The conflict between good and evil:** One of the troublesome impressions that the play leaves is that evil triumphs over good. How does this impression affect your assessment of Shakespeare's view of history? In order to discuss the idea of the conflict between good and evil, it is necessary to be able to recognize the two and to see how they differ.

Look for examples of evil behavior in the play. What defines them as evil? Similarly, look for examples of goodness. What defines the actions as good? Is there a greater preponderance of one over the other? What is the significance of that in terms of the ideas the play conveys? Remember that 2 *Henry VI* is only part of a story of the contest for power by a number of forces that unleash evil in pursuit of their goal. Even if evil is not defeated in this play, it is at the end of *Richard III*, if only for a brief moment in history.

Language, Symbols, and Imagery

The way characters talk and the images they use, if or when they do use imagery, reveals much about them. Look at the way Henry, Margaret, Cade, or any of the major characters speaks, especially when he or she is reacting to some event or presenting him- or herself to others. How does the language define the character? How does the nature of a character affect the words he or she uses?

Sample Topics:

1. **The Garden of Iden:** Environment is part of imagery. A writer can construct an essay contemplating the fact that Jack Cade is killed in a garden. Look at his dying words. How do they reveal Shakespeare's attitude toward Cade? How do they reveal his character? What is the significance of the fact that the last name of the landowner who kills him, the owner of the garden, is Iden, a pun on Eden, so that Cade, the man who promised a false utopia, is killed in the garden of Iden?

   Jack Cade and Alexander Iden both were actual historical figures. Iden killed Cade, and the name of the village, located in Kent, was and still is Iden. A writer may do some research to discover if this uncanny coincidence was noted at the time and regarded as significant.

2. **Recurring patterns:** When many characters use similar imagery, then certain patterns are formed that reflect something about the ideas the text is putting forth as well as aspects of particular characters.

   Look, for example, at the intensity of animal imagery in the play. What sort of images are they? How are they used? Who uses them? What does it say about that person, about the idea of human behavior or of human nature that the play projects?

Form and Genre

2 Henry VI has two principal subjects: history and the drama of history. Anatomizing the dramatic structure of the play, a writer can attempt to demonstrate that the form that history commonly takes as a set of dramatic narrative encounters is reinforced, in *2 Henry VI*, by the dramatic structure of the play, which is laid out as a progression of stories. In the play, Shakespeare creates and resolves confrontations and contests between shifting sets of characters, giving the play its form and presenting history as a story driven by human drama.

Sample Topics:

1. **History as comedy:** As it addresses issues of history, *2 Henry VI* encroaches on other genres, notably tragedy but also comedy. Neither history nor tragedy nor comedy is a "pure" category. In Shakespeare's plays, each frequently has an element of other genres evident in or integrated into it. This is apparent in the two plays devoted to the history of Henry IV in which the tavern scenes with Falstaff are comic but not exclusively so. The fate of Hotspur, likewise, borders on tragic.

   In *2 Henry VI*, the scenes of the London workers in the street are presented as if they were comedy, although they are not. You might consider an essay discussing the effect on the play or the effect the play is attempting to create by presenting those episodes as comic set pieces.

   Whatever purpose the scenes with Simpcox and his wife or with the apprentice, Peter, and his master, Thomas Horner, have as commentary on the action or on other characters of the play, they are also comic interludes. The word *interlude* suggests that they are presented like vignettes within the larger dramas of history and of a play.

2. ***2 Henry VI* as a didactic work:** Along with comic elements, *2 Henry VI* has tragic features. *Tragedy* is a term used to refer to various sorts of dramatic representations. Sir Philip Sidney

(1554–86), in his *Apologie for Poetrie* (1583, printed 1595), argued that tragedy concerns kings and queens and serves as a warning and guide to behavior for rulers. Can you show that the events of *2 Henry VI* can be seen as serving as examples and that the play in itself is a guide for how rulers, both kings and those close to them, ought to behave? Thomas Heywood, ca. 1570–1641, emphasized the grim and brutal displays of gory and violent action that he thought were at the heart of tragedy and argued that, by showing them in their terrible fullness, tragedy could help prevent them (*Apology for Actors*, 1608, printed 1612). This version of tragedy originated in the "closet dramas" (plays written to be read aloud rather than performed) of the Roman philosopher/playwright, Seneca (4 B.C.–65 A.D.). It is close to the genre typically called horror, of which there are many examples in *2 Henry VI*, as a count of the number of severed heads that grace the play will show.

These observations assert, then, that historical drama, especially its tragic elements, serves a purpose by teaching a lesson. What does *2 Henry VI* teach? Who are its lessons aimed at? From the scope of the play, there seem to be several targets. How does *2 Henry VI* teach the lessons it does? Look at the situations it presents, the way the characters speak, the pervasive images, the juxtapositions of scenes, the internal and interpersonal conflicts its characters face, the effects it has on you, and the reactions it appears to be attempting to provoke.

3. ***2 Henry VI* as drama:** *2 Henry VI*, like the body of Shakespeare's work, was written to be performed. Discuss the play's dramaturgical technique. How does it achieve dramatic effects? How does Shakespeare produce the tension and suspense the play depends on? How does he interweave the number of stories that form the total narrative of the play? How does he construct the play, set scenes in relation to one another, connect disparate actions, and show the dispositions of his characters toward one another? How does he reveal character through speech and how does he make speech appear to be the utterances of characters rather than a vehicle for ideas or a way to drive the action?

Compare and Contrast Essays

A conventional way to write a paper on a work of literature is to compare and contrast elements in the work, discover the similarities and differences between them, and then—this is a crucial and often neglected step—comment on those discoveries and come to some conclusion based on the analysis of the similarities and differences that you have made. Without a strong conclusion, comparison and contrast papers tend to turn into unambitious catalogs or lists of elements that are either the same or different.

Sample Topics:

1. **Henry and his adversaries:** In a comparison/contrast paper you can compare characters with each other, but you can also compare the situations that several characters find themselves in and consider how various characters respond to similar situations or go about achieving similar goals. Since Henry is at the center of all the action in *2 Henry VI*—nearly everybody but Gloucester is trying to overthrow him—it will be instructive to compare characters in the play with regard to their attitudes about Henry and their ways of plotting for power.

2. **Comparisons with other plays by Shakespeare:** One way of reading Shakespeare is to consider each play not only as a separate work but as an independent yet related part of one larger work, the entire body of his work. Either challenging or following this point of view, a writer can choose to compare characters (or other elements of the play like patterns of imagery, dramatic confrontations, or significant themes) from *2 Henry VI* with elements in other plays of Shakespeare—either within or between genres. How, for example, do the ambitions, actions, and plots of the characters in *2 Henry VI* compare to the ambitions, actions, and plots or contrivances of other Shakespearian characters? You can look at how Don John operates in *Much Ado about Nothing*, make note of how Edmund schemes in *King Lear*, or consider what drives Iago in *Othello* or Malvolio in *Twelfth Night*.

3. **The duke of York and his son, Richard:** Of particular interest to readers of *2 Henry VI* may be to compare the duke of York and his son, Richard, who will become Richard III. York appears in

the three parts of *Henry VI*, and Richard enters in *Part 2*, gaining importance in *Part 3* only to dominate his own play, *Richard III*. In making this comparison, a writer might begin by comparing the soliloquies both father and son deliver in order to observe the rhetorical similarities that give the language and the way of thinking that the father and son share a family resemblance.

Bibliography for *Henry VI, Part 2*

Arab, Ronda. "Ruthless Power and Ambivalent Glory: The Rebel-Labourer in *2 Henry VI*." *Journal for Early Modern Cultural Studies* 5, Fall 2005, pp. 5–36. *(Arab considers how Shakespeare's depiction of Cade and the rebellious workers offers an alternative vision of manhood that challenged the aristocratic construction of masculinity.)*

Bernthal, Craig A. "Jack Cade's Legal Carnival." *Studies in English Literature 1500–1900*, Spring 2002, vol. 42, pp. 259–74. *(Bernthal examines the influence of Elizabethan theater market forces and the injustices of the English legal system on the composition of* 2 Henry VI.*)*

Chartier, Roger. "Jack Cade, the Skin of a Dead Lamb, and the Hatred for Writing." *Shakespeare Studies* 34, January 1, 2006, pp. 77–90. *(Chartier considers the historical precedents for Jack Cade's condemnation of writing.)*

Dickson, Lisa. "Tent Him to the Quick: Vision, Violence, and Penalty in Shakespeare's *2 Henry VI*." *Renaissance Drama*, vol. 32, 2003, pp. 69–93. *(In an essay interpreting the role of punishment in* 2 Henry VI, *Dickson focuses on the prevalence of images of dismemberment and argues that punishment in the play does not serve to ensure social peace by enforcing social values but acts as a force that creates social dismemberment.)*

Fitter, Chris. "Emergent Shakespeare and the Politics of Protest: *2 Henry VI* in Historical Contexts." *ELH* 72, Spring 2005, pp. 129–58. *(Fitter argues that "many in the earliest common audiences of* 2 Henry VI *must have found their own contemporary grievances, military, political, and economic, channelled with eloquent anger into the play: would have recognized the democratizing ideology breeding among pirates and privateers: . . .*

and . . . would have decoded [contemporary Elizabethan political figures] in the terminally feuding figures of Gloucester and York.")

Laroque, François. "The Jack Cade Scenes Reconsidered: Popular Rebellion, Utopia, or Carnival?" *Shakespeare and Cultural Traditions,* edited by Tetsuo Kishi, Roger Pringle and Stanley Wells, pp. 76–89. Newark: University of Delaware Press, 1994.

(In a discussion of the scenes of popular uprising, Laroque argues that "The Jack Cade scenes in 2 Henry VI *provide the audience with neither comic relief nor with a credible alternative to the theme of the disintegration of the kingdom. Instead they present us with a vision of the world upside down, which is also a distorted mirror of authority as the commons blindly reenact the brutalities of the aristocracy. Jack Cade's political platform . . . is a mixture of utopian radicalism and festive traditions that aims at promoting his own pretensions to the crown as Lord Mortimer.")*

Owens, Margaret E. "The Many-headed Monster in *Henry VI, Part 2.*" *Criticism,* vol. XXXVIII, no. 3, Summer 1996, pp. 367–82.

(Owens discusses the iconic and political significance of severed heads in 2 Henry VI. *"More so than in any other history play of the period," she argues, "the severed head in* 2 Henry VI *functions as a site of contestation rather than as a sign of order restored. As this play seems to insist, the removal of heads does less to contain disruptive energies than it does to unleash them.")*

Sousa, Geraldo U. de. "The Peasants' Revolt and the Writing of History in *2 Henry VI.*" In *Reading and Writing in Shakespeare,* edited by David M. Bergeron, pp. 178–93. Newark: University of Delaware Press, 1996.

(De Sousa argues that in 2 Henry VI, *Shakespeare "closely studies the connection between writing, history, and power" and that "Jack Cade identifies writing as the power that authorizes and perpetuates social injustices. He sees all writing as oppressive for it confirms traditions and confers privileges from which the illiterate are by definition excluded." Cade's goal, de Sousa explains, is to "destroy rather than decipher or rewrite the code, thus attempting to restructure English society into a preliterate, ahistorical stage. Literacy, in this context, becomes a metaphor for the power of the dominant culture, the power to make history.")*

HENRY VI, PART 3

READING TO WRITE

THE HAPPILY-EVER-AFTER note on which *3 Henry VI* (ca. 1591) ends—as the newly installed King Edward IV proclaims, in the final words of the play, "our lasting joy"—is as short lived and unsteady as every other turn of political fortune in this last play of the three Shakespeare devoted to the life and reign of Henry VI. Edward's defeat of Henry is the prelude to his brother Richard's reign of cunning and terror that will be traced in *Richard III*, the concluding work in the eight-play chronicle recording the contest for England's crown, known as the War of the Roses, between the houses of York and Lancaster.

Unlike Henry VI, Richard III will openly dominate his play and give it unity by his presence. He pervades *Richard III*, directing its events and manipulating the other characters. Henry VI, even when not being contrasted to Richard III, is, as a force in his plays, almost a nonentity, an idea or a symbol rather than a person. Moreover, because as a person and as a character he seems weak, the idea he is supposed to symbolize, the monarchy, is weakened too. Rather than a stay against calamity and chaos, kingship in *3 Henry VI* is a commodity to be fought over. The action of *3 Henry VI* is the contest, the challenge that Edward, his brothers (especially Richard), and their followers mount against Henry's supporters for the crown. Henry himself is hardly involved in the action. He is at its center but passively so, a statue, a figurehead, a place holder to be revered or replaced, but he neither directs nor determines the action.

Without his strong presence as a king, the play seems to have no center. There are, instead, rival centers. One is Edward's camp; the other, rather than being called Henry's, is really that of his wife, Margaret. Henry, rather than being his play's director, more closely resembles its Chorus, as in act 2, scene 5. As Margaret and his son, Prince Edward, lead Henry's troops in battle against York's son, Edward, Henry sits apart, because Clifford, one of his supporters, has directed him to quit the field: "the Queen hath best success when you are absent." Margaret herself adds "Ay . . . leave us to our fortune." Henry, in consequence, sits on a molehill, commenting on the battle, so removed from the action and uncommitted to its outcome that he can say, "To whom God will, there be the victory."

The language of Henry's meditation is pastoral. Henry begins to think about the battle using the image of a shepherd blowing on his nails in the chilly moments when night and morning seem to be in a struggle for dominance. In this way, Henry describes the fortunes of the contenders in the battle and his own removal and dependency. He then describes the battle itself, drawing a picture of a raging sea contending with mighty winds. His thoughts then come to rest on him, his exclusion from the battle, and by extension, his lack of fitness for the role he was born to inhabit. He wishes, if it is God's will, for death and falls into a meditation about time, concluding with a familiar idea voiced by Shakespeare's kings. He contrasts a poor shepherd's easy sleep with a king's sleep, which is, he concludes, troubled: "care, mistrust, and treason waits on him." Both Henry IV and Henry V have expressed similar notions, but they had no ambivalence about their burden. Its weight added, for them, to their glory.

While fulfilling the function of a chorus, Henry is structurally removed from the action of the play. The content of his meditation adds to the distance. What follows his meditation takes him entirely out of the play. He becomes a member of the audience. As Henry sits considering his solitary lot, he witnesses two successive events that are dramatic interludes for us, corroborating narratives for him.

In the first episode, the king sees a son drag in the body of a man he has just killed in battle only to find, when he lifts the visor of the helmet, that the man is his father. In the second episode, the king and the audience witness the obverse, a father who realizes he has just slain his son in battle. These scenes have an obvious purpose. They show the human misery at the heart of war and suggest we are all one another's kin. The scenes also give a sense of the tangible reality that had been turned into an abstraction in the cavalier cry of self-regard with which act 2, scene 2 ends, when Edward boasts, in breaking off negotiations with Margaret, "These words will cost ten thousand lives this day."

The entirety—Henry's initial meditation, the two episodes witnessed by Henry and annotated by his commentary, all contained within our gaze as we watch or read the play—comments on the price of war and unites Henry's tender perspective with the audience's. By the design of the scene, Shakespeare has forged an identity between Henry and the audience just at the moment when Henry's sense of the value of the pursuit of power is entirely altered. It is from Henry's evolving point of view that we are to see the play. We are made to see it with him, through his eyes. The question is, what is his point of view? Or, more precisely, what does Henry represent?

Although he does not signify the model of a monarch in his person, not having the power of personality and a dedication to the use of power that a monarch needs to have, and although he has a forgiving rather than a vengeful attitude toward his enemies, Henry is not without symbolic significance. His soliloquy presented in 2.5 makes him a symbol of the contemplative temperament. He is a symbol of the things that the others in the play hold him in contempt for. He represents saintly resignation, bending one's will to God's before the events of the world and reflecting on them rather than engaging in them. In struggle with challengers, "frowns, words, and threats / Shall be the war that Henry means to use" (1.1.72–73). His is a submissive, quietist, pacifist position. As a king he is the model of a kind of behavior those below him shun. Their inability to frame for themselves the modesty of his disposition is the cause of war. A writer pursuing this thesis has many textual instances to cite that show how personal pride, belligerence, and thirst for revenge exert a pressure on those who experience them. This pressure then leads them to continue the cycle of violence Shakespeare describes in *3 Henry VI*. To see the play through Henry's eyes, from Henry's perspective, means to reject history and the hunger for power and self-assertion that seem to define and characterize it. Still, Henry is not drawn without complexity.

Just as there are two centers of power contending for primacy in the world of the play, there are also two centers within Henry apparently pulling against each other. His Christian docility, expressed through his willingness to resign himself to whatever earthly defeats are offered, what amounts to an imitation of Christ, is not his only attribute. Henry wants to be king. In act 1, scene 1, when Edward comes with overwhelming force to claim the throne from him, Henry keeps his crown by making a deal with Edward. Uncharacteristically, he first tells Edward,

> Think'st thou that I will leave my kingly throne,
> Wherein my grandsire and my father sat?
> No! first shall war unpeople this my realm.
>
> (1.1.124–126)

It was only 50 lines earlier that Henry had proclaimed that "frowns, words, and threats / Shall be the war that Henry means to use."

When the weakness of his claim and the inadequacy of his fighting force seem to give Henry no choice but to accede to Edward and to abdicate, he begs, "Let me for this my lifetime reign as king" (1.1.171), promising, if that condition is granted, he will disinherit his own son and make York his heir, effectively turning the monarchy over to the House of York. Although Henry recognized his obligation to continue the claims of his grandfather and his father, Henry IV and Henry V, respectively, to the crown, he surrenders the claim of his son and, in consequence, cuts off his father's and grandfather's line and claim as well.

It cannot be argued that Henry's agreement to be the last of his line is simply an example of his opposition to strife. What is apparent in this scene is his inability to make war, not his aversion to making it. If preventing war were his goal, and his contempt for his place as king were as firm as his words throughout the play suggest, Henry could have surrendered his own claim to the kingship as well as his heirs'. That would have had the same effect on his forebears and on his progeny as his retaining the office until his death. It is clear that Henry wants to be king himself and is willing to let war secure his desire. The play charts how enlightenment, if it is enlightenment that Henry achieves, is forced on him by his failure rather than by his wisdom and places him in a position to see the cost of war when he observes the two scenes of fathers and sons, on forebears and progeny. Failure schools Henry and sets him apart from the other characters in teaching him loving kindness rather than vengeance. The scenes of the father who killed his son and the son who killed his father resonate with him, particularly because he can identify in both roles. He is a son who has killed his father, in the sense that he has not been able to continue his father's line. He is a father who kills his son, in the sense that he has precluded his son's identity as king by disinheriting him. The institution of kingship and the pursuit of kingship are surrounded by murders.

Henry's renunciation of his son's right to the throne does not strengthen his reception as monarch or man. Clifford, Warwick, and Westmoreland all condemn him. Margaret, his queen, curses, berates, and denounces him. In addition, his bargain does not prevent ongoing war. Margaret assumes the power on the battlefield that ought to be his but that he cannot wield. He is effectively turned into a figurehead and a placeholder for the Lancastrians. At the war council before the battle with Edward's forces, all he can utter are words of Christian regret at seeing York's head on the gate, and a pious, homiletic reprimand to Clifford after he has rebuked Henry for abandoning his son's claim to the throne. Later on in the scene, when Henry tries to speak at line 117 of 2.2, everyone ignores him and he says nothing more until his molehill soliloquy.

After 2.5, Henry fades out of the play, to reappear only as a symbol of the king, whether he is being deposed and imprisoned or liberated and reinstalled as monarch. When he is onstage he is either a prophetic or a pathetic presence, often both at once. He blesses young Richmond and recognizes that he will become England's salvation, which he does, at the end of *Richard III*, when he defeats Richard and, as Henry VII, unites the Houses of York and Lancaster. In the last scenes of *3 Henry VI*, Henry is the sacrificial lamb, slaughtered by Richard after his imprisonment. With his death comes the resolution of the drama. Edward becomes king and momentarily ends the strife. But in Henry's end is Richard's beginning. As Richard murders him, Henry prophesizes the grief Richard will bring to the kingdom.

The problem the play presents is a weak central figure. Nonetheless, strength lies in weakness. That is the tragic lesson of the play. The weak King Henry is the strength of the play. His passive presence anchors the play and unifies its action. His resigned, quietist disposition affects the way the audience comes to be disposed to the ambition and violence that drive *3 Henry VI*. His passive opposition gives meaning to the battles waged and the passions unleashed by making them examples of how things ought not to be. War is not portrayed as heroic but as pathetic, engendering only cruelty and grief. The choice *3 Henry VI* presents is between the desire to exercise the power of an earthly ruler or to bear the duties of a heavenly servitor. Whether these positions are always mutually exclusive or not, in *3 Henry VI* they are.

The lack of a strong central character and a plot that seems episodic and lacking in a strong center can arguably been seen as the play's prevailing faults. Rather than seeing these elements as constituting faults, however, an essay on this topic could attempt to show them as the essential and unifying matter of the play. In the context of raging characters and terrible battles, *3 Henry VI* is a meditation on what constitutes weakness, what defines power, and on the compatibility or incompatibility of Christian values and earthly ambitions.

TOPICS AND STRATEGIES

Here are some suggestions for possible topics for essays on *3 Henry VI* and some general approaches to those topics. These suggestions offer a point of departure, not a master key to the perfect essay. One of the strongest ways for writers to start developing a viable topic and thesis is to find something that interests them, that they care to convey to others, that brings the play alive and gives it meaning. Use this material presented here to stimulate your own thinking.

Themes

Far more than an action play, *3 Henry VI* is an examination of values. What are the values that are examined and questioned, dismissed or endorsed both in the play and by the play? An examination of the themes of the play can lead a writer to an essay on the values implicit in the action of the play and to insights about what the play is saying. Perhaps the best way to spot the themes of the play is by forming a list and then free-writing about the entries generated. War, peace, power, ambition, resignation, succession, revenge, horror, cruelty, brutality, authority, loyalty, hatred, love, loss, or imperfection could be some of the themes listed. After the free association of this initial step, a more disciplined approach is necessary. What does the play say about any of these themes, and how does the play say it? To answer these questions, a writer must survey the play, seeking instances of when the play treats these themes, how it presents these themes, how it presents one theme in relation to another (resignation versus vengeance, for example, or loyalty versus betrayal), and how it shows their consequences.

Sample Topics:

1. **Brutality and horror:** How does the play present horror, and does it evaluate the use of violence and brutality? Does it judge those who are violent and brutal? If so, how does it convey that judgment? What does the preponderance of brutality and the presentation of the horror that results from brutality in the play suggest about history itself and about historical institutions, historical leaders, and national practices that are often honored? Does the play refashion a reader's regard for the great figures and the great actions of history? If so, how?

   To write an essay such as this, begin by identifying where the play presents, discusses, or shows responses to horrific examples of violence and brutality. Then look at the consequences of these acts of brutality and cruelty on their perpetrators, on their victims, on the general climate of the world that the play represents, and on the course of history. From this, a thesis can be developed about the way the play judges not only the morality of cruelty but brings the effects of cruelty on history and on personality into that discussion.

2. **The conflict between ambition and resignation:** Each by itself, ambition or resignation, can be treated as a theme in *3 Henry VI*. Taken together, as values in conflict with each other, they constitute what arguably is the central theme of the play.

   Writing about this conflict, the writer will not only seek examples of ambition and of resignation, which abound in the play, but also examples of the effects of ambitious behavior and of the attitude of resignation. For example, the scene of York's torment by Margaret and Clifford, although not a scene dedicated to dramatizing the workings and promptings of ambition, arguably demonstrates the effects of ambition on both victim and executioner.

3. **Love and hate:** As well as overt themes, there are implicit ones presented in the play. In order to argue that *3 Henry VI* is

essentially about love or hatred, a writer might cull a number of incidents and utterances from the play that can be shown as being at the root of hatred, for example, or that exemplify the results of its presence. Similarly, one can show the effects of the promptings of love on psychic disposition or the absence of love on historical circumstances.

4. **Fathers and sons:** The play is haunted by father-son relationships and describes a variety of them. What particular historical significance do they have? Consider the importance of the father-son bond not only in its psychological aspects but as the medium of dynastic succession and social order or disorder. Consider, too, what the obligations of the bonds entail and how they affect persons and personalities.

Writing about this topic requires a student to describe the nature of the father-son bonds as they are presented by the play, to show what significance the play attributes to the relationship, how the relationship is affected by war and ambition, and how it influences the course of history by keeping alive and renewing rivalries.

5. **Authority:** What constitutes authority in the play and makes it legitimate and true or false and illegitimate? What are the functions and purposes of authority? Where does *3 Henry VI* suggest that authority resides, in the spirit? in the sword? in a legal procedure?

Character

Essays that focus on questions of character development can target such questions as how Shakespeare makes each character recognizably him- or herself, how he distinguishes one character from another, how characters change or grow or fail to change or grow, or how characters and historical circumstances influence and affect one another.

Sample Topics:

1. **Henry's character development:** How does Henry change and grow over the course of the play, if in fact he does?

The writer's first task in developing a thesis on a topic such as this is to decide if Henry changes and grows over the course of the work and, if so, what those changes are. Evidence to support the thesis can come from Henry's soliloquy, the way he interacts with others, his attitudes about power, how others speak of him, and how he regards his right to be king and to execute its offices.

An obvious but valuable method to pursue is to look at the impression Henry makes on the reader or the spectators at the beginning of the play and at the end. If Henry can be described in both instances, for example, as weak, the question to be considered is whether it is the same kind of weakness in both cases or if there is a difference in the quality of Henry's weakness as it is presented at the start and at the conclusion of the play. What impression does the reader have of Henry at the beginning? At the end? How do these impressions differ? Has Henry achieved a human or a moral identity by the end of the play that he lacked at the start of it?

2. **Margaret's character development:** The nature of Margaret's character, a writer can propose, is tied to the circumstances of her life. She is one of the dominant characters in *3 Henry VI*, and she appears in all the three parts of *Henry VI* and in *Richard III*. Any complete discussion of her requires that she be seen as she spans the plays. How is her identity shaped and developed in each play and what circumstances cause it to evolve? A limited discussion is also possible. What is she like in *3 Henry VI*? What role does she play in setting the tone of the play, shaping its story and affecting the other characters? How do the events of the story shape her character?

A writer focusing on Margaret has a great deal of material at his or her disposal. Margaret speaks at great length in each of the plays in which she appears, and the way she speaks in each of the plays changes depending on her circumstances. A study of Margaret's character and the way it develops can be closely tied to a study of the changes in the rhetorical patterns of her speeches. A writer who chooses to compare the Margaret of *Part 2* with the Margaret of *Part 3* will need to rectify why she speaks differently or employs different verbal strategies in the two plays. What, for example, is the significance of the fact that in *2 Henry VI* nearly all of Margaret's utterances are lies, whereas in *3 Henry VI,* she speaks without guile?

3. **Richard:** Richard makes his first appearance in *2 Henry VI* and becomes the driving force of the eponymous *Richard III.* He is recognizably himself from his first appearance because of the way his speech reveals his character, shrewdness, wit, and self-awareness and by the cunning way he celebrates himself by confiding his thoughts and motives to the audience. A writer might use Richard's actions and utterances to describe the nature of that self, perhaps focusing on Richard's strong self-pity, which he is shrewd enough to express only through irony. A writer may consider if or how there is a causal relation between Richard's overbearing sense of his deformity and his overbearing pursuit of power. Richard's power is underlined by the fact that he is an important subject in the utterances of other characters.

A writer may choose to focus on Richard only as he appears in *3 Henry VI* or on his full career. In either case, a careful examination of his utterances will yield a great deal concerning one of Shakespeare's most popular villains. Despite his evil nature, or perhaps because of it, drawing the character of Richard provided Shakespeare with the opportunity to begin his probe of the psychology of character that deepens in his later plays. In Richard's case, one issue a writer may focus on—Richard mentions it more than once—is the connection between the inability to find satisfaction in sexual, romantic, or courtly love and the exercise of heartless power.

History and Context

As with all Shakespeare's English history plays, *3 Henry VI* has a twofold context, the period in which its action is set and the period in which it was written and first performed. Also as with the other English histories, its context is both historical and theatrical. The accuracy of historical presentation and the desire to produce exciting theatrical experiences for audiences are often at odds.

Sample Topics:

1. **The problem of succession:** At the core of all the conflicts in *3 Henry VI* is the problem of succession and continuity. The authority and legitimacy of the monarch are in question in the play because of the disputed claims to the crown.

England under Elizabeth I, in the 1590s, was faced with a monarch who had no heir. How this issue was being addressed by authors of the time is a subject for research a student writer must undertake in order to show how the disorder of the play might affect Shakespeare's contemporary audiences fearful that national stability might be at risk because there was no surety of royal succession.

2. **The accuracy of history and the demands of theater:** How accurate is Shakespeare as a historian? How important is it that he be accurate?

Circumstances, events, and characters are all subject to reinvention when they are removed from the historical realm and shifted to the theatrical realm. The historian's first loyalty ought to be to recounting what actually happened as exactly as possible and describing those who made it happen and who were affected by it as precisely as possible. A historian is in the service of history. History, on the other hand, is in the service of a dramatist. The dramatist uses history to reveal truths or establish legends and myths that can exist beyond the realm of history.

Examining the historical record and comparing events and characters as they apparently were with how Shakespeare used them can reveal much about Shakespeare as a craftsman and about how he used history to develop ideas that can be understood to be outside history.

Philosophy and Ideas

Philosophy addresses the problem not so much of how things are but of how we think about things. Notions of political power and personal conduct, among other issues, have preoccupied thinkers, scholars, and writers and certainly inform the fraught world of *3 Henry VI*.

Sample Topics:

1. **The active versus the contemplative life:** Implicit in the conflict presented in *3 Henry VI* is the collision between the active life as pursued by all the characters seeking to advance their power, their position, and their fortune and the contemplative life that Henry longs for and pursues at the expense of his effectiveness as a king.

   A writer who wants to examine the way *3 Henry VI* treats the conflict between the active and the contemplative life can examine what had been written in the centuries preceding the play and around the time of the composition of *3 Henry VI,* discovering what each mode was supposed to entail, how each was justified, and what the arguments against each were. Shakespeare does not openly present a thesis in the play. He dramatizes the struggle of opposing theses. Is there anything about the way the subject is handled that suggests the superiority or inferiority of one mode over another?

2. **Fixation:** Although the word does not appear in the play, nor is the concept a matter of the play's overt discourse or the characters' utterances, a writer may consider that a central idea to be derived from the play is the idea of fixation.

   A writer can attempt to demonstrate that each of the characters is fixated on an idea, image, desire, or self-conception that determines his or her action, his or her attitude concerning the other characters and the events that unfold. To begin exploring this thesis, a writer can examine the speeches of each major character to discover the engines of his or her behavior and to explore how steadfastly each adheres to his or her purpose. What then, a writer can inquire, is the effect of the inflexibility that characterizes each of the participants in the historical drama?

3. **Mutability:** Whereas the idea of fixation applies to the nature or psychology of character, the idea of mutability or change refers to the swings of fortune and the unpredictable nature of reality and outcomes. The idea of mutability was one of the

guiding notions in early English literature, going back to the work of Geoffrey Chaucer, who in the fourteenth century translated the fifth-century Roman treatise on power and the loss of power, *The Consolation of Philosophy*, by Boethius.

The power of mutability is, arguably, the guiding force in *3 Henry VI*. A writer wishing to demonstrate the importance of the idea of change in *3 Henry VI* can look not only within the play for examples of mutability at work and at how the narrative of the play is affected by the idea of change and transformation but also at a sampling of the writings of the time that deal with the idea of mutability.

4. **The problem of evil:** Beyond the problem of the political and military struggle for power that goes on between opposing forces, *3 Henry VI* introduces the idea of the problem of evil, especially of the power of evil, particularly but not exclusively as embodied in the figure of Richard.

A writer concerned with the problem of evil in the play can begin by showing how evil manifests itself, what its consequences are on the characters of the play and how powerful it is. Does the play offer a way to deal with what seems to be the inevitability of evil and its triumph? What, in the context of the play, represents true triumph? How is *3 Henry VI* a lesson in the cultivation of patience? To consider this issue, a writer could consider the play that follows it, *Richard III*, in which Shakespeare introduces the power conscience exerts over the strength of the will.

Language, Symbols, and Imagery

In a theater where there is no scenery and the plays are performed on an open platform in daylight, as the majority of Shakespeare's works originally were, the importance of the role of language cannot be overemphasized.

Sample Topics:

1. **Language as *mise-en-scène*:** As a means of communication between the characters of the play or as a means of reflecting

a character's thought, as in a soliloquy, language is a device for establishing mood and setting either through direct statement or through symbolic representation.

A writer might show how the language of *3 Henry VI* is used to compensate for a lack of scenery. Look, for an example, at the first lines of act 3, scene 1. How did Shakespeare's awareness of the realities and mechanics of theatrical production in his time potentially influence the creation of his works?

2. **Richard's use of language:** One area of investigation for a writer to examine is why it is that, orally, Richard is the most interesting character in *3 Henry VI*. By making citations to the play, a writer can show that Richard as an original and exceptional personality is constructed not through his deeds—the play is replete with characters who are not reluctant to use grotesque violence and cruelty to further their ambition—but through his utterances and the way he uses language to charm his interlocutors, the audience included.

A strong starting place is at line 22 in act 1, scene 2, when Richard convinces his father, York, to resume his campaign against Henry despite York's vow not to.

Form and Genre

Since *3 Henry VI* is part of a larger entity but also an entity unto itself, a writer concerned with its form might well focus on the problem of the play's unity, which essentially is the problem of its structural integrity or self-contained wholeness.

Sample Topics:

1. **The unity of *3 Henry VI*:** For Aristotle, the test of a work's unity is that it have a beginning, middle, and end. The beginning is the time before which nothing happened. The end is the time after which nothing happens. Strictly speaking, in the case of *3 Henry VI*, these definitions are impractical just because the play itself constitutes a middle section in the overall tetralogy. A writer must show that the play constitutes one complete and

discrete action with a beginning, middle, and end, even if that action can fit into a larger structure.

To prepare to write on this topic, a writer can concentrate on the first and last scenes of the play, showing how something that was begun at the beginning is, in fact, concluded at the end, even if related events have preceded and will succeed the action recounted in the play. The first scene shows York's camp after a battle, as York and Warwick discuss how Henry evaded captivity by leaving his troops in the field, essentially abandoning them and his role as their king and leader. The last scene of the play shows York's son Edward celebrating the death of King Henry. The body of the play concerns the contest for Henry's place. The action of the play is contained within its beginning and ending.

2. *3 Henry VI* **as horror:** Although *3 Henry VI* is, by genre, a history play, it is defined by strong elements of horror. As a genre, horror is gratuitous. It seems to offer nothing but the thrill of barbarism and the shock of hatred. History as a genre, on the other hand, is a didactic drama. We are supposed to learn from the past so that we do not repeat its errors and so that we can emulate its triumphs. What is accomplished by the combination of history and horror inside one dramatic structure? How does each genre affect the way we perceive and receive the other?

For this topic, a writer could cull examples of each genre from *3 Henry VI* and analyze how the incidents bear on each other and reinvigorate or devitalize each other. What effect does the presence of elements of both genres have on how readers or viewers of the play understand the work overall?

3. *3 Henry VI* **as drama:** *3 Henry VI* is a stage play not a tract or a history lesson, although a reader may derive insights from it about the struggle of good against evil, right against might, or the self-propelling quality of violence. As a drama, the play's first obligation is to interest its audience and to keep its audience's attention. Writing about *3 Henry VI* as drama requires that the writer identify those aspects that "play well," explain what it is about the particu-

lar aspects that gives them dramatic excitement, analyze the play's articulations, and show how one scene or episode is connected to another in a meaningful way that advances the plot of the play. It will be useful to recall E. M. Forster's distinction between a story and a plot: "[A] story [is] a narrative of events arranged in their time-sequence. A plot is also a narrative of events, the emphasis falling on causality" (86). Plot is what gives story meaning because it shows the relationship between the parts of the story and among characters. It shows connections, how one things leads to another or derives from something else, and it accounts for the central conflicts. The dramaturgy, the way the plot is constructed and expressed, is what gives rise to meaning, ideas, themes, and patterns in the work.

A writer interested in *3 Henry VI* as drama should seek to show how the parts of the story are arranged, how the characters are made to interact, and how connections between the parts are made. The writer will then likely have discovered a thesis: "Henry is the unifying principal of the play," or "Acts of violence provoke further acts of violence in a spiral of vengeance," or "The drama of the play is effected through the interplay of cruelty and charity."

Compare and Contrast Essays

In a comparison/contrast essay, you might compare characters in the same play with each other: How does Henry VI compare to Richard or to Clifford? How does Margaret compare to York or to Elizabeth Grey? You could also compare characters (or other elements of the play, such as patterns of imagery) in *3 Henry VI* with characters or other elements in other plays, whether by Shakespeare or other writers—either within or between genres. For example, how does Hamlet's disposition compare with Henry's? Do Clifford and Brutus in *Julius Caesar* have anything in common with each other? Clearly, they are both engaged in an armed struggle for the power to determine the nature of the government, whether of ancient Rome or late medieval England. What differences define them? Why are these differences important?

A comparison/contrast paper becomes meaningful when the comparison between the figures under examination reveals something that is not confined only to them. It can be the realization of a psychological or social perspective, or it can be an insight into the way Shakespeare developed as a playwright and an explorer of the human character. Why is Brutus so much more formidably human a character than Clifford, who hardly becomes more than a vibrant action figure?

Sample Topics:

1. **Comparing attitudes to adversity:** There is hardly a character in *3 Henry VI* who does not undergo terrible suffering.

   Compare and contrast the kinds of suffering the play documents and the kinds of responses the various characters offer to their suffering. Does the play judge the various responses? If so, in what way?

2. **Comparing the characters' attitudes about ambition:** Probably the principal cause of suffering in *3 Henry VI* is the ambition that motivates the majority of the characters in the play.

   Comparing and contrasting attitudes about ambition and the force of ambition may reveal how characters who seem to be in conflict with each other are, in fact, driven by similar forces.

3. **Comparing Shakespeare's Henry VI with Jean Anouilh's Henry II:** Jean Anouilh's play *Beckett, or The Honor of God* (1959) presents the story of the friendship and the rivalry between Henry II of England and the Archbishop Thomas à Beckett. Of particular interest to readers of *3 Henry VI* is Anouilh's depiction of Henry II, like Henry VI, as a weak king.

   A writer pursuing this approach can analyze the circumstances of each play and of each king's response, paying attention to the nature of virtue (or vice).

Bibliography and Online Resources for *Henry VI, Part 3*

Colon Semenza, Gregory M. "Sport, War, and Contest in Shakespeare's *Henry VI.*" *Renaissance Quarterly*, Winter 2001, vol. 54, no. 4, pp. 1251–73.
(Colon Semenza argues that "War and political conflict are a sort of royal sport in the world of Shakespeare's Henry VI *plays. Though authors had*

emphasized the similarities between sport and war for centuries, Shakespeare struck out in a notably original direction by appropriating sport in order to condemn the evils of modern warfare.")

Hunt, Maurice. "Unnaturalness in Shakespeare's *3 Henry VI*." *English Studies* 80, 1999, pp. 146–67.
(Hunt argues that the unity of 3 Henry VI *is the result of the proliferation of unnatural actions, indicated by Henry's disinheriting his son Edward in favor of York.)*

Moretti, Thomas J. "Misthinking the King: The Theatrics of Christian Rule in *Henry VI, Part 3*." *Renascence: Essays on Values in Literature*, Summer 2008, vol. 60, no. 4, pp. 275–95.
(Moretti argues that the principle theme of 3 Henry VI *is the conflict between Christian values and sovereignty.)*

Petrarch, Francis. *De Vita Solitaria/The Life of Solitude*, translated and with introduction and notes by Jacob Zeitlin. Urbana: University of Illinois Press, 1924; reprinted Westport, CT: Hyperion Press, 1978.
(The Web site http://www.hermitary.com/solitude/petrarch.html *contains Petrarch's meditation on solitude, in which he speaks of the virtues of the contemplative life from a humanist point of view rather than from a traditional Christian perspective.)*

Extract from St. Thomas Aquinas's *Summa Theologica*
http://www.newadvent.org/summa/3182.htm
(In question 182, Aquinas considers "The active life in comparison with the contemplative life," and deals with these four issues: 1. Which of them is of greater import or excellence? 2. Which of them has the greater merit? 3. Is the contemplative life hindered by the active life? 4. Which takes precedence over the other?)

Text of Boethius's *The Consolation of Philosophy*
http://etext.virginia.edu/latin/boethius/boephil3.html
(This meditation on power and the loss of power is by Boethius, ca. 480–524 A.D., a Roman official, stripped of his office in 523, jailed, and executed on suspicion of disloyalty to the emperor Theodoric. In prison, Boethius wrote The Consolation of Philosophy. *It became one of the guiding texts of the Middle Ages in regard to mutability and was frequently translated from the Latin. Geoffrey Chaucer was one of its translators.)*

RICHARD III

READING TO WRITE

ALL THE destructive energy that was let loose by the conflict between York and Lancaster in the War of the Roses gathered in the figure of Richard III. For the House of York, having vanquished the House of Lancaster, nothing remained but to feed on itself and thereby demonstrate how evil comes to be the engine of its own destruction. *Richard III* (1592–93) presents the twilight of the gods of civil strife; Richard himself embodies the vengeful frenzy of their self-destruction. He is the final manifestation of brutality (as the ruling power) and of selfish ambition (as the ruling passion) in England. All the contenders of the previous three-part *Henry VI* who waged war against one another converge and contract into the single personage of Richard III. Shakespeare constructs him not only as the dramatic representation of a historical process and an iconic representation of the devil but as a psychologically motivated individual.

Because of his character, Richard dominates his play as nearly no other figure in the seven plays preceding *Richard III* has. Consequently, his will, his actions, and their repercussions occupy the entire space of the play, excluding anyone else. In *Richard II*, the story of Richard's descent is matched by the story of Bolingbroke's ascent. In both parts of *Henry IV*, several plot strands are interwoven to form the action of the play. Falstaff is set against King Henry. The plays trace their stories as well as the progress of Prince Hal to the kingship and his resulting self-construction, a process shaped by his responses to his father and to Falstaff as well as to the burden of history he was born to bear. In addition, *Part 1* tells the story of Hotspur and *Part 2* of Justice Shallow.

There are competing points of view presented in these plays and several centers of interest, just as there are in the three parts of *Henry VI*, which is characterized by a sprawling cast and a cavalcade of episodes. *Richard III* is only about Richard. Even the story lines concerning Buckingham, or Anne, or Queen Margaret, or the murdered princes in the tower are really much more part of or an extension of Richard's story than theirs.

Henry V, although it bears the ghostly echo of the absent Falstaff, is nearer to *Richard III* than the other histories. A single, strong figure dominates the play. However, it is the kind of figure portrayed that makes the difference between the two plays. Henry is a part of the action of his play, the English response to a French challenge. Richard fabricates and directs the action of the play that bears his name until he is killed. A writer considering an essay contrasting *Richard III* and *Henry V* or each play's eponymous leading character might begin by asking how those two kings are similar to, and how they are different from, each other

After reviewing both plays for substantiating material to sustain your description of what each character is like, and before turning what you have discovered into a thesis, in order to formulate that thesis, you, as a writer, will need to consider what the contrast between the two figures reveals about each character, about each play as a drama, about engaging the emotion of an audience, about the nature of power and kingship, and about the role of motive in determining the value of an action or policy. A writer might argue that both Henry V and Richard III are similar in their ruthless pursuit of power, are both masters of policy, both Machiavellians, despite the fact that Shakespeare's Henry V, for many spectators, shines with honor whereas Shakespeare's Richard III, charming as he is, is recognized universally as wickedness incarnate. What keeps Henry V from seeming wicked, if you think he actually is wicked, or from being wicked if you think that he is not? What makes Richard III extraordinary, the paragon of evil, in a world rampant with the cruel, selfish, and brutal men and women who populate the three parts of *Henry VI*? What keeps Richard III from being a heroic figure? Despite the full title of the play, *The Tragedy of Richard III*, is he actually a tragic figure the way King Lear, Hamlet, Othello, Macbeth, and even Hotspur, for example, are? What, if anything, is frightening about Henry? What is it that makes Richard the frightening character that he is? What makes him diabolical?

The significance and the value of the comparison of Richard to Henry depend on the writer's ability to draw a strong conclusion from the juxtaposition. Certainly one crux for both men's lives is the notion of power, the desire for and use of it, the responsibilities that accompany it, and the effect of one person's pursuit of power on his world and the people who occupy it.

What do Henry and Richard have in common? For an audience, as for a reader, the most important aspect of a play, the first thing that is noticed, and the thing that keeps a spectator's or a reader's attention and interest is the drama of the play. What does drama consist of? In essence, dramatic works are made up of two essential elements, action and character. Drama is created by the interaction of characters. Action and character are composed of, are constructs of, language. A comparison between Richard III and Henry V is, fundamentally, a comparison of their language, of the selves they construct and the action they advance by the way they speak. A writer seeking to compare these two figures and the dramatic engine of each play will first notice how both Richard and Henry are masters of rhetoric and masterful in their manipulation of others through the use of language. They both use speech not only to express their wills but to bring others, despite their subjects' and associates' own hidden self-interests, over to their own side. What Richard and Henry have in common is their desire for power and their willingness to kill for it. Yet, audiences surely respond differently to how each uses power, speaks of power and, consequently, why each hungers for power or sees himself as a purveyor of power. The differing responses, certainly, are the result of differing circumstances but equally of the way each character is presented and the way each character presents himself through his way of speaking.

What differentiates Richard and Henry as rhetoricians? To consider this question, a writer should attend as much to the way in which both men speak as to what they say. Richard's speech is self-referential. He is always talking about himself, calling attention to himself. Henry's speech is not self-referential. He speaks of himself as England's agent in the accomplishment of glory. He is at the center of the spectacle. He gives himself over to it, but the spectacle is not about him but about his vision of England. In his references to himself, he presents himself as an example, a guide, a force to direct others to participate in his projects. Henry's speech is inclusive. He binds his interlocutors in what is laid out as a noble project to which they and the king are to be mutually devoted, an enterprise in which they are united as "a band of brothers." Henry uses his rhetoric to inspire his supporters and to defy his enemies. Richard binds people to him, as if through hypnosis, casting a spell with his words in order to advance his cause by deceiving them. His words do not arouse, excite, and inspire those to whom he speaks. Rather, his words subvert them and compel them to do his bidding. Henry V energizes his listeners with his words. Richard III subdues them with his.

It would not be accurate to say that Henry V is never self-referential. He is, once, in the wooing scene with Kate in act 5, scene 2. His strategy is to denigrate himself as a romantic figure and make much of his shortcomings as a lover. In this way, he not only wins Katherine's consent to be his bride, but he wins the audience, too, with a charming, boyish assurance that can remind audiences of his earlier incarnation as Prince Hal. There are odd resemblances between the way he and Richard woo a desired love object, and a writer might probe them in order to define something about the art of persuasion and the exercise of power each man employs.

At the root of Henry's charm is his sincerity. He is a consummate actor, but his acting is not a craft of deception but a method for heightened expression. He performs the man he is and wishes to be. Even at the height of his engagement with Falstaff in *1 Henry IV*, when Hal already knows what Falstaff may already fear, that Hal will abandon Falstaff, Hal admits it frankly in the four words—"I do. I will"—that he utters when Falstaff, in his rapturous role pretending to be King Henry IV, admonishes the future king not to banish his friend Falstaff.

Henry V does not manipulate others. He inspires and commands them. He does not deceive others the way Richard does, even when he goes disguised through his camp and argues with his troops. He shows himself truly as he is and as he evolves. He always reveals the power of his personality. That is his charm. It is the same sort of charm that Richard III has only filtered through a different personality. Henry wants to join the human community through his role as king. Richard wants to rise above the human community and be like a god in relation to it. Richard, too, is a consummate actor, but unlike Harry, he is insincere, sincerely insincere.

At the root of Richard's charm is his breathtaking hypocrisy. He performs the man he wishes others to see. He is always lying, but he dissembles so well—he fundamentally means his lies as they are necessary for his advancement—that his lies are captivating. They are irresistible dares that triumph over his interlocutors' doubts. That, of course, is what gives him his diabolical quality, for the devil is a figure of deception and challenge.

Ostensibly, Richard has a purpose in lying, as Margaret, for example, in *2 Henry VI*, where she hardly utters one true word, also has a purpose in lying. Like her, Richard is advancing his cause. Henry V is doing the same when he speaks honestly. Unlike Richard, Henry publicly says what he will do and does what he says. Richard III, however, unlike Henry or Margaret, the reader may surmise, is less excited by advancing his cause than in having a cause that he can advance by lying. Lying, for him, is not simply a means to an end; it is an end in itself. The triumph of his personality exists in the success of his lies and the enjoyment he derives from framing and constructing them. Margaret lies for a purpose: to attain power. Richard lies for the delight of deceiving and manipulating the truth and experiences the thrill of power in the very process of lying. Richard molds reality through the power he achieves by the exercise of lying. Power for Richard is not, as it is for Henry V, the ability to serve an ideal but the power to rejoice in the obliteration of any ideal, of anything at all but his own will.

Richard shares his pleasure in his duplicity with his audience, with us. He is honest with us about his lies. Without stepping out of his role, he steps out of the action in order to share with the audience how he will shape that action or, more fittingly, how he will misshape it. Most ingratiatingly, he admits that he distorts and takes pleasure in doing so because of his own misshapen body and spirit (1.1.14–31). Here is a man who seems to know himself, and he is clever enough to make us his confidants and co-conspirators rather than his judges. We conspire in his plots by the interest we take in watching him unfold them. Because of his self-knowledge, Richard acts as both a character and as the Chorus in his play.

That duality is one of the things that differentiates him from Henry V. In *Henry V*, there is an actor, not the king, who plays the role of Chorus. At the beginning of each act, he guides the audience into the action and shapes our perception. Henry V is a character inside the play who never threatens to cross the border that separates the audience from the actors and from the action. Richard's strange power comes from his ability to dissolve that boundary and from his perceived identity as a divided man. Henry is not divided but single minded, an integrated person. He always says what he means, and he means what he says. Richard approaches directness and honestly only when he is flattering or manipulating the audience. Otherwise, he hides what he means in order to make his way to what he wants, often through the help of characters who do not wish to help him.

A writer may consider several questions. If Richard appears to have the Socratic wisdom and knows himself, despite being evil, what good is knowing yourself? What does it say about the nature of the self in general? What self does Richard know? Does the play postulate 1) that human beings are essentially evil or 2) that there is another self beyond the person Richard believes himself to be and know? If *Richard III* postulates the existence of either—can it postulate both?—how is the play able to accomplish that? Can you, from Richard's own utterances, talk of a missing self that is Richard's real self, that Richard is haunted and motivated to evil by the sense of his own absence or incompleteness?

Richard shows that he is a divided man by the simple fact that he talks to himself. Henry V talks to himself, also, but does not, at the same time, talk to the audience directly as Richard does. When Henry talks to himself—as he does in *Henry V* in his defensive musing "Upon the king," and in *1 Henry IV* in his equally defensive Machiavellian apologia to himself, "I know you all"—although it indicates a division or a conflict in him, it is a staged presentation of his thoughts. Through these soliloquies he works out and repairs whatever division he feels in himself. His single-minded pursuit of the war with France is his proof that he has vanquished his inner division and wed himself to his duty. When Richard talks to himself, it is as if he is talking to a co-conspirator—he is not working out a conflict—and he is letting the audience in on it, if not actually turning the audience into that co-conspirator. By these addresses to the audience, he shows his confidence in the invincibility of his evil. That makes him frightening and, in fact, confirms his evil status. He is so sure of himself that he does not feel the need to hide his wickedness. His pursuit of power is not the result of a dedication to duty but to the acquisition of raw, self-aggrandizing power.

Yet Richard is, in the end, consumed by his evil. It is not only Richmond in the field who defeats Richard. It is Richard's own conscience, the sense of guilt that clings to him and undermines him despite his brazen denial of morality. At Bosworth Field, the night before the battle, his conscience overwhelms him as the memory of all those he killed haunts him in the shape of spirits that revisit and depress him. Similarly, the memory of Richard's crimes forges a sense of confidence in Richmond, as he recalls them in his sleep, through the use of the same dramatic device.

The disturbance of Richard's equilibrium shown in his dreams is set up earlier in the play. Twice in act 4, scene 4, Shakespeare shows Richard as less the master of himself and of the situation than he had consistently been before. These outbreaks of confusion, when Richard forgets what he is doing, indicate that his assurance that he knows himself is, in fact, mistaken. The self, he discovers, is something more than what he thinks it is in his arrogant villainy. The part of him that he had not detected or that remained hidden reveals itself to him in his troubled dreams before his final battle. He acted as if he believed he was immune to the gnawings of conscience, but he discovers he is not. If the invisible power of divine providence is not at work in *Richard III,* then the hidden psychology of the human unconscious seems to be.

TOPICS AND STRATEGIES

Punctuated by a number of remarkable confrontations, featuring a cast of well-defined characters, taking as its subject the subversion of goodness and decency by a diabolical disregard for humane or even human consideration, *Richard III* offers writers a wealth of topics and analytical directions to explore. Some of its themes reflect the themes of the history plays that precede it, like power, ambition, and the pain, suffering, and grief they can be responsible for. Other themes are more particular to the play, such as the theme of cunning and hypocrisy as tools used for achieving power or the theme of bitter remorse and irreversible disaster. The power of providence as opposed to the power of human will is an especially potent thematic conflict that plays out in *Richard III.*

Themes

Of particular interest in *Richard III* is the problem of evil. Shakespeare introduces and examines it indirectly as he illustrates and contemplates two competing ways of thinking about how the world operates. The belief that history is the work of providence had been the dominant view in the God-centered world of the Middle Ages. The Renaissance brought with it the belief that the human will can shape the world through the cunning, daring, self-assertion, and intelligence people possess. Divine providence negates evil by employing it for the ultimate triumph of the good. The fall of Adam is rectified by the rise of Jesus. Human will, as a governing force, left to its own proclivities, does not have the divine principle to guide it. That is the point Shakespeare seems to make with the character Richard III.

In Richard, evil is the result of the human will, not the mysterious dispensation of the divine, but Richard is not the sole force of the play. Richmond appears. Perhaps he is the agent of providence. Or is Richmond's success less about providence and actually the result of Richard's final attack of weakness? A writer can argue that Richard is undone by an unwanted realization of the evil of his actions. Nearly without notice the evil he has unleashed in his climb to the top takes a toll on him that he never anticipated. Richard made a deal with the devil, that is, with himself, and overlooked, as Faustian bargainers do, that there would be a time when the power would wear off and payment would fall due. Even if there is no providence, there is conscience. Richmond has as his ally in his fight with Richard the assault Richard's conscience has also mounted.

Sample Topics:

1. **Grief:** It is not surprising nor, a writer may argue, is it accidental, that after the immense brutality and heartlessness charted in the preceding three *Henry VI* plays grief is a pervasive theme in *Richard III.*

   How does *Richard III* represent grief? What purpose does the representation of grief serve in the play? What sort of commentary, if any, does it make on the action or on some of the characters of the play, or on the previous plays to have grief as prominently represented in *Richard III* as it is? Does grief have a purgative power in the play? What does *Richard III* seem to be saying about grief and its relation to inhumanity? Is grief, as it is presented in the play, shown to be unalloyed? Is it a pure emotion? Does it also represent anger?

A writer considering the theme of grief will find actual scenes of grieving to study, but he may also think about how grief permeates the play's other scenes and find examples of scenes, actions, or speeches that express grief or that arouse grief in other characters or in us as readers or members of an audience. What connection does the play make between grief and remorse?

2. **Power:** What insight does *Richard III* offer into the nature of power, into the desire for power, and into the pursuit of power? How does the play portray the possible uses of power? Are there contradictory ideas about power presented in the play? A writer might contrast Richmond with Richard, focusing on their speeches to their armies and on their motives as they are described in the play. A writer can also look at what the play seems to say about the power of words. Does the play suggest that there are different kinds of power?

Look at what Richard says, at what he does, how often he uses the power of persuasion or of manipulation rather than brute power. Look at how power is described in dreams. Examine Richard's own explanations of his behavior, other characters' comments concerning his deformity, and his mother's descriptions of his birth and his form at birth.

3. **Ambition:** Richard is driven by ambition. How does the play depict the effects of ambition or ambitious characters on the world they live in?

An essay on this topic might start by looking closely at how Richard talks about his desire to be king. Once he becomes king, does he enjoy his position? Another source of evidence to base a judgment on would be the effects of Richard's successful rise on the kingdom he comes to rule. Is he a tyrant because he is ambitious or because of some other flaw that makes him use his ambition in a particular way?

4. **Omens:** *Richard III* refers to omens on several occasions. What is the role of omens in the action of the play?

To address this topic, look at the number and kinds of references to omens in the play and who makes them and how much credit is given to omens. Richard uses a false prophecy. Stanley's messenger brings the report of his ominous dream to Hastings in 3.2. Hastings ignores it at the price of his life. What effect does the existence of omens have on the drama of the play, on expressing the worldview of the play in regard to a guiding providence?

Character

By separating and defining some of the various characters Shakespeare featured in his play, by showing their particular attributes and their differences, a writer can bring clarity and definition to the play and show the human context in which Richard's evil plays out.

Sample Topics:

1. **Richard's character development:** Before writing about how Richard's character does or does not develop, it is helpful to describe that character in its complexity and to substantiate that character analysis by citations from the text. Does Richard change over the course of the play? If he does, how? What are the changes? What seems to cause them? If Richard does not change over the course of the play, how do we know he does not? Are there reasons for his not changing? What keeps him from changing? Is it possible that Richard does and also does not change, or changes without being aware that he has changed?

To develop a thesis on a topic such as this, the writer must first decide (based on at least one rereading of the play) what, if any, changes happen in Richard's character. Evidence for this can be drawn from his soliloquies, from his conversations with and actions with regard to other characters, and from things other characters say when he is not present. One way to begin thinking about Richard's development is by comparing his opening soliloquy with his last long speech, "His Oration to his Army." What has happened in between these two points to cause whatever changes there are in Richard's presentation of himself?

2. **Richard's effect on the character of others:** Such is the power Richard exerts in the play that the other major characters are essentially defined by him and by their reactions to him. Their identities are contingent on his view of them and are determined by their responses to him.

Focusing on a series of characters such as Anne, Buckingham, Margaret, Elizabeth, the Duchess of York, Hastings, Stanley, and the young princes, a writer may show how they are fashioned and their fates determined by how Richard conceives of them and how he regards their usefulness to his career.

By examining their responses to him, a reader can seek to uncover what it is about them that makes them yield to his influence and thereby discover a source of his power. What element in people is open to manipulation by a demagogue like Richard?

History and Context

Shakespeare's portrait of Richard III is a tribute to the author's ability to overtake our imagination, but is Shakespeare's Richard true to the historical Richard? Josephine Tey in her 1951 detective novel, *The Daughter of Time*, presents a different Richard from Shakespeare's, a decriminalized Richard. After some necessary research about the historical Richard, your own consideration of the differences between the actual Richard and Shakespeare's villain may be used to examine or explain Shakespeare's dramatic purpose. How is history adjusted to the dramatic needs or conventions of the play? How has Shakespeare helped shape the way we think about history in general?

1. **What kind of king was Richmond (Henry VII)?** From Henry IV through Henry VIII, Henry VII was the only one of Shakespeare's Henrys who was not given his own play. He appears briefly as a child whom Henry VI recognizes as the realm's

future salvation, and he appears in that role at the end of *Richard III.*

What kind of king did he actually become? Is the way he is presented in the play true to the actual man?

2. **Richard III as a reflection of Elizabethan politics:** Do the characters, situations, and practices drawn from the latter half of the fifteenth century have any relevance to the late sixteenth century? What were the politics of the decades of Elizabeth's era like, especially with regard to political intrigue, power conflicts, and the exercise of guile and brutality?

Although not often presented as part of the great pageantry and Renaissance luminosity of Elizabeth's reign, there were a number of political power conflicts as well as powerful spy and torture networks employed by the crown. After researching the political climate and the "secret police" operating under Elizabeth, can you show that there is a way to read *Richard III* as Shakespeare's attempt to address forbidden subjects by indirection and thus without risk?

Philosophy and Ideas

One of the reasons Shakespeare has exerted the grip on the human imagination that he has is because of the number of ideas and conflicting ideas that are embedded in his work. Problems of identity, loyalty, determination, power, obligation, reality, and agency are woven throughout *Richard III.*

Sample Topics:

1. **The power of the will:** Richard astonishes us and the people in the play repeatedly by his ability to make people perform actions that are against their own interests. He is able to bend people to his will. What does it say not just about Anne or Elizabeth that Richard can subdue and seduce them and win their cooperation when they have every reason to defy him? Is it only his power, or is there something in human nature that longs to cower before a force it knows intellectually to be repulsive but yet is emotionally or even sexually attractive? A

writer may use the instances of Richard's influence to consider the problem broadly.

The twentieth-century German poet Rainer Maria Rilke has written in *The Duino Elegies* that beauty and terror have a similar power over us because they both can destroy us. People who have been held as hostages or in captivity have sometimes been known to identify with, love, and admire their captors. This psychological condition is known as the Stockholm syndrome, so called because of the response of people held hostage in a Swedish bank in 1973. Battered and abused spouses or offspring sometimes continue to love the person who beats and reviles them. What is attractive about Richard's power, and what does it suggest about relationships between those with power and those without it?

2. **A world without God:** Richard seems to believe that he is or can be the master of events, the creator of his own and other people's destiny, that he is a free and independent actor in a world with no moral center or guiding intelligence. While he seems to be a master of irony, he really is a victim of irony if he is wrong about the lack of providence in the direction of history.

   What does the existence of a man like Richard say about the nature of history and especially about the nature of providence? Does the play suggest that the appearance of Richmond demonstrates that the world is governed by providence, however strangely? If Richmond's appearance is not a matter of providence, what is the play saying about the existence of good and evil? You may want to refer to Henry VI's recognition in *3 Henry VI* of Richmond's future greatness as contributing to a sense of something greater than individual effort in the working of history.

3. **The problem of meaning:** What does *Richard III* say about whether the world is meaningful or meaningless? Does it offer any help in the way we can think about what makes the world meaningful? Is there a connection in the play between grief and meaning? Does lamentation, for example, suggest that the world

has meaning or even imbue it with meaning? Is meaning something that exists independent of us or is meaning created by us as we struggle with one another to impose the meaning we see?

Consider Richard's actions as a project to create and impose a particular meaning and to subvert other meanings. Consider the grieving and laments of the women as a way they bring meaning to a world in which meaning has been lost for them.

Language, Symbols, and Imagery

Language, when Richard uses it, becomes a weapon. He uses it against others and often overcomes them not by the force of arms but by the force of his tongue. To show Richard's facility with language and the way language reveals his character and duplicity, a writer can focus on the first two lines of the play and the way Richard manipulates meaning, turning it inside out, and subverts the expectations he initially sets up. In the same way, he manipulates people.

The scenes with Anne and Elizabeth, as well as his interactions with Margaret and his mother, can also be read with a focus on how Richard creates himself and demolishes others with language. His use of language is not always sophisticated. In act 3, scene 7, in conversation with Buckingham, Shakespeare shows Richard can use simple slander for his purposes. A writer may also discuss those instances when Richard is reluctant to use language at all and speaks in hints, as, for example, he does when he speaks to Buckingham in act 4, scene 2 and Buckingham, for the first time, neglects to understand him.

Sample Topics:

1. **Animal imagery:** As a play about inhumanity and brutality, *Richard III* can be expected to present the reader with a great deal of animal imagery.

   Can you argue that such imagery serves not only to sharpen our sense of the viciousness of brutal behavior but also, paradoxically, in a world where human goodness is excluded, can suggest the actual goodness of humanity? What are examples in the play of evil acts attributed to beasts, with which the human evildoers are stripped of their humanity and defined as animals? A careful reading of the play will present the student writer with an abundance of animal imagery. How is it incorporated into the play? What does it suggest?

2. **The magical aspects of language:** Instead of seeing language used in *Richard III* as a tool with which to manipulate others, as Richard uses it, a writer may focus on the magical intentions of language in *Richard III.* It is a mode of language, especially employed among the women, of lamentation and cursing.

An essay can be written about the uncanny power of speech to bring into existence the things the words refer to and conjure. As such, language seems to signify a force above or beyond the speakers. A writer may examine the false prophecy Richard uses ("that 'G' of Edward's heirs the murderer shall be") to facilitate Clarence's execution. It is, in fact, not false, only misinterpreted, for Richard (Duke of Gloucester) is actually the murderous "G" referred to. A writer may also consider such eerie pronouncements as Hastings's, beginning at line 64 of act 3, scene 2. It is an example of an unconscious premonition expressed through the language of irony.

A writer may also consider the function of irony in the language of *Richard III* and what relation irony has to the instability that Richard's duplicitous nature brings to his world.

Form and Genre

According to its full title, *Richard III* is a tragedy. It is also a history, the concluding chapter in a chronicle that spanned some 150 years of English history. What is the difference between a tragedy and a chronicle of a tragic history? If we say that a history is concerned with the story of a nation and that a tragedy is concerned with the story of a person, do Shakespeare's histories and tragedies bear out that distinction? What is it that makes a person or personal story tragic? Can there be a tragic villain just as there is a tragic hero? What would make Richard III a tragic villain rather than just a villain? As a villain, what makes him different from the other villains in Shakespeare's history plays? Considering *Richard III* as a tragedy, then, requires a writer to consider Richard's role in the play and his character and how it is revealed.

Sample Topics:
1. *Richard III* **as drama:** *Richard III* is a stage play, written originally not for study but to be performed before an audience. While it recounts English history, or, at least, one reading of English history, and while it explores human personality and human responses to forces ranging from ambition to grief, in order to be effective, *Richard III* must be dramatic. It must rouse the interest, emotion, and excitement of the people watching it. How does Shakespeare bring drama to the events of the story he is telling?

A writer concerned with this issue might think of writing an essay that would view *Richard III* as a drama of confrontations. In order to pursue this topic, a writer can examine the nature and number of confrontations that are presented in the play and show that nearly every scene is a portrayal of some dramatic confrontation between Richard and another character, a confrontation a character has with him- or herself, or a confrontation between two or more characters.

2. **The use of spectacle and acting:** A writer can argue that the source of the dramatic power that Richard brings to the play lies in his ability to create reality through stagecraft.

In order to pursue this thesis, a writer needs to show, with textual citation and example, how Richard is a master dramatist, an actor, a director, a scriptwriter, and a purveyor of spectacle in the play named for him, how he effects his aims through the practice of these arts, and how the presentation of this theatricality affects the drama and reception of the play itself. Richard provides plenty of information in his direct remarks to the spectators. There are also dramatic examples. Consider the scene of Richard with his Bible on London's walls.

Compare and Contrast Essays

Comparisons and contrasts become meaningful when they reveal something essential about the work(s) the elements being juxtaposed are part of. How does a study of Clarence illuminate Richard? A study of Elizabeth illuminate Anne? A study of Buckingham illuminate Stanley? A study of

Tyrrel, the murderer, illuminate the personalities of the other murderers? To understand what kind of tragedy *Richard III* is, a writer can compare it to other tragedies by Shakespeare or to a play such as Sophocles' *Oedipus Rex.* Comparing Richard to characters such as Othello, King Lear, Antony, Iago, Edmund, Faulconbridge, or Hamlet can reveal what kind of character Richard is as well as provide insight into Shakespeare's development as a creator of living characters and dramatic situations.

Sample Topics:

1. **Self-awareness and psychological acumen:** In order to compare him with other Shakespearean characters, a writer might first choose one of Richard's particular and outstanding traits and compare him, with regard to that trait, to another character. Usually, but not always, the characters with a keen sense of self-knowledge are Shakespeare's villains. Locate instances where Richard's understanding of himself is verbalized. Consider Richard, then, in comparison to several of Shakespeare's famous villains, Edmund in *King Lear* or Iago in *Othello,* for example. What does a study of these characters reveal about the value and the use of self-knowledge?

   Shakespeare's supreme villains are also masterful psychologists. Richard is no exception. They understand others, what makes others behave as they do, and how to manipulate them, better than the other characters in the play. What does this power of theirs suggest about the context in which perception is a virtue? How can it become a vice? Compare Richard as a psychologist to Edmund or Iago. How do these fundamentally similar figures differ? What do they have in common?

2. **Richard's incomparability:** Often, a writer can compare characters within the same play. Focusing on their orations to their armies, for example, a writer can compare Richard and Richmond. Is it possible, however, to argue that Richard is not really comparable to any of the other characters in *Richard III?* What textual passages suggest his incomparability? In what way is he fundamentally different from the others? Is it his self-knowledge? Or is it something else, like his daring to defy what seem

to be the limits of humanity? Consider the thesis that the difference he constructs is the result of a prior difference over which he has no control.

Richard dominates his play so thoroughly that other characters seem to exist in the play not to relate their personal stories but in order to show how Richard behaves with regard to them. A writer might argue that, dramatically, Shakespeare "uses" Anne or Buckingham as much as Richard does, using them to advance his plot, as Richard does, rather than to tell their stories. A writer might attempt to compare Richard with Shakespeare the author, both being fashioners of plots and manipulators of character.

A writer might also focus on some of the secondary characters, comparing them to one another, with regard to how each interacts with Richard. Compare, for example, Richard's scene with Anne and his scene with Elizabeth, focusing on how he seduces each and how each responds to his seduction.

Bibliography and Online Resources for *Richard III*

Kehler, Dorothea. "Shakespeare's *Richard III*." *The Explicator*, Spring 1998, vol. 56, no. 3 pp. 118–22.
(Keller argues that Elizabeth, in the second seduction scene in which Richard attempts to get her consent to marry her daughter, does not capitulate to Richard the way Anne did in the first seduction scene, rather defeating him in their rhetorical contest.)

Levith, Murray J. "*Richard III:* The Dragon and St. George." *Shakespeare Newsletter*, Summer 2003, vol. 53, no. 2, 39–42.
(Recalling the English legend of St. George and the dragon, Levith reads Richard as the dragon and Richmond as St. George. He also suggests the possibility that, while Shakespeare flatters the Tudor account of history, in which Richmond, as the first Tudor, overcomes and resolves the strife between York and Lancaster, he also subverts it by suggesting through Richmond's emblem of a fiery dragon that the House of Tudor will become a dragon too.)

Marche, Stephen. "Mocking Dead Bones: Historical Memory and the Theater of the Dead in *Richard III*." *Comparative Drama*, Spring 2003, vol. 37, no.1, pp. 37–58.

ders whether Richard III *is a history or a tragedy and the role of characters in determining its genre.)*

_..ta. "Richard III's Animalistic Criminal Body." *Philological Quarterly,* Summer 2003, vol. 82, no. 3, pp. 301–25.
(*Olson reviews the animal imagery used to describe Richard and sees in the disgust that others express in regard to his deformed body a perverse source of their attraction to him.*)

Reynolds, Paige Martin. "Mourning and Memory in *Richard III.*" *ANQ,* Spring 2008, vol. 21, no. 2, pp. 19–26.
(*Reynolds argues that "memory . . . actually determines the outcome of the battle" in which Richmond defeats Richard and that "[i]nsofar as they have borne the burden of memory throughout the play [by their incessant mourning], the women of* Richard III *bring about Richard's downfall.*")

Tiffany, Grace. "Richard III's Sinister Aesthetics." *Shakespeare Newsletter,* Fall 2007 vol. 57, no. 2, pp. 59–72.
(*Tiffany writes about Richard's power as a seducer who does not disguise his own evil but uses it as the very tool of his seduction.*)

Van Elk, Martine. "'Determined to prove a villain': Criticism, Pedagogy, and *Richard III.*" *College Literature,* Fall 2007, vol. 34, no. 4, pp. 1–22.
(*In an essay designed to help teachers study* Richard III *in the classroom, van Elk discusses the various ways the play addresses the idea of identity, the way identity has been and is conceived of being constructed, and the way the play has been approached in three films of the second half of the twentieth century.*)

"A Performance History of Shakespeare's *Richard III*"
http://www.r3.org/onstage/drunk.html
(*Margaret Gurowitz offers a history of stage performances of* Richard III, *one of Shakespeare's most frequently performed plays.*)

HENRY VIII

READING TO WRITE

AT THE end of act 2, scene 3 of *Henry VIII* (1612–13), Anne Bullen tells a confidante, identified only as Old Lady, not to "deliver" to the queen, Katherine, "what here y'have heard." What the Old Lady has heard and seen was that the king, Henry VIII, has bestowed on Anne Bullen the title of marchioness of Pembroke and an annuity of 1,000 pounds. The king's gift is announced directly following a conversation between Anne Bullen and the Old Lady in which Anne asserts that "By my troth and maiden-head, / I would not be a queen," and the Old Lady challenges her saying, "I would, / And venture . . . so would you." Anne again denies that she would, and the Old Lady again challenges her demurral. This argument continues until the Chamberlain arrives with the king's gift, which Anne accepts. (It would be an act of contempt not to accept the king's gift.)

The Old Lady adds, after the Chamberlain departs, that loftier gifts for Anne are yet to come. Although Anne again denies her wish to be elevated in any way or to rise above the queen she serves, she, like the rest of the court, is aware that Henry's queen of 20 years, Katherine, has fallen out of favor, and because of the king's gifts, Anne is aware, too, that his favor has now transferred to her. He is thoroughly smitten with her. Thus as Anne and the Old Lady leave the stage to be with the "comfort-less" queen, Anne admonishes the Old Lady to say nothing of Anne's new fortune, thus showing the loyalty and courtesy of her own character and her awareness of the importance of place in the court. The Old Lady, for her part, being commanded not to tell the queen of Anne's advancement, responds, "What do you think me?" implicitly promising her silence, but also suggesting that malicious behavior, gossip, intrigue, and backstab-bing constitute some part of the culture of the court.

Folded within this conversation is one of the play's primary themes, the theme of betrayal. The idea of betrayal itself suggests a social orga-nization based on competition for pride of place. Passive as she is in the process of the queen's deposition, simply by being the object of the king's desire, despite her own will, Anne is disturbed by her role in it as well as by the queen's ill fortune. That ill fortune is a result of betrayal, and Anne's behavior indicates that she does not wish to be a partner in that betrayal.

The plot against the queen has been spun by Cardinal Wolsey, the king's intimate and fully trusted adviser and officer, his lord chancellor. Unlike Anne's, however, Wolsey's entire career is built on a series and a variety of intrigues and betrayals by means of which he advances and raises himself. The theme of betrayal is represented in the play by Wol-sey's actions. The way Wolsey works his betrayals defines the nature of the era in which Shakespeare and his apparent co-author, John Fletcher, set Henry's court.

Henry VIII represents an era recognizably different from the era of contention that Shakespeare had chronicled in the eight plays begin-ning with *Richard II* and concluding with *Richard III*, a series he had completed approximately 13 years before the composition of *Henry VIII*. The world of cutthroat violence that is re-created in those plays, a world of wars and warriors, humiliation, cruel executions, and cun-ning plots by unscrupulous men and women—whose lust for power makes them monstrous—has all but vanished in *Henry VIII*. Instead of through bloodletting, usurpation, and barbarities, the operation of Machiavellian power-lust and rivalry for pride of place occurs in the realm of bureaucracy through factional intrigues and alliances veiled by procedure and rank. The king is no longer threatened by contenders for his position but is at the head of a government of self-aggrandizing men competing with one another for the power that comes with prox-imity to him and from being the agents of his authority. He is threat-ened by unscrupulous officers—Woolsey mainly, not a man of the battlefield but of the Star Chamber—who use their proximity to Henry and their offices to strengthen their power rather than his, the law's, or his subjects'.

Cardinal Wolsey perpetrates the only act of violence in *Henry VIII* reminiscent of the kind of thing that went on in the earlier plays, but it is accomplished within the framework of bureaucracy. Wolsey engineers the trial and execution of the duke of Buckingham, a critic of his policies and, consequently, a threat to his office. Unlike the power-hungry contenders before him, Wolsey does not accomplish the deed with his own hand or hire murderers: He uses the judicial system to further his ends. The king remains innocent of the injustice, having been manipulated and deceived by Wolsey. The evidence brought against Buckingham comes through betrayal. The surveyor employed by Buckingham, in service to Wolsey now, testifies that Buckingham had spoken treason against the king. Whether Buckingham is actually guilty or not is never definitively revealed by the text, although the dramatic presentation strongly gives the impression that he is not guilty. This ambiguity, whatever political considerations or fears of offending powerful forces that may have given rise to it at the time of the play's presentation, also suggests the web of tensions and the veiled and ambiguous nature of truth and trust present in the bureaucratic system by which Henry's court is run.

While Henry is gullible, Katherine, his queen, recognizes mischief, noting, "You were the Duke's surveyor, and lost your office / On complaint o' th' tenants. Take good heed / You charge not in your spleen a noble person" (1.2.172–74). While Katherine's intervention goes unheeded by the king, it is noted by Wolsey—who has, indeed, been accumulating personal wealth by overtaxing the people—much to her disadvantage. Her honesty being a threat to his power, Wolsey, as is his common practice, undertakes to remove her as an obstacle to his authority and advancement. It is his policy to eliminate the people he deems to be impediments to his continuing accumulation and exercise of power.

Katherine rankles him not just because of her insight and clarity but because Wolsey, for his own purposes, wants her out of the way. He wishes to arrange to have the king marry the French king's sister, the duchess of Alençon. Henry, however, wishes to marry Anne Bullen, with whom he has fallen in love. Consequently, Wolsey tries to hold up the divorce in order to prevent that marriage. Wolsey plays an intricate game, attempting to manipulate several competing issues to his advantage. He promotes a divorce he also attempts to stall.

In order to unseat Katherine, Henry commissions Wolsey to secure from the pope permission for Henry to divorce her. When the pope's representative, Cardinal Campeius, comes from Rome to Henry's court in order to participate in Katherine's trial, he asks Wolsey in a private conversation about "one Doctor Pace," in act 2, scene 2, starting at line 111. Pace had been Henry's secretary, but he was, according to the court gossip, driven from his office by Wolsey and replaced by Gardiner, a man whose primary loyalty is to Wolsey. Wolsey does not deny the charge, explaining to Campeius that Doctor Pace "was a fool, / For he would needs be virtuous." Shifting then to the new man—his own puppet, Gardiner—Wolsey says, in contrast, "That good fellow, / If I command him, follows my appointment." He caps the comparison with this conclusion: "I will have none so near else." He is deliberate in the choice of his underlings. They must be his followers, never his equals. It is a point of pride with him. "We live not to be griped by meaner persons." Pride is the source of his treachery. Bureaucratic manipulation is the tool of his treachery. Buckingham, Pace, and Katherine are his victims because they stand in the way of his self-assertion, as does the king himself.

Undoing the king's authority is a trickier business than eliminating potential rivals, for he must supplant the king without unseating him. This Wolsey attempts to do by joining his own interests with the pope's, but his treachery miscarries for no other reason than a bureaucratic slip-up. As Wolsey is preparing, in 3.2, to rid himself of another rising competitor, Cranmer, the king uncovers Wolsey's disloyalty to him because Wolsey has inadvertently included certain documents, inventories of the wealth he has covertly accumulated and letters to the pope, not intended for Henry to see, in a packet of other papers that were intended for the king.

The theme of bureaucratic treachery continues to drive the action of the play even after Wolsey's fall, repentance, and death. When Henry's ruling courtiers jealously bring charges against Cranmer, who is archbishop of Canterbury, one of Henry's favorites and a man whom Henry believes to be wrongly accused, their malicious bad faith is dramatized by the fact that they keep Cranmer waiting in the antechamber for half an hour before admitting him to the council chamber. This is the essence of the display of bureaucratic power, as Kafka shows in *The Trial:* to keep people waiting. Bureaucracy, as Henry will reproach them with regard to their treatment of Cranmer, violates the ethics and aesthetics of *noblesse oblige* or the responsibilities that come with royal power. The pettiness of their motives and proceedings is set against the generosity of Henry's royal prerogatives and exercise of power.

Against the theme of betrayal, *Henry VIII* sets the theme of the importance of steadfast and wise authority, embodied by Henry himself, who grows into it, and by the birth of his daughter, the future monarch, Queen Elizabeth I, and her successor, King James I. Of Elizabeth, at her christening, Cranmer says,

> all the virtues that attend the good,
> Shall still be doubled on her. Truth shall nurse her
> Holy and heavenly thoughts still counsel her.
> She shall be lov'd and fear'd: her own shall bless her;
> Her foes shake like a field of beaten corn,
> And hang their heads with sorrow. Good grows with her.
> In her days every man shall eat in safety,
> Under his own vine,
>
> . . . .
>
> God shall be truly known; and those about her
> From her shall read the perfect ways of honor.
>
> (5.5.27–37)

James, the reigning king at the time of *Henry VIII*'s initial performances, Cranmer says,

> Shall star-like rise . . .
> And so stand fix'd. Peace, plenty, love, truth, terror,
>
> . . . .
>
> Shall then be his, and like a vine grow to him.
> Wherever the bright sun of heaven shall shine,
> His honour and the greatness of his name
> Shall be, and make new nations. He shall flourish,
> And, like a mountain cedar, reach his branches
> To all the plains about him.
>
> (5.5.46–54)

The contention, then, in *Henry VIII*, is not the bloody dispute that divided warring rivals in their pursuit of supreme power. Rather, it is the contention between monarchy and bureaucracy, between the stability of monarchy and the disorder inherent in the intrigues and quests for power characteristic of bureaucracy. In *Henry VIII*, monarchy emerges victorious because the king is presented as a wise superior able to control the abuses of petty men who vie with one another for supremacy in his service. Yet the future that Shakespeare and Fletcher could not see, the events that succeeded their death and the death of King James, and the events that defined the reign of King Charles I showed that victory to be an unstable one.

TOPICS AND STRATEGIES

While most of the preceding history plays were concerned with the chaos resulting from the breakdown of the social order and the battles and intrigues waged between contending parties hoping to gain control of or to retain social power through bloody means, *Henry VIII* is concerned with the problem of maintaining a peaceful social order despite the existence of varying factions and interests. The challenge the play presents to a writer is its apparent lack of the kind of action and intrigue that characterize its predecessors. There are no battles, no bloody set pieces, no fascinating villains, no charismatically troubled heroes, and hardly any real drama. Things seem to happen between the lines and offstage. There is a considerable amount of narration presented through conversations between secondary characters.

One of the main sources of the unity of the play is its focus on social virtues. The concern with betrayal previously discussed, by implication, suggests an equal concern with loyalty. The character of Katherine, for example, is not only set against Wolsey dramatically but also thematically. He represents betrayal and evil. She represents loyalty and faithfulness.

Themes

Many themes in *Henry VIII* can be subsumed under the larger, more overarching theme of social order, either as contributing to it or threatening it. A writer can examine the play for instances in which order is threatened or strengthened, examining plots and spectacles, actions and attitudes.

Sample Topics:

1. **Pride:** How does the play represent and evaluate pride? How does it judge the proud? How does the play show pride to be a threat to the social order?

   To write an essay about pride as a theme of the play, begin by identifying where the play either represents or discusses pride, which characters are shown as being proud, and how their pride is judged by its results. What are the consequences of pride for them and for others? What kinds of judgments concerning pride do other characters offer? Which characters represent the opposite of pride, and how do they affect the social order? From this, a thesis can be developed about the role of pride in the play and the play's evaluation of pride.

2. **Chastity/virginity:** How important are chastity and virginity in the play, and why are they important? Is there any connection between chastity and virginity and the concepts of pride or treachery? What is the relation of chastity or virginity to the social order?

   For an essay on the role and significance of chastity and/or virginity in *Henry VIII*, a writer ought to examine the nature of the characters who represent chastity and virginity and the role(s) they play in *Henry VIII* and qualities they represent. It would also be important to consider the play as a harbinger of Elizabeth's reign and a tribute to it. She was known as the Virgin Queen. In the context of *Henry VIII*, why is virginity or chastity (which may be defined as the extension of virginity into marriage) of great significance? Must the concepts of chastity and/or virginity be confined to sexuality, or can they be extended to represent an attitude about behavior and relationship? Are there any characters in *Henry VIII* who seem explicitly not to be chaste? What, then, is the opposite of chastity? When Queen Katherine defends herself by reminding the king of her chastity, what else is she saying about herself?

3. **Self-interest:** While *Henry VIII* purports to be a play about how English identity was formed and a benevolent central government was solidified, what does the play show about the role, consequences, and importance of self-interest in the characters' lives and for the health of the state?

An essay on this topic might start by looking closely at the role that self-interest plays in shaping the personalities and the actions of the major characters in the play and what effect the practice of self-interest or of self-sacrifice has on the nation itself.

4. **Penitence and forgiveness:** *Henry VIII* is a play about people who do wrong and people to whom wrong is done. Much of the wrongdoing is deliberate. Some of it is not. Obviously, the play does not support wrongdoing, but what does the play say about reactions and responses to having done wrong and having suffered wrong? How does the play show the value of penitence and forgiveness, and how does it define and describe these practices and show what good is accomplished by either penitence or forgiveness?

In order to write about this subject, a writer's primary focus would be on the two principal opponents, Wolsey and Katherine, but consideration of Buckingham, Anne Bullen, and Cranmer is also useful. What about Henry? How is he wronged? Does he wrong others? If he does, how is that presented, judged, accounted for—particularly because the play seems to be a celebration of Henry and his daughter, Queen Elizabeth, and her successor, James I, in other words, English monarchy itself as it was shaped by Henry?

Character

Consideration of character in *Henry VIII*, it can be argued, can be most fruitfully pursued by focusing on types rather than on individuals. Even when there is a change in the attitude or behavior of a character, it seems to be a change from one type of attitude to another. Can you show that the internal experience and the drama of character transformation that accompany outer change are not developed or made part of the action of

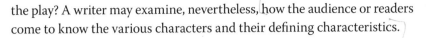

the play? A writer may examine, nevertheless, how the audience or readers come to know the various characters and their defining characteristics.

Sample Topics:

1. **Wolsey's development:** How does Wolsey change, and what causes the change?

   Does his change seem to come from something within him, or does his change reflect a particular "agenda" that the play seems to be advancing? If so, what is that agenda and what in the play seems to indicate the presence of that agenda? What does Wolsey himself say about his fall? How does that commentary shape a reader's opinion of his character?

2. **Henry's character:** Is Henry a fully developed character or a less differentiated, symbolic figure? What is it that makes him one or the other? What is the significance of his being either an individual or a figure? Is there a difference between the king as a man and the king as a figure in the play? Does the play give any insight into his character, or is he part of a theatrical pageant? Does Henry change or grow in the course of the play? If so, how, and what accounts for his change?

   Do Shakespeare and Fletcher show the man or use him as didactic example, as part of a lesson in the way a king ought to be? What is Henry's dramatic function in the play? Can one draw any lessons about how a king ought to behave from Henry's portrayal? From consideration of these questions, a reader might construct a thesis about what the play presents as the proper role and nature of royal authority.

3. **Evaluating Katherine as a character:** What kind of figure is Katherine? How is she presented? How does the way she is presented affect a reader's response to her? Is she an individual or a figure designed to define the ideal wife? What about her presentation determines your response? Consider how she responds to attacks against her, to her suffering, and to her adversaries. Consider her death. Does the play give any indications of her

intelligence, her dignity, her insight, her political or religious beliefs, or her sense of what is right? What does the way she is portrayed say about the world she inhabits and about the limits that the play must respect?

As with the king, is she drawn as a person or as a role model? Structurally, what is her importance as a counterpoint to Wolsey? How does the portrayal of Katherine affect how a reader responds to other characters in the play?

4. **The presentation of Buckingham:** How is Buckingham presented in the play? Is he a sympathetic character? Is he guilty of what his surveyor accuses him of? Is his innocence ever absolutely indicated?

You might consider an essay arguing that whether he is guilty or innocent actually does not matter for he is used to convey the nature of Wolsey's handling of power.

5. **The representation of character in general:** A writer might address in an essay the issue of how important to the play the development and presentation of character are in general. Although they are of key importance in many of Shakespeare's great plays, are they beside the point in this one?

A writer may examine what is the common way the play presents or refrains from presenting character and how the way character is represented in the play affects the meaning and drama of the play.

History and Context

Henry VIII, first performed in 1613, is an account of events that occurred in the 1530s. Consequently, the play represents one of the ways a historical period was viewed by another. There are several approaches a writer interested in history and context can, therefore, take when writing about the play.

Sample Topics:

1. *Henry VIII* **as history:** Shakespeare and Fletcher took considerable liberties with history in *Henry VIII*, with regard to sequence and with regard to the intrigues and alliances that defined the interrelations of characters. How does the play differ in the presentation of events from how they actually occurred? What does the play accomplish by altering time sequences and relationships? What historical information or information about characters does the play omit, and what effect does that have on the drama and the mood of the play?

Can you argue, for example, that far from being a historical chronicle, *Henry VIII* is a mythological revision of history? What elements in the play seem less appropriate for a history play and more characteristic of a romance or mythic play?

2. *Henry VIII* **in 1613:** Can *Henry VIII* be seen to be as much a play for 1613 as it is a play about the 1530s? What were the nature of political intrigues in 1613 in the court and concerning England's international relations?

In 1612, Prince Henry, the much esteemed and highly regarded, strongly Protestant prince of Wales died apparently of a fever, although perhaps by poisoning, at the age of 18. His death was a cause for national grief. How might *Henry VIII* be read in regard to that death and its consequences?

3. *Henry VIII* **and King James:** Can you read *Henry VIII* as a didactic play that offers lessons in statecraft and governing that might be applicable to James?

Select passages that seem to involve lessons in governance focusing on mistakes Henry makes as well as virtues he displays. Through research, discover some of the issues confronting James that the words and actions of the play might help him in handling.

Philosophy and Ideas

The themes of a play and the ideas and philosophy it contains are not necessarily very different from each other. The themes of betrayal, pride, forgiveness, penitence, chastity, loyalty, and humility that are pervasive in the play are ideas that the play explores, and the conclusions the play seems to come to about those ideas can be understood as the play's philosophy. It is important when examining any work of art, and certainly the plays of Shakespeare, which are known for their complexity and inexhaustibility, to be wary of seeing absolutely resolved and exclusive philosophical positions. The nearer a work of art is to the truth about ourselves and our world, the further that work is from being a manifesto, a doctrine, or a work of propaganda for any position or viewpoint. A good and careful reader can find in a complex work of art a variety of truths about the human condition. What do you find in *Henry VIII*?

Sample Topics:

1. **The responsibilities of a monarch:** Although *Henry VIII* is not explicitly a handbook for kings, can you find in it a philosophy of governing or ideas about what virtues and qualities a king ought to have and what pitfalls a monarch ought to avoid? These ideas may be presented implicitly, allowing you to draw them out from the events of the play.

   What are Henry's weaknesses as a king? They are downplayed but obvious, especially in his early carelessness with regard to Wolsey. From a consideration of his faults, derive a sense of the virtues a king ought to cultivate.

2. **Self-transcendence:** The idea of self-transcendence, an essay can postulate, is central to *Henry VIII* and is most forcefully exemplified by the two major antagonists of the play, Katherine and Wolsey. Wolsey, the emblem of overweening pride and of treachery, and Katherine, the model of submission and fidelity, both meet disgrace for different reasons, and both transcend their conditions. How do they achieve the grace, if they do, that is granted them at the end of their lives? Searching the way they talk about themselves and their actions and their fates is a use-

ful way to begin, as well as noting how others speak of their deaths. Seeing if other characters—Buckingham is worth considering—share their final beatitude is also useful.

Can you draw from these instances a philosophical idea about how one ought to behave and how one ought to encounter the fickle nature of fortune? Ideas about penitence and forgiveness will be useful here, and this topic will give a writer the opportunity to examine the play's evaluation of those ideas. In addition, an essay on self-transcendence can consider the relationship between the individual and society and how such transcendence affects an individual's relation to eternity.

Form and Genre

The genre of *Henry VIII* appears to be history, but a comparison with the actual history the play purports to represent may leave a reader wondering how accurate a descriptor that is. Beside the content, the form of the play may yet add to an uneasiness in designating the play a history. *Henry VIII* is drama, yet much of that drama can fall under a subcategory, spectacle or pageant. The action of the play seems to be moving toward the final spectacle. Spectacle and pageant suggest myth or even propaganda rather than outright drama. Drama is marked by conflicts and their resolution. Spectacle and pageant are relatively free of both since a spectacle or a pageant is a form that essentially celebrates the end of conflict and, indeed, the conclusion of a historical episode. There is no tension for a Christian watching a Christmas or Easter pageant. One celebrates a transcendental birth; the other the triumph over death. In such pageants, conflict is merely an element of spectacle. The obstacles to the already known ends are simply embellishments of the spectacle, not dramatic elements.

Sample Topics:

1. *Henry VIII* **as spectacle:** How does the degree of spectacle in *Henry VIII* affect the drama and meaning of the play? How does spectacle make *Henry VIII* a particularly English play? What part does nationalism or British patriotism contribute to the fabric of the play? How does spectacle transform history into mythology?

To write about this topic, a writer might contrast the business of the court with the visionary material the play presents.

2. *Henry VIII* **as a didactic work:** This topic asks the writer to think about what the purpose of the play might be in light of its particular form and genre. Does the play contain a lesson for both rulers and the ruled, for monarchs and subjects, particularly because of the spectacles it introduces?

If the entire play can be seen as a pageant, how does that affect it as a drama, and what effect does it have on the presentation of characters? Every play is spectacle, but not all plays are designed for the audience to see them as spectacles as they are watching them. What is the effect of Henry VIII's being self-consciously presented as a spectacle to its audience? A writer might start by considering the function of the account of the meeting of the French and the English kings that begins the play.

Language, Symbols, and Imagery

The drama of *Henry VIII* is largely symbolic of the monarch's majesty, and the play is replete with heraldic imagery. The play itself, it can be argued, is designed to present and celebrate the insignia of monarchy and is itself a kind of symbolic language of assertive spectacle.

1. **Double authorship:** It was primarily through linguistic analysis that the division of *Henry VIII* was made, some portions attributed to Shakespeare and some to Fletcher.

Can you find and describe significant differences in diction, syntax, grammar, style, and the use of metaphor and imagery in several sections of the play to substantiate the hypothesis of two writers?

2. **Spectacle:** In *Henry VIII,* symbolism and imagery are not confined to the language of the play but are largely presented through spectacle.

How do the spectacles affect the way an audience understands the characters involved in them or the social context? How do they affect the meaning of the play and an audience's attitude in regard to monarchy?

Compare and Contrast Essays

Considering the histories preceding *Henry VIII*, there is a wealth of possible essay topics for compare and contrast essays. After reviewing some of the other histories, choose a particular one. The play you pick will help shape your topic and what aspect of the plays you write about. You may also consider comparisons with some of Shakespeare's nonhistory plays.

Sample Topics:

1. **Comparing *Henry VIII* with *Henry V:*** Such a comparison may suggest writing about the variety of ways to present and to understand nationalism. Is nationalism seen as a function of history or of myth? Similarly, are the historical characters presented portrayed as heroes or as legends?

   A writer can focus on the role of the king in each play, the nature and meaning of spectacle, the attitudes of subordinates, and the differences in the kind of speeches that occur in each play. Consider the significance and the effect of the absence of comic characters in *Henry VIII* and their presence in *Henry V*.

2. **Comparing *Henry VIII* to *Henry IV, Part 1:*** Comparing these apparently quite dissimilar plays may stimulate you to think about the difference between drama and spectacle and between complex characters and well-defined roles. Consider the contrast between Wolsey and Falstaff.

   Are there ways in which these characters are similar to each other? What do they have in common? Both represent a strong self-centeredness, and both abuse whatever power they have. Both, in effect, are thieves and have no compunction about swindling. Both, in the end, are rejected by their kings. Yet there are major differences that distinguish them from each other. What are those distinguishing characteristics? How do these differences reveal and affect the nature of each play?

3. **Comparing the function of the play within a play:** The royal pageantry and Katherine's vision may be regarded as plays within the play, a common feature in much of Shakespeare's work. Compare and contrast how the device of the play within a play is used in *Henry VIII* and in another of Shakespeare's plays and the effect it has on *Henry VIII* and the other play(s) you choose. How is the purpose the play within the play serves in *Henry VIII* different from the purpose it serves in the other plays?

You can refer to several of the English histories, *Richard II* and *1 Henry IV*, for example, as well as to plays like *Hamlet, Cymbeline, The Tempest,* and *A Midsummer Night's Dream.*

4. **Comparing the scene of charges brought by the surveyor against Buckingham in *Henry VIII* with the scene of charges brought against Thomas Horner by Peter Thump in *2 Henry VI*:** Although the men involved in *Henry VIII* are aristocrats and the men in *2 Henry VI* are working-class artisans, the two situations, a subordinate bringing evidence of treason against his master, in each play are parallel situations. Show the similarities and differences between the two situations.

How can a reading of one scene affect a reading of the other? What significances and implications can be drawn from reading the two scenes in relation to each other? In relation to a statement about the nature of mankind?

5. **Comparing *Henry VIII* and *The Winter's Tale*:** On the face of it, these two plays are quite different from each other. Yet, there are strong similarities in their plots despite the obvious generic, linguistic, and stylistic differences.

How are these plays similar, and how are they different from each other, particularly with regard to their apparent similarities? What do these differences tell us about each play? Pay particular attention to the relationship between Leontes and Hermione and to Henry and Katherine, to Perdita and Elizabeth, and to the fates of Hermione and Katherine.

Bibliography and Online Resources for *Henry VIII*

Alter, Iska. "'To Reform and Make Fitt': *Henry VIII* and the Making of 'Bad' Shakespeare." In *"Bad" Shakespeare: Revaluations of the Shakespeare Canon,* edited by Maurice Charney, pp. 176–86. Rutherford, N.J.: Fairleigh Dickinson University Press, 1988.

(Reviewing a history of stage performances and adaptations, Alter argues that the common impression of Henry VIII *has been shaped by how the play has been presented over the centuries rather than by the actual text, which, she argues, is concerned with "the details of internal governance [hardly the most vivid matter for performance] rather than with the grand or grandiose posturings of battle.")*

Glimp, David. "Staging Government: Shakespeare's *Life of King Henry the Eighth* and the Government of Generations." *Criticism,* Winter 1999, vol. 41, no.1, pp. 41–65.

(Glimp views Henry VIII *as addressing an Elizabethan anxiety about the destructive influence of theater on individual morality and social institutions; he suggests the play attempted to turn that threat around and make theater an ally rather than an adversary of government.)*

Jackson, MacDonald. P. "Phrase Lengths in *Henry VIII,* Shakespeare and Fletcher." *Notes and Queries,* 44 (242):1, March 1997, pp. 75–80.

(Through statistical analysis, Jackson attempts to distinguish which parts of Henry VIII *were composed by Shakespeare and which by John Fletcher.)*

Kezar, Dennis. "Law/Form/History: Shakespeare's Verdict in 'All Is True.'" *Modern Language Quarterly,* March 2002, vol. 63, no. 1, pp. 1–31.

(Kezar offers a "reading [of Henry VIII *that] is concerned with the struggle between literature and history (between fictional form and factual content)" and "with literature's struggle . . . to provide a normative mechanism whereby facts, however literary, can be judged" and truth can be distinguished from historical fact.)*

Knight, G. Wilson. "Henry VIII and the Poetry of Conversion." *The Crown of Life: Essays in Interpretation of Shakespeare's Final Plays,* pp. 256–336. London: Oxford University Press, 1947.
(Knight celebrates Henry VIII *as a play giving ritual and, consequently, religious expression to the presence of peace after an era of war, essentially through a valorization of law.)*

Richmond, Hugh M. "The Resurrection of an Expired Form: *Henry VIII* as Sequel to *Richard III*." *Shakespeare's English Histories: A Quest for Form and Genre,* edited by John W. Velz, pp. 205–27. Binghampton, N.Y.: Medieval and Renaissance Texts and Studies, 1996.
(Richmond argues for Shakespeare's exclusive authorship of Henry VIII *by attempting to demonstrate that, in* Henry VIII, *Shakespeare integrates the methods and plots of his early English chronicle histories, particularly* Richard III, *with the mystical temperament of his late romances such as* The Winter's Tale.)*

Vanita, Ruth. "Mariological Memory in *The Winter's Tale* and *Henry VIII*." *Studies in English Literature, 1500–1900,* Spring 2000, vol. 40, no. 2, pp. 311–37.
(Comparing the portrayal of the women in The Winter's Tale *and* Henry VIII, *Vanita argues that as they are made victims of patriarchal injustice, Hermione in* The Winter's Tale *and Katherine in* Henry VIII *gain moral stature and reflect and recall the role of Mary in the Christian narrative.)*

Waage, Frederick O. Jr. "Henry VIII and the Crisis of the English History Play." *Shakespeare Studies,* 8, 1975, pp. 297–309.
(Waage argues that Henry VIII *is covertly a play reflecting the grief that followed the death of Henry, prince of Wales, in 1612. In addition, contrasting Shakespeare and Fletcher's* Henry VIII *with three other Henry VIII plays presented in 1613, he argues that history plays that could appeal to the whole English nation were no longer possible because of the developing political factions within the government.)*

Wasson, John. "In Defense of *King Henry VIII*." *Research Studies* 32, no. 3, September 1964, pp. 261–76.
(Wasson's "defense" entails reading Henry VIII *as a history play rather than as a tragedy and is particularly useful because he provides an outline of each genre and a discussion of their respective differences.)*

Wegemer, Gerard. "Henry VIII On Trial: Confronting Malice And Conscience in Shakespeare's *All Is True*." *Renascence: Essays on Values in Literature,* Winter 2000, vol. 52, no. 2, pp. 111–30.

(Wegemer reads Henry VIII *as being structurally shaped by a series of trials, each of which concerns malicious intentions against the authority of the king; he argues that the king's own actions are driven by a hidden wilfulness and are, in fact, tyrannical.)*

INDEX

Characters in literary works are listed by the name followed by the work in which they appear.